PRIVATE BANKING

Private Banking

An Introduction

Edited by

Sujatha B
Nancy John

2010

Icfai Books
The Icfai University Press

PRIVATE BANKING: AN INTRODUCTION

Editors: Sujatha B and Nancy John

First Edition: 2010
Printed in India

Published by

The Icfai University Press
52, Nagarjuna Hills, Punjagutta
Hyderabad, India – 500 082
Phone: (+91) (040) 23430–368, 369, 370, 372, 373, 374
Fax: (+91) (040) 23352521, 23435386
E-mail: info@icfaibooks.com, icfaibooks@icfai.org, ssd@icfai.org

ISBN: 9788131407486

Editorial Team: Sushuma G and Srinivas Reddy G
Quality Support: M Manorama and J K Vadana

CONTENTS

OVERVIEW

The Indian economy is rapidly integrating with the world economy through extensive economic reforms. Among the emerging markets, India is considered a key player in terms of fast growth, rise in high net worth individuals, rapid urbanization and change in spending patterns. When compared with other emerging economies, India's dollar millionaires' club has grown by 19.3% in '05 with financial assets of Rs.4.5 crore and above.

Private banking in India is gradually growing and both domestic as well as foreign players are targeting clients of the highest social level, popularly known as High Net Worth Individuals (HNIs). Mostly, HNIs comprise doctors, lawyers, businessmen, celebrities and CEOs of corporations and commodity merchants etc. These individuals lack time to manage their extra assets and hence place their demands on their private bankers and banks. They seek expert advice to manage their assets wisely. According to Abhay Aima, country head, equity and private banking group, HDFC Bank, "Essentially, private banking is for people who do not have the time to study the various investment instruments or have access to information from Reuters, Bloomsberg, CNBC, CNN, Crisil or his own research database to take an informed decision."

Private banking is however still at a nascent stage. "The threshold of private banking has not evolved as per international standards, where the limit is usually $1 million," says DSP Merrill Lynch, executive vice president (debt and private clients group) Pradeep Dokania. The threshold limit for a HSBC customer in India is Rs.1.5 crore, which is lower than the bank's international threshold limit of Rs.4.5 crore ($1 million). In general, private banking in India caters to HNIs who have excess wealth ranging from Rs.10 lakhs to Rs.2 crores or more and desire that their wealth is protected from market risks.

Today, private banking is moving from providing traditional banking services to building relationships beyond financial matters. Hans J Baer, a Zurich private banker stated, "Private banking is the full range of services that a client may wish to obtain and this therefore extends way beyond wealth management". Private banking is the means of managing private clients' money by providing various services like efficient wealth management, savings, inheritance and tax planning. Over time, private banking builds deeper relationships between the banker and his client.

The emergence of many new derivative products, mutual fund schemes, declining interest rates and the rising wealth of individuals in India has paved the way to the growth of private banking. Private Banking is an industry that is under constant pressure due to the unpredictability of the markets. In such a scenario, banks face new challenges in catering to the services demanded by their rich clientele. The private bankers are also seeking innovative ways to satisfy their wealthy customers.

Private banking clients are growing more astute and demanding as they seek professional advice and wealth preservation beyond the plain-vanilla investment ideas. This has given rise to the recent trend of interest in alternative products. Alternative products include private equity, hedge funds, property and "investments of passion," such as classic cars, masterpieces of art, stamps and fine wines, etc. The World Wealth Report points out that, "alternative investments have become mainstream investment vehicles as HNIs around the world strive for better performance and portfolio balance." These new asset classes have been found to yield better returns over the long term.

Against this backdrop, this book seeks to focus on the emerging opportunities for private banking in India. It highlights the factors driving the growth of private banking in the country and the region, debates the sustainability of domestic and foreign private banks and analyzes the performance of private banks. The book is split into three sections. The first section covers the emerging opportunities for private banking in India. The second section takes us through the driving forces behind such growth and analyzes the performance of the private sector banks in India and discusses their sustainability. The final section discusses the regional trends and the lessons to be learnt.

Section I: Emerging Opportunities

The evolving global environment of financial services has led to demand for greater flexibility and specialized services. The first section discusses about the emerging opportunities in private banking.

The first article **"Private Banking Industry: New Insights"** by *Sujatha B,* provides new insights into the private banking industry, its growth and future, emerging opportunities for private bankers and their clients and the challenges for private banking in the face of money laundering laws and regulatory measures. It brings out how private banking industry is witnessing substantial growth with the increase in the number of high net worth individuals. It traces the global and the regional trends in private banking, and discusses some of the key players in the industry and their strategies in this context.

Wealth management and Private banking business is growing by leaps and bounds in India. The second article **"Banking on the Rich"** by *Raghu Mohan,* discusses the private banking market in India. The author says that in India, the market is still evolving and ICICI and HDFC banks are the major Indian players in wealth management and private banking business. It concludes that the local economy is expected to be the third largest after China and the United States in the next 30 years. The value addition **"We Consider Ourselves as an Investment Bank for Individuals"** by *Nilanjan Dey,* gives excerpts of an interview with Mr. Sandeep Sharma, Head, SG Private Banking India, on the promising wealth management market in India and outlines SG Private Banking strategy.

The third article **"Private Banking in India: Millionaires Calling"** authored by *Amit Singh Sisodiya* and *Sanjoy De,* describes how private banking and wealth management services in India are gaining momentum as the number of high net worth individuals is escalating. The article reveals that rising customer demand, coupled with increased competition among wealth managers will result in the introduction of more sophisticated products and services. It also brings out that the wealth management market in India is still evolving; and the penetration level of wealth management services in India is only 10%. **"Desi Millionaires: 83,500 and Rising"** sourced from *The Economic Times* is a value addition to this article. It talks about how India's dollar millionaires' club is growing faster than most other economies and that the rise in millionaires has given a fillip to the private banking business in India.

The next article **"India Beyond Outsourcing: The Opportunities for International Banks"** by *Janmejaya Sinha, Christian de Juniac* and *Saurabh Tripathi,* deals with the Indian banking market. The authors emphasize that India's banking market is one of the fastest growing in the world due to increase in foreign investment, favorable demographic profile and regulatory changes. Retail financial services businesses—such as mortgages, personal loans, wealth management, and asset management—have enormous potential in India. It has also been observed that foreign institutions that entered India have gained higher returns than their home countries.

The last article in this section **"Wealth Management and Private Banking: Key Themes for Future"** written by *Anita Iyer*, discusses briefly the wealth management industry in India. The wealth management industry, though in a nascent stage, is experiencing rapid growth in terms of the number of providers, clients and assets under management. It also highlights that the changing investor demands and tax regulations are helping banks in providing a complete portfolio advisory module in addition to traditional banking products. The value addition **"Wealth Management and Private Banking – Building a Proactive Model"** by *Ajay Mahajan,* highlights that attracting and retaining clients, places an enormous demand on expertise, technology and product capabilities. The challenge lies in dynamic implementation of investor suggestions and feedback and building a proactive model.

Section II: Prospects and Performance

Indian banking industry is undergoing a radical transformation due to globalization, liberalization and privatization. To increase the efficiency and profitability of the banks, the banking sector is opened up for new private sector banks. New private sector banks have brought with them state-of-art technology for business processing and service delivery, besides being efficient in catering to the customers' demands. The second section analyzes the performance of private sector banks in India and deals with private banking activities.

Productivity, profitability, professionalism, introduction to technology, competition from foreign banks and PSBs, innovation of new products and services, etc., have set in and necessitated dramatic changes in providing private banking services. The first article in this section **"Private Sector Banks in India – A SWOT Analysis"** written by *Chowdari Prasad* and *K S Srinivasa Rao,* attempts to undertake SWOT analysis and other appropriate statistical techniques, to rank 30 private sector banks from the financial data collected for three years. The article ranks the banks using the overall performance. The authors conclude that with increased usage of technology, best utilization of manpower resources, along with professional management adopting corporate governance principles, private banks will continue to give their best and evolve in the Indian financial system.

In the second article **"Performance of the New Indian Private Sector Banks: A Comparative Study"** by *Sanjay J Bhayani*, the author analyzes the performance of new private sector banks in providing better private banking services through the help of the CAMEL model. Based on the analysis, it is concluded that the competition among banks is tough in providing varied private banking services and the consumer benefits from it. The article brings to light that there is a tremendous growth in the retail segment and there is a lot of untapped potential in the market for private banking.

The next article **"A Comparative Study on the Service Quality and Customer Satisfaction among Private, Public and Foreign Banks"** authored by *Rengasamy Elango* and *Vijaya Kumar Gudep*, analyzes the level of awareness and customer satisfaction of the three major banking sectors of India. Indian banking industry is undergoing radical transformation due to globalization, liberalization and privatization. The study revealed that the foreign banks have topped the list in delivering qualitative customer service. It also showed that the private sector banks are competing successfully with the foreign banks to provide better banking services in tune with the changing global competitive scenario.

Growing acceptance of Foreign Banks is partly due to the high aspirational value attached by the consumers to banking and associating with a foreign brand. Robust systems, well-defined processes of their global network and an attractive market have enabled these banks to move from a 'dipping the toe' strategy to establishing and cementing their foothold in the Indian market. The fourth article **"Sustainability of Foreign Banks in India – A Statistical Analysis"** written by *Chowdari Prasad* and *K S Srinivasa Rao* studies the sustainability of foreign banks existing in India and the working of foreign banks that have newly entered and identifies the foreign banks which are vulnerable and the reasons thereof. It also analyzes each of the foreign banks and its development on various parameters/ sub-parameters under CRAMEL.

HDFC Bank, the first Indian private bank, offers private banking as a comprehensive and exclusive service to select high net worth individuals and institutions. The next article "**HDFC Bank – Fostering Relationships through Private Banking**" by *Sushuma G* gives a brief introduction about HDFC Bank's private banking operations in India, traces its growth and performance, highlights its strategies and future plans.

The sixth article "**ABN-Amro's Private Banking in India**" by *Nancy John* briefly talks about ABN-Amro's private banking operations in India, its growth and performance and tries to highlight the bank's strategies and plans for the future. ABN-Amro's private banking division handles assets worth $60 billion worldwide. The bank's private banking section provides a complete range of advisory services to HNIs to help them in financial planning.

Section III: Lessons from Regional Trends

The final section of the book deals with private banking operations in different regions like Europe, Asia and Latin America. This section provides learning lessons to India with references to private banking operations in various regions.

Asia's high net worth individuals are getting rich quicker than elsewhere in the world due to wealth management. *Indu Prasad* in the next article "**Private Banking in Asia: Wealth from Wealthy**" says that private banking in Asia, though performing well, is still facing some challenges such as talent, awareness of private banking capabilities and complexity of markets and products. Private banking now is about making returns and finding solutions. Hence development of this sector would ultimately depend on the sustenance of customer faith.

Private banking in Asia is growing faster than any other region in the world. Business in Singapore is rolling because most of the Asians are keeping their wealth in the region. The second article "**Private Banking in Singapore: Riding on Asian Economic Boom**" by *D Satish* ponders on whether Singapore, which has a congenial environment for the growth of wealth management companies, will emulate Switzerland as the most favorable nation for private banking. The value addition "**Singapore: A Private Banking Tiger**" by *Michel Benedetti* is about how Singapore has been developing as a further centre of financial advisory and other services to high net worth individuals.

The private client wealth management industry in Europe remains relatively fragmented, although a few major players have emerged and consolidation is an ongoing theme in the sector. It has been estimated that the top 10 private banks in Europe manage around 20% of HNI wealth, and within a country, no player has more than 5% of the domestic private banking market. The third article "**Private Banking in Europe – Getting Clients and Keeping Them!**" written by *Philip Molyneux* and *Anna Omarini,* examines the features of private banking business in Europe and focuses on the key roles of client segmentation, retention and acquisition. It also illustrates important themes relating to the wealth management service proposition. The value addition "**Private Banking in Switzerland**" compiled from various sources briefly talks about private banking operations in Switzerland and the transformation that is taking place in the private banking sector.

The next article "**Wealth Structuring for Latin American Clients**" authored by *Richard J Hay* and *Robert L Reymond,* reviews the opportunities for private bankers in the Latin American region, which have arisen in recent developments. It provides an overview of the major drivers of change, including a review of the impact of worldwide taxation on structuring for offshore investments maintained by wealthy families resident in Mexico, Venezuela, Argentina and Brazil. Finally, lessons from the experiences in the region are considered for their impact on the strategy for institutions with global private banking businesses.

SECTION I

EMERGING OPPORTUNITIES

1

Private Banking Industry: New Insights

Sujatha B

While the bull market of the '90s gave the impetus to wealth creation, the bear market that followed highlighted the significance of wealth preservation. Hence, the focus of major international financial institutions is now on private banking, or the business of looking after rich people's money.

"Money is a singular thing. It ranks with love as man's greatest source of joy. And with death as his greatest source of anxiety."

— John Kenneth Galbraith, American Economist.

Private Banking – The Sizzler among Financial Services

The private banking industry is booming fuelled by the surge in the number of wealthy individuals. As per the World Wealth Report 2006, published by Capgemini[1] and Merrill Lynch[2], the number of High Net Worth Individuals (HNWI)[3] stood at 8.7 million in 2005 growing by 6.5 per cent over the previous year. The report also revealed that the Asia-Pacific region witnessed a faster growth

---

[1]   Capgemini is one of the world's foremost service providers in Consulting, Technology and Outsourcing.

[2]   Merrill Lynch is one of the world's leading financial management and advisory companies providing investment management services.

[3]   HNWI refers to individuals with net financial assets of over US$1 million.

in terms of wealth creation and also as an attractive investment region. The growth in wealth creation is backed by a consistent growth in real GDP and market capitalization. The bullish market and increasing use of stock options further gave rise to a new class of affluent employee millionaires. Unlike the previous generations of wealthy individuals who had inherited wealth and were primarily concerned with preserving it, the new breed of self-made millionaires are more demanding and seek active management of their wealth. They are not only well-informed and sophisticated, but also seek active participation in wealth building. This elite group has people from all walks of life and includes professionals, celebrities and CEOs. One thing that is common amongst them is their.quest for professional advice to manage their wealth in tune with their requirements. As the number of wealthy individuals is rising, more banks are scrambling to woo the privileged. And, they have a good reason to do so.

The increase in wealth to be managed gets translated into growing fee income for the banks. Private banking customers contribute to a sizeable percentage of the banks' fee-based income. The Swiss private banking major UBS announced a rise of over 50 per cent in its second quarter earnings in August 2006. Hawaii banks reported a 63 per cent increase in income from private banking services during the first three quarters of 2006. Citigroup's private banking division reports to have captured half of Asia's billionaires as its clients, and is further expanding its operations in India and China. Credit Suisse, the second largest Swiss bank, reported huge inflows from private banking clients and is further expanding into the Middle-East and Singapore. Booming Asian economies and the rising demand for professional wealth management services have prompted international bankers like JP Morgan Chase and HSBC to increase their focus on wealth management and private banking. Christopher Wheeler of Bear Stearns[4] considers private banking to be the fastest-growing area of financial services, with a compound annual growth rate of 24 per cent between 2002 and 2005[5]. A Credit Suisse report shows that about 20 per cent of the HNWIs in Asia use private banking services. Didier von Daeniken, Credit Suisse's head of private banking for South-East Asia and Australasia, predicts that private wealth management there may grow by 25 per cent.

---

[4]   Bear Stearns, a worldwide investment banking and securities trading and brokerage firm.

[5]   "Rich Pickings", *The Economist*, August 17, 2006.

Global Trends and Emerging Opportunities

The global wealth management and private banking industry is thriving as revealed by KPMG's Global Private Banking and Wealth Management Survey, 2005. It points to Asia Pacific being the most dynamic region accounting for 38 per cent of transaction activity followed by North America with 37 per cent, with Europe's persisting decline in transaction activity for the fourth year. The survey reveals the trend towards organic growth in the relatively younger Asia-Pacific market as against a trend towards growth through acquisitions in the more mature American markets. One more interesting trend in the global private banking industry is the shift towards onshore financial centers, indicating a growing preference for local private banking service providers.

The Asia-Pacific region proves to be the most promising destination for private banking institutions. The region still has a low degree of penetration of private banking laden with tremendous growth potential. The Monetary Authority of Singapore, the country's central bank, estimates the assets under management by private banks at US$200 billion, which is reported to be growing at 20 per cent per year. The strategic location of Singapore, the Government's efforts to promote the island as an offshore base for financial services, prevalence of a favorable regulatory environment and legal system, and the availability of trained manpower are some of the factors that weigh in favor of Singapore as the next Switzerland for the private banking industry.

India is second only to South Korea in terms of growth in number of HNWIs. The number of dollar millionaires in India grew by 19.3 per cent in 2005 to 83,500. There are only a few players like ABN Amro, BNP Paribas, Deutsche Bank, DSP Merrill Lynch and SocGen catering to the high-end private banking market in India. During the first three years since it launched its private banking operations, HDFC Bank, India's leading private bank, has reported 100 per cent year on year growth in its private banking clientele. Reports state that roughly 30 per cent of the private banking market has already been captured by private and foreign banks and the rest of the potential is yet to be tapped. That explains why international players like UBS and Credit Suisse are eyeing this segment with interest. Multiplicity of investment options, introduction of derivative products and complexity of financial instruments, falling interest regime and growing wealth are some of the factors driving the growth of private banking in India.

Private banking is catching up in Australia with the spurt in the number of HNWIs, estimated at around 50,000 by the Boston Consulting Group. The BCG report showed the combined wealth of Australians at $1260 billion in 2005, rising by 6.3 per cent. The rising share market and the increasing sophistication of the wealthy Australians have given a fillip to the private banking activity in the region. The big four Australian banks – NAB, CBA, ANZ and Westpac – have initiated measures to target different segments of the HNWI market. To meet the tall demands of the sophisticated clients, banks are opting for a strategy of "co-opetition", tying up with other providers so that they can present their clients with the best of breed products, not necessarily with their brand or tag.

A survey conducted by PricewaterhouseCoopers in Russia in 2005, forecasts a 30 to 50 per cent growth per year for the private banking industry. The survey estimates the current number of private banking accounts at not more than 10,000 and the value of privately managed funds at around $12 billion. The market is highly segmented and competition is far from fierce. The survey further reveals the trend towards higher minimum thresholds for wealth management, with an anticipated 10 per cent rise in income from new clients.

Products and Services

Private banking products and services can be broadly grouped under three categories:

- Basic banking products and services that include deposits and cash accounts, money market instruments, lending products and foreign exchange, payment and custody services.

- Private banking products and services include investment research and portfolio advisory services, in-house mutual funds and brokerage services.

- Wealth Management products and services include structured products, hedge funds, retirement planning, family office, estate planning, trust and fiduciary services.

Private banking service providers are focusing on redefining their product offerings to fight commoditization and differentiating their product lines by tailoring them to provide holistic solutions to suit client needs, sometimes even from a multi-generational perspective. Most private banking services focus on the following five key areas:

- *Asset Management* – Designing client specific asset allocation and investment strategies in line with clients' objectives and risk preferences.

- *Debt Management* – Structured payments, arranging for security lending, handling trust administration in line with the financial goals of the clients.

- *Tax Planning* – Devising appropriate strategies for tax planning, retirement planning that accommodates the clients' style and standard of living, succession planning for the clients' business, estate planning and transfer of wealth to the successive generations, and even includes hiring professional help to achieve the above.

- *Risk Management* – Protecting clients' wealth and net worth by planning for comprehensive risk coverage through insurance products and also through a structured portfolio of assets that exhibit the clients' risk preferences, guiding the heirs to takeover the family business, etc.

- *Philanthropy Planning* – Drawing up plans for the clients' charitable activities, taking into account the tax implications and vehicles for implementing them in accordance with the clients' priorities.

Strategies of Key Players

Most of the key players in the market focus on improving service through innovative solutions and building stronger relationships with their clients, as revealed by the 2005 Survey of the European Wealth and Private Banking Industry by IBM Business Consulting Services. The survey findings pointed to the need for stronger customer insights, a more pro-active role in portfolio management, seeking clients' feedback through surveys and inviting clients to events to stimulate their interest. In order to maintain profitability and sustain their fee-based incomes, the banks must involve their product specialists and senior management in blending innovative and high value into holistic solutions tailored to the clients' business and personal requirements. Banks also need to be open to a more flexible arrangement that provides for partnered solutions. The key would be to invest in the long-term value of the client-base and promote a culture of customer advocacy that maximizes customer trust. A classic illustration in this context would be that of the USAA Insurance, which was adjudged the best company for customer advocacy by Forrester Research. USAA Insurance took the opportunity to win over the trust of its credit card customers by dropping interest rates on credit card dues, waiving late fees, deferring payments and offering unsecured loans to victims of the Florida hurricane in 2005.

Pampering the Plutocrats

Private banking service is all about building deep relationships and bonding with the client, often extending beyond the financial advisory role. It calls for addressing the financial and human needs of the client. Private bankers provide solutions ranging from investment guidance, tax planning, estate planning, philanthropy advice and help in establishing charitable foundations. As service providers, they pamper their rich clients through gestures, subtle and vivid – by calling on them at their convenience, asking the right questions about the client's family, sending flowers and sweets to wish the client on birthdays and anniversaries, sending the front row tickets for the client's favorite music concert, providing unusual services that may even go to the extent of helping in finding a suitable match for the client's daughter, or choosing the right architect to build the client's dream home. As relationship managers, their bonding with the clients becomes close-knit and they often grow to be one among the family and a trusted confidante. Private banking grows roots into successive generations fostering relationships with family and not just individual clients. Citigroup Private Bank and UBS organize training sessions in wealth management for their clients' heirs to help with succession planning of family business. UBS even offers tips and advice on the art market to its wealthy clients.

Challenges for Private Banking

A survey of 34,000 Americans under the name "A Penny Saved", in 1995 revealed a low degree of sophistication about money among the respondents, wherein 77 per cent had no knowledge of their father's earnings during their childhood; 70 per cent had no idea of their parents' rent or mortgage; 77 percent had no clue of the family insurance details. But this is no longer true of the new generation individuals. They are more sensitized about money matters and are very sophisticated, demanding a multitude of products and alternative investment propositions. In this context, the private banks face a multitude of challenges such as knowing the client, client acquisition and retention amidst competition, issues related to open architecture, shortage of skills, a changing tax and regulatory regime. Figure 1 below depicts the key challenges identified by the participants in the European Wealth and Private Banking Industry Survey 2005.

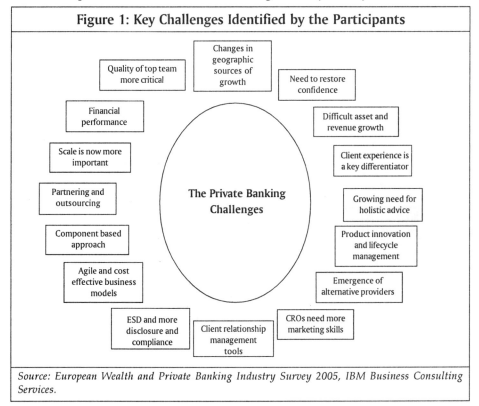

Figure 1: Key Challenges Identified by the Participants

Source: European Wealth and Private Banking Industry Survey 2005, IBM Business Consulting Services.

Differentiation – The Holy Grail for Wealth Managers

The increasing sophistication of the clients and the growing competition presses private banking players to differentiate their product line with value added propositions. Banks are battling to maximize the share of wallet from existing clients as well as winning over clients from their competitors. While winning over new clients ranks as the top strategic priority with CEOs, retaining existing clients is the second most pressing issue. Survey reports point out personal relationships and quality of staff to be the key differentiators of the various banks. Providing holistic wealth management solutions and investment performance are also seen as significant differentiators. Investment in training relationship managers and brand building are seen as essential strategies for customer acquisition and retention. Banks need to focus on appropriate strategies to target each segment of the customer band ranging from the 'affluent' ($100000 to $500000) to the 'ultra high net worth' (>$50 million). The Global Private Banking/Wealth Management Survey 2005 by PricewaterhouseCoopers findings in respect of the assets under management for the various client bands are illustrated in Figure 2.

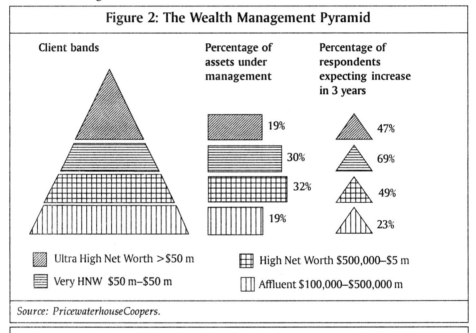

Figure 2: The Wealth Management Pyramid

Client bands	Percentage of assets under management	Percentage of respondents expecting increase in 3 years
	19%	47%
	30%	69%
	32%	49%
	19%	23%

Ultra High Net Worth >$50 m   High Net Worth $500,000–$5 m

Very HNW $50 m–$50 m   Affluent $100,000–$500,000 m

Source: PricewaterhouseCoopers.

"Experience Immersion" – A New Initiative at Credit Suisse

David McQuillen, Vice President, Customer Experience initiated an "experience immersion" process at Credit Suisse which enabled the bank to think differently about its clients. As part of the exercise he urged customer executives to take up visits to local branches, talk to customers and find out their requirements. During the two-hour branch visits, the executives are taught to watch customers, complete customer tasks like filling out forms, visiting the bank's website or participating in actual transactions playing the role of the customer and finally getting the customer's feedback through face to face interactions. The exercise resulted in bringing about

Contd...

Contd...

minor changes or improvements that went a long way in creating an impression amongst customers.

Taking into consideration the fact that the average Credit Suisse private banking client was 67 years old, David McQuillen emphasized that the bank be more empathetic to customers with disabilities. He organized an event for the bank's senior managers wherein he arranged for small exercises such as making them spend time in a wheelchair and eat lunch in the dark to give them a first-hand experience of the clients' state. Such efforts had a direct impact on both the service providers and the customers. The immersion process soon attracted the attention of other players like ABN Amro, Capital One, Safeco, and Telecom New Zealand, who were interested in trying it out themselves. To quote the COO of Credit Suisse's private-banking unit, Christoph Brunner, "in some cases, we actually make it hard for customers to do business with us. [I saw] that little things make a big difference. For example, just having signage that people understand. Having friendly and helpful employees. As a bank, we often think that only the financial products themselves matter—but there is so much more that goes around that."

Source: www.fastcompany.com

Future of Private Banking

The private banking industry has undergone comprehensive change in an evolving global environment. It has to shed the hood of secrecy in the wake of organized crime and is under pressure to comply with anti-money laundering laws and transparency regulations. There is an increasing shift towards onshore locations. Therefore, only those players who possess the ability to leverage global scale and reach will sustain. As the industry heats up with growing competition, the demand for greater flexibility and customized services becomes a key determinant of the banks' growth strategies. The private banks that endeavor to think out of the box and adapt their services to fit the evolving needs of the clients will have the edge over their competitors. The ultimate winner is the customer who is assured of the best value for his money. As Andrew Carnegie says, "And while the law [of competition] may be sometimes hard for the individual, it is best for the race, because it ensures the survival of the fittest in every department."

(Sujatha B is Consulting Editor at IBS Research Center, Chennai. She can be reached at suja1209@gmail.com).

References

1. Considerable Growth Forecasted for Russia's Private Banking Sector, *http://www.pwc.com*

2. Don Peppers, Martha Rogers, Tying trust to customer value, *http://searchcrm.techtarget.com*

3. European Wealth and Private Banking Industry Survey 2005, IBM Business Consulting Services.

4. Friend, confidante – and private banker, *http://www.business-standard.com/special/bankannual/2003/private.htm*

5. Global Private Banking/Wealth Management Survey 2005, PricewaterhouseCoopers.

6. *http://pacific.bizjournals.com*

7. *http://www.cio.com*

8. Hungry for more? Global Update 2005, KPMG.

9. Ian Wylie, Talk to Our Customers? Are You Crazy?, *http://www.fastcompany.com/magazine/107/business-at-its-best.html*

10. Lachlan Colquhoun, The rise and rise of competition and 'co-opetition' in private banking, *Financial Times*, Oct 30, 2006.

11. Neel Chowdhury, Bespoke Banking, Aug 21, 2006, *www.time.com*

12. Neel Chowdhury, How to clone Switzerland, Aug 21, 2006, *www.time.com*

13. Private Banking in Singapore – A new treasure island, *The Economist*, Aug 17, 2006

14. World Wealth Report 2006, *www.us.capgemini.com*

2

Banking on the Rich

Raghu Mohan

Wealth Management and Private banking business are growing by leaps and bounds in India. IBM's survey says that they will grow by 25 to 100% over the next two years. Foreign banks like Citibank are leveraging their international expertise and gaining business. They are providing a wide array of products to the customers based on their needs and requirements. ICICI Bank and HDFC Bank are the major Indian players in this business. Goldman Sachs says that India will be the third largest economy in the next 30 years. So, there is immense scope for Indian banks to enrich their bottom line through wealth management services.

If you thought making money is tough, there is a lot in the banking industry that finds managing it tougher. Their reasons range from being too busy making money, to having no time to manage it; sometimes the sums involved are so large that they anyhow require professional help, they say. Whatever be the case, the good news is that help is on hand. Enter wealth management and private banking, which are fast emerging as lucrative business propositions. And in recent times, financial intermediaries like banks, asset management companies and broking firms have jumped onto the bandwagon.

Source: Business India, November 8-21, 2004. © Business India. Reprinted with permission.

IBM consulting services' second edition of *Indian Wealth Management and Private Banking Survey 2003-4* forecast that growth rates for local wealth managers estimated at between 25 and 100% over the next two years, still holds good. That the industry is growing in terms of number of players as well as number of high networth individuals; and the number of respondents or practitioners of the art stood at 19. Notes Ravi Trivedy, partner (financial services, strategy and technology consulting), IBM Business consulting services: "There has been significant growth in incomes and wealth levels over the past few years. Financial services industry players have begun to recognize the potential of wealth management as a profitable business." The industry, though at a nascent phase, is experiencing rapid growth in terms of the number of providers, clients and assets under management. IBM had acquired the member firms of PricewaterhouseCoopers in October 2002. Why? To service customers in the financial services industry: Wealth management and private banking in particular.

Others like Deutsche Bank's head for private wealth management Nikhil Kapadia point to The Merrill Lynch and Capgemini Ernst & Young Survey on wealthy individuals in India which states that there are approximately 60,000 people who have financial assets of a minimum of Rs.4.5 cr or about a million dollars. The survey further states that this segment is one of the fastest growing in Asia on a relative basis. The National Council for Applied Economic Research says that there are 24,000 households with annual incomes of Rs.50 lakh in

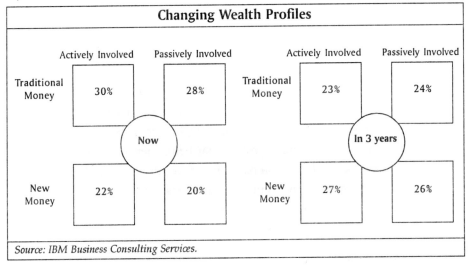

India. And even as numbers of the wealthy swell, changes in the macroenvironment are also influencing the way clients look at managing their wealth.

Says Kapadia: "The market segmentation includes 'old wealth' (inheritance) and 'new wealth' (creators). The 'new wealth' is the driving force. The changed composition of the GDP where services now account for nearly 50% demonstrates the impact of the new wealth being created. Some examples of new wealth creators are stock options enjoyed by Indian professionals in multinationals, stake sellouts by business process outsourcing ventures, and initial listings by companies like Biocon, NDTV or Bharti Televentures".

At Citibank it is understood that easy and passive options like deposits are no longer attractive given the low interest rates. That clients need to invest in options that give them higher yields, and these come with higher levels of risk. This is where the need for professional wealth managers becomes more pronounced. With the rising number of investment opportunities, increased number of market players, and more evolved products, the advantage is well set to move in favor of professional wealth management markets as trends have been in the more financially-developed countries.

Yet another factor driving private banking is the changing nature of financial intermediation itself. Explains ICICI Bank's head of private banking Arpit Agarwal: "The banking model itself is undergoing a change with importance accorded to

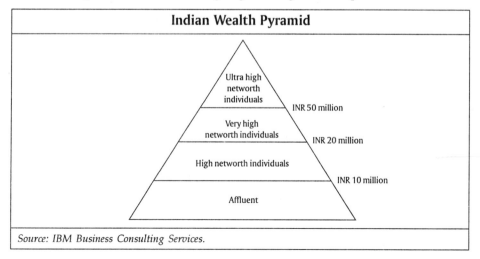

Indian Wealth Pyramid

Ultra high networth individuals — INR 50 million

Very high networth individuals — INR 20 million

High networth individuals — INR 10 million

Affluent

Source: *IBM Business Consulting Services.*

banking relationships, which is enabling cross-selling. Financial deregulation and global linkages are supplementing wealth creation, prompted by emergence of globally competitive industrial sectors like software, pharmaceutical and automobile sectors. An expanding middle class and relatively young population unlike say Japan, France, or the United States where a dominant old population is constraining public finances are generating demand-led growth. Lifestyles have also undergone change, with the demand for quality investment advisory on the rise as investment climate turned volatile with the September 11, World Trade Center attacks which was followed by a weakening dollar. This is one of the fastest growing businesses in India with several organizations experiencing 30 to 50% growth rates."

As in the case of any emerging business line with wallet-share being the name of the game, harping on the potential has also led to confusion by those offering such services. The media too has played a role in this. Priority and preferred banking are being positioned as private banking by most banks. Essentially, these banks have relationship managers who offer a customized service. They will deliver cash to the customers' doorstep, pre-approve a credit card or a loan up to a specified amount; sell a mutual fund or an insurance cover. All of this is available at a market segmentation of Rs.25 lakh. If you have a deposit that ranges upwards of Rs.25 lakh, in most cases you qualify to have a relationship manager at these banks who give you priority or preferred services, and hence, the nuance of private banking.

Then again, wealth management and private banking is used synonymously. Agarwal explains that globally, wealth management, which relates to investment planning by and large, is interchangeably used to represent private banking. Along with a whole lot of banking convenience, the private banking model normally covers wealth management, tax advisory, trust services, estate planning and host of other services. Dedicated and skilled relationship managers backed up by research, reliability, dependability, trust, reach, regulatory compliance and continuity in business are its hallmarks. The presence of a banker enhances credibility and lasting partnership. In matured markets, capital account convertibility and developed nature of various market segments have resulted in various product offerings, both domestic and sourced from overseas.

In India, private banking is mostly viewed from two completely different angles: Banks are viewed as superior banking services, and brokers and/or investment bankers are viewed as capital market experts. Most banks are trying to develop expertise in capital market advisory, and brokers are getting into strategic tie-ups with banks to complete the range of products and services. In India, banks are only allowed to undertake advisory services on a non-discretionary basis.

A Holistic Approach

So at one end of the spectrum—not indicative of quality or capability—there is HDFC Bank or ICICI Bank, and at the other, a Deutsche Bank or Citibank which has segmented the market at a much higher level. The latter's market segment doesn't want credit cards, loans, or cash delivered as "core offerings". They want wealth management centered around mitigating risk, asset allocation, capital preservation, and succession planning. In other words a more holistic approach to the wealth that they might have created or inherited. At Deutsche Bank for instance, the minimum cut-off levels are upwards of Rs.1 cr to start such a relationship and moves towards a minimum relationship size of Rs.5 cr.

In more mature markets, a wider product suite is offered and the levels of sophistication in both private bankers and customers, in terms of knowledge and skill sets, is higher. Additionally, entry norms are stringent. Service providers need to have a brand, minimum capitalization, or full service capability. In India the market is still evolving. Products are limited, and this has resulted in commoditization and the entry barriers are not as daunting as in overseas markets.

The need is now not just to have products, but to offer innovative solutions created with the clients' needs in mind. Says a Citibank official, "In a solution like CitiGold Wealth Management, the dedicated wealth managers step in to satisfy this need by following a disciplined and scientific financial planning process. The wealth manager first profiles the customer to understand his financial status, risk profile, needs and long-term goals based on which asset allocation is formulated."

And these products could range from capital guaranteed products (bonds and term deposits) to market-linked products (MFS, insurance and asset products like loans against MFS, mortgages). Furthermore, these customers are exposed to global products and privileges, and expect the same back home as well. Therefore, service providers are leveraging on their global expertise and presence outside India to offer similar products and service experiences to these select customers. The recent Reserve Bank of India (RBI) ruling allowing Indians to invest up to $25,000 overseas brought forth one such opportunity for the service providers. Citibank was the first to make this available to its customers through the "Global deposit" product, within hours of the RBI ruling, through Citibank Singapore.

In addition to products, such high net-worth customers also appreciate a range of advisory services, which the financial services corporation or bank can offer on a self or referral basis with experts in that field. Citibank, for instance offers real estate, tax- and art-advisory services to its CitiGold wealth management clients through such a referral arrangement. Apart from products and services, exclusive benefits which befit the special status of the client are offered to the customers to give a differentiated experience.

In the case of ICICI Bank, private banking services is only an extension of its already existing products and services to its high-end client base, ICICI Bank, apart from its corporate and retail banking outfits that cater to all kinds of banking relationships, uses its trading platform *ICICI Direct.com* for online equity and debt investments, its own broking subsidiary, a presence in both life and non-life insurance and asset management through group companies. The bank claims that its advanced technology platforms, branch and ATM infrastructure, phone banking and web-based delivery channels makes it a preferred option for Private Banking clients. Incidentally, the private banking business at ICICI Bank has three levels: Rs.5 lakhs, Rs.25 lakhs and Rs.50 lakhs, and offers various products and services to its private banking clients.

It is pointed out that new money clients are largely from the IT and IT-enabled services industry. This category typically includes professionals and entrepreneurs who are time-constrained and need a wealth manager to proactively manage the same. At the same time, the trick for the private banker is to get a larger share of the wallet. Says Trivedy: "What we have learnt is that most clients allocate between 41-60% of their investible wealth. This figure is an estimate, as it is difficult to know the customer's total wealth given the reluctance to disclose a full portfolio."

Rise in Client Awareness

But there is no denying that despite this reluctance, client awareness is on the rise. Explains Kapadia: "People have lost money in periodic boom and bust cycles. Experience is driving people to be more cautious and demanding. Also with the advent of business channels on TV and the media in general where several frontline business papers and magazines cover investment and feature wealth management articles, exposure has been magnified several times over in the last few years. Additionally, Indians are travelling abroad and the exposure gained from such travel through the foreign media has aided the development of knowledge. The presence of a number of foreign-owned investment firms in India where investment information is available has also contributed".

Seconds Agarwal: "Greater media coverage of financial markets, global exposure of clients, increasing levels of education with each new generation, financial education programs conducted by organizations and the basic drive of clients for making informed investment decisions and actively participating in decision-making are major driving factors for the ever-increasing sophistication of client behavior".

The local private banking business is in its very early stages of development and many players have not even completed five years in this area. The ones that have been around for many years have only a handful of relationship managers. Good private bankers are people who have dealt with a large number of clients across various market conditions and asset classes. As the majority of players are relatively new, old and experienced private banking manpower is in short supply and poaching is a common practice for hiring. "A good private banker can be compared to an experienced doctor, who after handling hundreds of operations develops credibility," says Agarwal.

The industry, sources say, has great potential given that the local economy is expected to be third largest after China and the United States in the next 30 years, as forecast by Goldman Sachs. Says Trivedy: "With rising incomes and the growth in the number of entrepreneurs, there will be a growth in wealth... wealth managers who have the reach and the ability will reap significant gains."

Agarwal at ICICI Bank observes that openarchitecture, which allows for providing unbiased advisory services to clients so that clients have access to many choices, is the recommended way going forward. What is being nuanced here is that most wealth managers are moving beyond proprietary products. And that means servicing with third-party products. It is in the interest of the client as they have access to many product manufacturers under one umbrella and is like going to a supermarket. The credibility of the player would be determined by the choice of products that they choose to display and the due diligence and service levels they maintain in selecting them. "Art-advisory and similar services would be only effective if they are to have a matured and transparent market and are scaleable in nature. Offering niche products may give a short-term advantage in terms of product differentiation, but the real challenge lies in providing every product displayed to all clients on a scaleable and sustainable basis," he says.

One fallout though will be that run-off-the-mill retail banking will also stand to benefit. "Traditionally retail and private banking have been looked as a fast food joint vs. an exclusive restaurant. With innovations in technology, introduction of self-service channels and the ongoing elevation of service standards, this boundary is no longer so distinct. A good private banking service can only happen if the organization genuinely believes that all client service standards should be of the highest quality," concludes Agarwal.

We Consider Ourselves as an Investment Bank for Individuals

– Nilanjan Dey

India is becoming an increasingly attractive market for many industries – wealth management is no exception.

The time for private wealth management has arrived, feels Mr Sandeep Sharma, Head, SG Private Banking India. The latter, part of French financial services group Societe-Generale, is in the country since last December.

"The promising wealth management market here is a reflection of India's exceptional economic performance", he states.

Excerpts

What are the emerging trends in wealth management in India?

Real estate and private equity are increasingly becoming important asset classes for high net worth individuals (HNIs). The demand for realty is on a high growth path on account of the burgeoning economy. The real estate market, growing at about 30 per cent annually, is projected to touch $50 billion by 2008.

While a few realty funds have been launched, we believe retail investors have been left out as only HNIs and institutional players have the capacity to participate in these.

However, equity participation will be ensured by the introduction of real estate mutual funds, which are fairly common in developed countries.

How is the private equity scenario developing?

Alternative investments including private equity allow HNIs to broadbase their portfolios. Though at a nascent stage, private equity in India is on the rise because of maturing financial sophistication. Secondary research highlights that in the developed markets, there is a growing conviction among HNIs that investments in fundamentally strong businesses are a very dependable wealth management strategy.

Is the client base expanding? Is it becoming more expensive for people to mandate a private wealth manager?

India is becoming an increasingly attractive market for many industries – wealth management is no exception. There is a promising onshore wealth management services sector here.

Driving the development has been the country's exceptional economic performance over the last decade. The booming economy has led to innumerable opportunities and pushed individual wealth growth.

According to one estimate, India has seen about 19 per cent growth in HNI population in 2005 *vis-à-vis* the world growth rate of 6.5 per cent. The fee structure here is yet to be developed and is currently accrued from brokerage fees and commissions on the services rendered.

What is SG Private Banking India's strategy?

We consider ourselves as an investment bank for individuals. There are a large number of affluent individuals who are not being served by competitors. They present our pool of potential clients. Our growth pattern reflects SG's global development of private banking, in which Asia Pacific plays a key role. We have offices in New Delhi and Mumbai. Besides, there is a comprehensive IT operation in Bangalore.

How can a wealth manager create a difference in prevailing market conditions?

Wealth management is a highly specialised service, covering all asset classes. Asset allocation helps determine an optimal mix of asset classes, ranging from equity, debt and real estate to

Contd...

Contd...

alternatives. The latter may include 'investments of passion' – even fine art and collectables – as well as structured products and hedge funds. Clients' life goals, time horizon and risk tolerance are three vital factors on this front.

How Can Technology Help?

There is a need for systems, which can provide a single view of a customer's entire portfolio with the wealth management services provider. There is a need for online financial planning tools. Clients are eager to be in control of their portfolios and are often active in selecting products in line with their asset allocation strategy. Overall, technology is beginning to play a more critical role.

Source: www.thehindubusinessline.com © The Hindu Business Line. Reprinted with permission.

3

Private Banking in India: Millionaires Calling

Amit Singh Sisodiya and Sanjoy De

A sharp spurt in the number of millionaires is transforming India into a private banking hotspot.

Private banking unlike retail banking is the means of managing private clients' money by providing various services like efficient wealth management, savings, inheritance and tax planning. These banks promise to maximize returns and minimize risk along with the tax burden of the clients through careful allocation of their money.

As the private wealth around the world is surging up and the number of High Net worth Individuals (HNIs) is escalating, private banking and wealth management services are gathering momentum. In fact, it is now the fastest growing area among all financial services. This niche service sector has tremendous growth potential and is increasingly alluring the private banking majors and wealth managers internationally who are uninhibitedly venturing into this promising segment.

The reason behind the present euphoria over private banking is the increase in the number of super rich, globally; especially in the Asia-Pacific region.

Source: Chartered Financial Analyst, October 2006. © *The Icfai University Press. All rights reserved.*

According to the World Health Report published by Capgemini, a global consultancy firm, and Merrill Lynch, a bank, the number of HNIs (with assets greater than $1 mn) has increased by more than 20% in the past five years and by more than 90% in the past decade. Interestingly, in terms of HNI gains, the emerging market economies like India, China and the Middle East have outperformed their more mature western counterparts. In fact, the number of Asians who reached the status of HNIs hit 2.4 million last year, up 7.3% from 2004. This figure is close to Europe's 2.8 million where the growth rate was 4.5% in the year 2005 as compared with 2004. According to the report, South Korea's high net worth population increased the most, by 21.3%, during the same period, while India registered a growth of 19.3%. Russia, South Africa, Taiwan, Hong Kong and Indonesia posted the next biggest hikes in HNI numbers. However, in the US, the growth rate plummeted to 6.8% in 2005 from 9.9% of the previous year. Banking analysts estimate that China and India will drive the growth in the private banking industry at least for the next five years. On the other side, the falling rate of the US HNIs can be attributed to their domestic investment bias. On the contrary, a continuing shift to international holdings in Asia-Pacific (including India and China) and the Middle East is largely responsible in fueling the growth of the assets of the world's wealthy to $33.3 tn.

Enter the Millionaire Club

In India, dollar millionaires' club is growing faster than most of the other economies. According to the World Wealth Report, the number of HNIs in India reached 83,500 in 2005 as compared to 70,000 in 2004. The number of HNIs grew by 19.3% in 2005 with individuals having financial assets of Rs.4.5 cr. Indeed, private wealth in India has never been so great and this combined with an investment astute population is giving a tremendous fillip to the private banking and wealth management industry. According to the global consultancy firm KPMG, India's economy is growing at 8% per annum through a transformation to the next level of maturity. This enables double digit returns on most asset classes, which is not the case in a majority of other countries, thereby making India a preferred private banking destination. The robust and liquid financial market in India is really conducive to wealth management. Moreover, the emerging trend of high savings rate due to high earning levels augurs well for private banking industry.

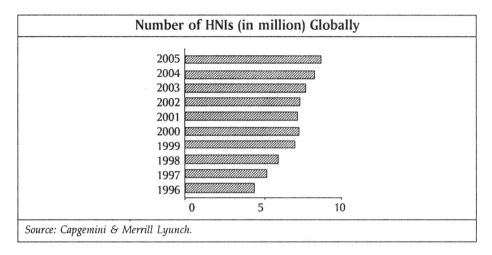

Source: Capgemini & Merrill Lyunch.

In India, the private banking and wealth management sector is indeed getting hot. Some of the major international private bankers operating in India are Citibank, UBS, HSBC, Deutsche Bank, ABN Amro and Merrill Lynch, to name a few. These banks have not however made significant strides into the market so far, but are now planning to enter the entire wealth management chain, and are eager to offer niche services like financial planning, wealth protection, estate planning and even family office management. UBS, the largest private bank in the world, has a significant presence in the Asia-Pacific region with full service branches in Hong Kong, Singapore and Taiwan. But it has not been able to make strides into the Indian market significantly.

DSP Merrill Lynch, a leading global investment bank that caters to selective HNIs, has a client base of 450 Indian families, which is an increase of 50% over last year. ABN Amro, the Netherlands-based bank, had about 500 client groups in 2000 and plans to target 3000-4000 client groups every five years. For designing the financial plans of the clients, ABN Amro initiated a model which entails tax implications and risk-return profile so that the clients get optimum return on assets. Realizing the potential in this segment, HSBC too has thrown its hat into the ring and started its private banking operations in India in May 2005. HSBC *Premier,* which caters to the need of people with a deposit of more than 25 lakhs, offers a range of benefits which combines global expertise with local understanding. HSBC *Premier* relationship managers are accessible 24/7 to assist the clients in managing their wealth, taking into consideration the current needs, risk profile and future financial goals of their esteemed clients.

A helpline has been set up by Citibank that extends support services which include home maintenance, purchase of movie, train or air tickets. According to BNP Paribas sources, "We offer all solutions from cradle to grave like banking, investment, tax management, legal solutions and transmission of wealth to the next generation." In fact, BNP Paribas is the first private bank which is planning to offer trust services for those who inherit wealth; an idea that is yet to catch on in India. Sensing the immense potential of this sector, indigenous private firms are also pretty eager to enter this arena. Presently, there is only one indigenous private firm operating in India—the Delhi-based Pioneer Client Associates, which is offering services to HNIs and ultra-wealthy families. This four-year-old firm, which started with only six families, now has a client base of 160 each with average balance sheet size of $2.5 mn. While the foreign banks and firms like Pioneer Client Associates are providing services to the cream of the Indian community, a few of the new generation private banks like ICICI and HDFC too have entered the field of wealth management. However, these retail banking giants are trying to adopt a different type of model. According to HDFC, "We do not go by the deposit size of the customer and accept deposits as low as Rs.10,000. We need to be flexible, as the Indian market is different from international markets and wealth management is still evolving here." But, the public sector banks are still shaky and staying away from this market.

Customization is the Key

Growing client sophistication and fierce competition for client business will require wealth managers to deploy sector-specific customer satisfaction and retention strategies. Only those wealth managers, who can develop an indepth understanding of their customers, will be better-positioned to retain and enlarge business by deploying specific strategies for marketing, pricing and servicing. So the wealth managers have to consider non-financial criteria for categorizing the customer according to behavioral and psychometric considerations. To meet the increasingly sophisticated demands of clients, the wealth managers need to provide efficient and niche services. To keep up the standard, modern and up-to-date training to the wealth and relationship managers encompassing the areas of marketing, relationship management, regulation, compliance and product knowledge will become *sine qua non*. Presently, in India the banks are less interested to train their advisors on market and economic trends. In most of the cases, only the newspapers and industry newsletters are the only sources available to the advisors to enhance their skills. Imparting regular updates on the market trends in the form of internal newsletters or intranet helps advisors a lot in analyzing the current state before counseling their clients. Moreover, only a handful of banks have the so-called product specialist to guide their wealth managers and clients. This product specialist can play an important role by guiding both the internal advisors and clients in identifying market trends and opportunities well in advance.

These emerging "newly rich" individuals lack the time to manage their serious money and will increasingly delegate it to professional wealth managers. According to the IBM Business Consulting Services report, the "new money" and the affluent sections will experience the highest growth. These new customers are time constrained, technology-savvy and will be the major users of wealth management services. Only those wealth managers who are geared to service this segment in terms of reach, technology, products and efficient staff will reap significant market share and profitability.

In fact, sophisticated financial products and services are no longer viewed as value proposition by this ultra-rich class, as these similar products with little variation are available from almost all the players in the market. To differentiate it from others, products and services should incorporate personal touch and technological finesse.

Rising customer demand coupled with increased competition among wealth managers will result in the introduction of more sophisticated products and services ranging from gold, real estate, commodities, art, hedge funds, insurance and pension. In this backdrop, for mere survival, the wealth managers will need to innovate and offer appropriate products and services to meet the needs of the wealthy in times of economic boom as well as depression.

As far as the level of sophistication and quality of services are concerned, Indian wealth managers are not at par with their developed counterparts. In fact, the wealth management market here is still evolving; and given the fact that the penetration level of wealth management services in India is only 10% when compared to, say, Europe where it is around 60-90%, we can safely say that the prospects for private banking in India are nothing but bright.

(Amit Singh Sisodiya is Deputy Editor, the Icfai University Press, Hyderabad,

Sanjoy De is Research Associate, the Icfai University Press, Hyderabad.)

Desi Millionaires: 83,500 and Rising

India's dollar millionaires' club is growing faster than most other economies. The number of HNIs grew by 19.3% in '05, the second best performance after Korea's 21.3% – though Korea is growing on a lower base. The number of dollar millionaires – individuals with financial assets of Rs.4.5 crore and above – in India now stands at 83,500 as compared to 70,000 in '04, according to the World Wealth Report from Capgemini and Merrill Lynch.

- No. of millionaires in India up by 19.3%, second only to S Korea
- India had 83,500 millionaires in '05, up from 70,000 in '04
- US has maximum millionaires – 2.67 million
- 1 in every 100 Americans is a millionaire, compared to 1 in 13,000 Indians

While high net-worth individuals (HNIs) are on the rise across the world, Asia-Pacific is the only region where they generated a larger amount of cash through investing. The rational behind a faster growth in wealth creation was a faster growth in real GDP and market capitalizations in the Asia-Pacific region.

The report states that over the previous decade, financial wealth among HNIs had grown from $16.6 trillion to $33.3 trillion. Currently, the number of HNIs across the world is nearly 9 million, compared to 4.5 million in 1996, growing at 8% CAGR (see table). These financial gains were particularly strong in Latin America, Eastern Europe, Asia-Pacific, Africa and the Middle East, where emerging markets continue to play a moderate game of "catch up" with major markets.

The number of ultra HNIs too is on the rise. Ultra HNIs are defined as individuals with financial assets of $30m plus (Rs.135 crore plus). The total number of these ultra HNWIs now stands at 85,400, a 10.2% increase in '05, compared to an 8.9% increase in '04. According to the report, these gains show that while market returns and economic indicators signaled that a deceleration was under way in many regions of the world, HNIs were still able to find select pockets of high performance in '05.

The rise in millionaires has given a fillip to the private banking business in India. Currently, only a handful of entities cater to the high-end of private banking in India. These are ABN Amro, BNP Paribas, Deutsche Bank, DSP Merrill Lynch, SocGen. Others like UBS, Credit Suisse are also looking at launching their private banking in India.

ABN Amro Bank executive vice-president and head of private clients (Asia), Barend Janssens, said, "We foresee an expansion in the need for wealth management services in India due to deregulation of markets and our target base in India includes diamond merchants, large corporates and small and medium enterprises."

One area where HNIs found significant opportunity was in the Asia-Pacific region, where the twin drivers of market capitalisation and GDP continued to deliver high rates of growth.

Latin America and the Middle East also exhibited strong growth, which benefited HNIs investing domestically and from other parts of the world. Alert to cooling real estate and capital markets, HNIs continued to reassess their market opportunities and investment strategies. Generally speaking, HNIs remained guarded with respect to real estate and mature markets, however, their portfolio balancing act varied from region to region.

4

India Beyond Outsourcing: The Opportunities for International Banks

Janmejaya Sinha, Christian de Juniac and Saurabh Tripathi

India is the most important emerging market for some foreign institutions like Citibank and Standard Chartered Bank providing higher returns than their home countries. Foreign banks that have entered India more recently have focused on such niche segments such as wholesale, investment, and private banking—and have done so profitably. India is widely expected to become the third-largest economy in the world by 2035, behind China and the United States.

India's banking market is one of the fastest growing in the world. The reasons are numerous: a burgeoning national economy, financial-sector reforms, foreign investment that has risen in step with an easing regulatory climate, and a highly favorable demographic profile, to name a few.

Some leading international banks have already demonstrated that it is possible to establish a presence in India and achieve profitable growth amid local competition. But India's potential is so vast that significant opportunity still awaits foreign banks that have not yet explored the country. It is an opportunity that few can afford to ignore.

Fueling India's banking growth is greater than $600 billion economy that is expanding at about six percent per year, stimulating per capita incomes and consumption. Large numbers of households are shifting into the middle class, creating booming markets in housing, motor vehicles, televisions, computers, mobile phones, and other products—most of which require financing. Total banking assets have doubled over the past five years, and industry profits have tripled over the past three years. The current profit pool of about $4.8 billion could climb to $20 billion by 2010 and may reach $40 billion within a decade— resulting from a rapid expansion of revenue that will parallel that of the overall financial-services sector.

What is more, about 60 million new households should be added to India's bankable segment by 2009. And the country will likely have a surplus of 47 million people aged 15 to 59 by 2020—a time when most other large economies will face a shortage in this age bracket. Infrastructure gaps, although glaring in some areas, are improving, and a stable political-reform consensus bodes well for continued economic growth.

Of course, entering India's banking market is no small task. More than a few foreign institutions have tried to secure a foothold, found the going slippery, and departed with not much to show for their effort and investment. But the fact that success is attainable should make international banks take notice: India in the 21st century is about far more than outsourcing and offshoring. The 33 foreign banks currently doing business in India collectively earned more than $500 million in aftertax profits in 2004, with the three most established players accounting for most of that profit. For some foreign institutions—Citibank and Standard Chartered Bank, for example—India is the most important emerging market, providing even higher returns than their home countries.

Given India's potential over the next decade and beyond, it is imperative for international financial institutions to consider entering the country. Moreover, foreign banks already present in India should explore ways of expanding onshore in order to ride the growth in the domestic market. Naturally, part of any bank's debate about India should begin with an exploration of where the country's best opportunities currently lie.

Opportunity Knocks

Retail financial-services businesses—such as mortgages, personal loans, wealth management, and asset management—have enormous potential in India today, given their relatively low levels of penetration.

Retail lending, for example, at about $40 billion in 2004 and growing at roughly 30 percent per year, still represents only about 20 percent of industry advances and less than seven percent of GDP—a much lower percentage than in Thailand (18 percent), Malaysia (33 percent), and South Korea (55 percent). India's demographic profile makes it likely that this rate of growth will continue for the foreseeable future.

Consider India's mortgage business. Bolstered by low interest rates, mortgages currently account for half the retail asset market. And, there is significant room for further development, with volume rising possibly to $50 billion within the next few years. Or take the wealth management sector. India is among the top six Asian countries in terms of net investable assets (NIA). According to various estimates, there are around 400,000 Indian households with NIA above $250,000, 150,000 households with NIA above $500,000, and more than 60,000 households with NIA above $1 million.

In the broader asset-management arena, the roughly $35 billion in assets being professionally managed in India is quite low, representing just under six percent of GDP. Nonetheless, the value of assets managed by private and foreign-owned players (which now account for more than 75 percent of the market) has grown by 60 percent annually over the past five years. With more than $180 billion in long-term fixed deposits in banks and low penetration in the pension market, sustained growth is expected. What makes the opportunity especially attractive is that many private institutions above a certain critical mass are earning a return on equity of more than 30 percent.

India's billion-strong population, demographic profile, and rising degree of affluence also bode well for other retail products currently in their infancy, such as credit cards and life insurance. India's credit-card base has risen to about 10 million, for example, but only two players are earning appreciable returns.

Moreover, since the insurance sector opened up, growth in new premiums underwritten by private players has increased from $56 million in 2002 to $550 million in 2004. Yet, penetration still lags that of most emerging markets, and life insurance is just beginning to shed its image as solely a tax shelter. With a regulatory limit on foreign ownership of 26 percent, most domestic private-sector life insurers—amid explosive growth in the sector—involve alliances with international players such as Prudential UK, MetLife (UK), Bajaj Allianz, and Royal & SunAlliance Insurance.

The Peculiarities of the Indian Market

India's growth story is unfolding across a business landscape that has more than a few special features, which international banks should be aware of.

The first concerns the overall structure of India's financial-services industry. Long-entrenched state-owned institutions are the incumbents, dominating business within most segments. (See Figure 1) But these institutions are deeply constrained in their autonomy and in their ability to adhere to a market-based human-resources strategy. Moreover, in the short to medium term, they are not likely to be available for acquisition.

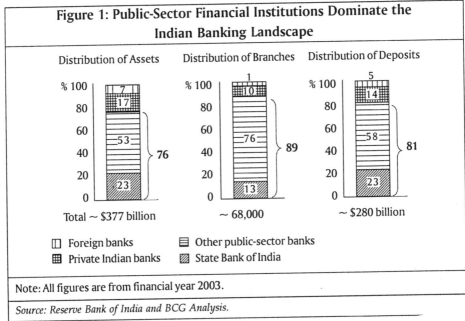

Figure 1: Public-Sector Financial Institutions Dominate the Indian Banking Landscape

Distribution of Assets   Distribution of Branches   Distribution of Deposits

Total ~ $377 billion   ~ 68,000   ~ $280 billion

☐ Foreign banks   ☰ Other public-sector banks
⊞ Private Indian banks   ▨ State Bank of India

Note: All figures are from financial year 2003.

Source: Reserve Bank of India and BCG Analysis.

Second, the bulk of the Indian financial-services industry is concentrated in urban areas. Indeed, there are really two ways to look at the Indian market: inside metropolitan areas and outside their boundaries in rural regions. Most of the recent growth has come in urban areas, with the 20 largest cities currently accounting for 50 percent of the financial-services market. Similarly, 80 percent of housing loans originate in 20 percent of the country's urban residential districts. Markets outside metropolitan areas have not yet been fully explored.

Third, banks in India typically have a very high volume of small transactions, requiring an operating platform that can support very low breakeven levels. The global operating platforms of international banks appear to be disadvantaged compared with those of new private-sector players that have entered the market since 1994.

Fourth, India's information infrastructure is still evolving. Information capture, especially with respect to risk, is gradually getting more attention as banks embrace technology. For example, a credit bureau for retail businesses has just been set up. Yet banks have to use considerable finesse in working around the problems that still exist in this area.

Doing Things Right

It is critical to note that the twists and turns on the road to success in India—although tricky to navigate—have not prevented some international banks from proving that they can arrive in the country, set up shop, compete with local players, and be profitable. Consider two noteworthy early entrants to India: Citibank and Standard Chartered Bank. Their success at tapping the country's potential in the off-shoring and outsourcing arenas has overshadowed their remarkable achievements in the domestic banking market, where they have taken leadership positions in particular market segments.

Citibank has 35 branches in 25 cities across India and coverage of more than 50 cities through a distribution subsidiary. It is active in most retail, corporate, and investment banking services, and has turned a relatively modest investment in India into a $7 billion asset book and more than $200 million in aftertax profit in 2004. With an impressive return on assets (ROA) of more than 2.5 percent, India is clearly a key franchise of Citibank.

Initially, with a limited number of branches, Citibank focused on niche segments. Over time, it captured 35 to 40 percent of India's credit-card profit pool. It also went after select small-to-medium-enterprise clusters, retail assets, and investment services for retail customers. Citibank today is moving away from this niche strategy toward a more widespread, mass-market business model and has very ambitious growth aspirations. Elements of the institution's success have included its careful choice of profit pools to enter (and exit), innovation in product design and in the use of technology, and deft harnessing of India's managerial talent pool.

Standard Chartered Bank is the largest international bank in India today, with 76 branches and 158 ATMs in 26 cities. With an $8 billion asset book and ROA of more than two percent, India is Standard Chartered's third most profitable market, after Hong Kong and Singapore. An important element of Standard Chartered's success in India has been its highly successful acquisition of Grindlays Bank (from ANZ Bank) in 2001. The acquisition consolidated Standard Chartered's position, and its current premier status includes a strong presence in major cities and in nearly all product segments.

Foreign banks that have entered India more recently have focused on such niches as wholesale, investment, and private banking—and have done so profitably. Given the robust growth in India's financial-services industry, many of these institutions are now evaluating whether to venture into additional segments.

ICICI Bank, a top domestic private-sector bank, provides another example of how dramatic growth is possible in India. ICICI—using loan fairs, aggressive pricing, and direct sales for customer acquisition—has tripled its market share to more than 20 percent over the past four years and has secured its position as a leading mortgage lender. Indeed, with lower technology and factor costs, as well as lower profit aspirations, Indian private-sector banks have been able to take share away from both foreign and Indian public-sector banks. One element of their success has been their ability to structure their business models and operating platforms to suit the requirements of low breakeven levels in different products.

Seizing the Moment

International banks that have succeeded in India have a good deal in common, and institutions that aspire to enter the country can learn from their experiences. Most success stories indicate that potential entrants should

- evaluate profit pools to target where global presence, scale, and product expertise can provide competitive advantage over domestic players

- be flexible in striking a balance between localizing business models and operating platforms, and integrating them into global standards and platforms

- use Indian managerial talent—typically bright, highly educated, experienced in the local market, and widely available—to the fullest

- understand and inform the regulatory environment, and seize opportunities—both organic and inorganic—as they become available.

Ultimately, forward-thinking international financial institutions need to explore strategies for banking in India. The country may not be a solution to the short-term global banking problem of slow growth, but it can be a significant medium-term opportunity that is relatively easily accessible at a reasonable level of risk.

Banks can begin to evaluate the opportunity by asking themselves the following questions:

- Where are our current growth possibilities?

- What percentage of global incremental banking-revenue pools will originate in India in the short, medium, and long term?

- Which customer and product segments in India might be most attractive for our institution?

- What is our understanding of India's risks?

- Could the India opportunity be relevant for our bank?

- What are we risking by not evaluating the opportunity?

India is widely expected to become the third-largest economy in the world by 2035, behind China and the United States. Leading international banks will not be able to ignore it. Indeed, a stark choice may be looming: enter India now at relatively low cost, or enter later and pay heavily for the delay in terms of investment and lost opportunity.

(Janmejaya Sinha is a vice president and director and Saurabh Tripathi a manager in the Mumbai office of The Boston Consulting Group. Christian de Juniac is a senior vice president and director in the firm's London office. They could be reached at: sinha.janmejaya@bcg.com, tripathi.saurabh@bcg.com and de.juniac.christian@bcg.com respectively.)

5

Wealth Management and Private Banking: Key Themes for Future

Anita Iyer

Wealth managers, who develop an in-depth understanding of their customers, will be well-positioned to retain and grow business by deploying distinct strategies for marketing, pricing and servicing.

In India, there has been a significant growth in income and wealth levels over the past few years. Financial services industry players have begun to recognize the potential of wealth management as a profitable business. The wealth management industry, though in a nascent stage, is experiencing rapid growth in terms of the number of providers, clients and assets under management. IBM Business Consulting Services undertook IBM's second Indian Wealth Management and Private Banking Survey in the period between November 2003 and February 2004. IBM is of the view that the wealth management industry is poised for tremendous growth in India. We have developed a few key themes that we believe will prevail in the future.

Source: Chartered Financial Analyst, October 2005. © The Icfai University Press. All rights reserved.

There will be further growth in the number and type of wealth management players in India

The wealth management industry in India will continue to grow rapidly in the next few years. We believe that more financial services players will enter this industry and provide distinct and structured services. Financial institutions are increasingly looking at private banking and wealth management to augment their revenues, for they are regarded as profitable, less risky and not overly competitive. In addition to banks, asset management companies and brokering houses, the other entrants into the wealth management arena include independent financial advisors and investment banks.

There will be a significant increase in the number of wealthy individuals in India

The Indian economy is projected to sustain its current growth and performance, resulting in an enhancement of incomes and wealth in the country. The BRIC (Brazil, Russia, India, and China) report, an economic research paper by Goldman Sachs, forecasts that India will be the third largest economy in the world, after China and the US in the next 30 years. With rising incomes and the growth in the number of entrepreneurs and professionals, the wealthy individuals segment will grow rapidly across the country. These 'newly rich' individuals lack the time to manage their money and will delegate it to professional wealth managers. In our view, the 'new money' and mass affluent segments will experience the highest growth. These customers are time constrained, technology-savvy and will be the major users of wealth management services. Wealth managers who are geared to service this segment in terms of reach, technology, products and knowledgeable staff, will reap significant gains in market share and profitability.

Increasing deregulation will enable customers to diversify their wealth locally and globally

Regulatory changes on the horizon include full capital account convertibility resulting in customers having wider choices for their investment, savings and protection needs. Successful wealth managers will be able to foresee and prepare for deregulation by designing products and services that incorporate specific features. For example, a number of banks have introduced a foreign currency product for resident Indians taking cue from a recent regulatory change. Some players have introduced a mutual fund scheme for global investments.

Increased client sophistication and competition for client business will require wealth managers to deploy segment specific-customer satisfaction and retention strategies

Wealth managers, who develop an in-depth understanding of their customers, will be well-positioned to retain and grow business by deploying distinct strategies for marketing, pricing and servicing. This will require wealth managers to consider non-financial criteria for segmenting their customers including behavioral and psychometric segmentation. In our view, customer retention will become a critical issue going forward. Wealth managers, who have a formal mechanism to measure customer satisfaction (in-house and external surveys, complaint monitoring, etc.) on an ongoing basis and implementable customer retention strategies, will succeed in the long-term. Referrals and strong service performance will continue to remain the key factors for selecting a wealth manager.

Competition for key wealth management resources will require wealth managers to address staff satisfaction, compensation and retention strategies

There will be a huge demand for wealth management personnel in India, due to the growth of wealth management providers and wealthy individuals in the next few years. Wealth managers will need to provide trained resources to service increasingly sophisticated, discerning and demanding customers. In our view, training will become a critical requirement encompassing the areas of marketing, relationship management, regulation and compliance and product knowledge. Competition for scarce, competent, specialist wealth management personnel will increase. Wealth managers equipped with appropriate human resource policies covering the areas of compensation (monetary and non-monetary rewards and incentives), staff satisfaction and retention will succeed.

Increased customer demand for sophisticated products will result in wealth managers offering a wider array of more complex products and services

Growing customer demand and increased competition among wealth managers will result in the introduction of more sophisticated products and services spanning across asset classes. In our view, wealth managers will innovate and introduce products and services encompassing gold, real estate, commodities, art, hedge funds, structured products (e.g., inverse floater notes, principal protected notes, etc.), insurance and pension. The success of the wealth management industry is dependant on global and domestic economic factors. Wealth managers will need to innovate and offer appropriate products and services to meet the needs of wealthy individuals in times of economic boom as well as depression.

Wealth managers will introduce profitability models and tools to measure and enhance their performance

We believe that wealth managers will need to formulate strong profitability models and invest in MIS tools to understand profitability at all levels in the wealth management business. Wealthy clients typically generate more fees, but also incur higher costs due to higher levels of service required. Hence, wealth management providers need to strike an optimum balance between increased revenues and higher costs. Performance could be monitored by measuring client, household, product, relationship manager and distribution channel profitability. This analysis will enable wealth managers to refocus their efforts on high value customer segments and rethink their strategy on unprofitable clients, channels or products.

Technology tools will be critical for both enabling revenue generation as well as achieving operational effectiveness

IBM believes that successful wealth managers will need to formulate and implement appropriate technology strategies for their wealth management business. Technology tools covering the areas of financial planning, straight-through processing, product and account aggregation and performance monitoring will enable wealth managers to enhance their service quality and responsiveness. These tools will assist the relationship manager as well as clients who prefer self-directed planning.

IBM views aggregation, i.e., the ability to collect client data internally across the organization and externally across other organizations, as a key focus area. Account aggregation tools will enable the customer to access account information across multiple providers from a single wealth manager's website. Wealth managers in India will need to address the issues of both internal and external aggregation to move ahead. Product aggregation tools will enable the wealth manager to provide products from different suppliers to their clients from their own website. IBM believes that the Internet will become a very important channel to conduct business in the future. Wealth managers, who are early adopters, will be successful as they integrate the Internet with their other channels and business models.

In conclusion, we believe that the wealth management industry is poised for tremendous growth in India. Successful wealth managers with a clear vision and strategy, and equipped with supporting people, processes and systems, will reap significant gains.

(Anita Iyer, Managing Consultant, IBM Business Consulting Services. She can be reached at anita.mehta.iyer@in.ibm.com).

Wealth Management and Private Banking – Building a Proactive Model

– Ajay Mahajan

The quality of advice and level of service play an important role in building a winning business model for banks.

Wealth management and private banking divisions are increasingly gaining importance in the banking sector, as banks in India are being considered a one-stop shop for providing financial solutions by the customers. Changing investor demands and tax regulations are helping banks in providing a complete portfolio advisory module in addition to traditional banking products. The structure of the banking industry is shifting by attracting talented advisors and helping in client retention and penetration aspects.

Banks are currently looked upon by both corporate and individual investors in providing innovative financial solutions like selection of best managed products and structured products.

Differences between the traditional type banking players and complete solutions providers can be noticed in the existing industry players based on the fee income these players generate from wealth management and private banking services. The quality of advice and level of service play an important role in building a winning business model for banks.

Various wealth surveys conducted in the recent past suggest that investors need broader wealth management advice on tax planning, business succession planning, international investments, art, real estate and other innovative investment options. Managing investor needs, aspirations and goals are the three key drivers for all the players to ensure customer retention and further penetration. Customer confidentiality is increasingly gaining momentum in the Indian space and is being promoted as important criteria by most players in their positioning.

Sophisticated financial products and solutions are no longer seen as value proposition by the ultra affluent investors, as these products with little variation are available from all the players in the market. The real difference stands out in the personal touch and technology of the service provider. Offering investors online purchase, sale and tracking capability in addition to personal touch are critical drivers of this business.

Trends suggest that banks are increasingly being considered as trusted advisors by the high net worth clients for all their investments needs. Trends also suggest that investors are now contemplating whether independent advisors can be credible across a whole range of investment products.

Right quality of advice and experience of the advisor are two important drivers of wealth advisory business. With more number of banking players now offering advisory services, attracting the right quality of advisors with good understanding of capital markets and experience becomes critical in developing a strong advisory model. Unfortunately, many players are experimenting with new talent in this space as there is a shortage of experienced talent.

Currently, banks are investing very little in training their advisors on market and economic trends. Most of the advisors are dependant on newspapers and industry newsletters. Very few players have invested in developing internal on-the-job training grounds for their wealth advisors. Imparting regular updates on the markets and trends in the form of internal newsletters or posting important data on the intranet helps advisors in analyzing data before counseling their clients.

Moreover, very few banks have the so-called product specialist to guide their wealth advisors and clients. Product specialists help both internal advisors and clients in identifying market trends and opportunities well in advance. Portfolio regular reviews with product specialists helps in building the client's confidence and re-balancing the portfolio on regular intervals.

Contd...

Contd...
Tracking the investment portfolio helps in timely corrective action of the investments not delivering the returns as per the assumptions/expectation. Most players today, are still working on providing this vital tool to their investors for enabling them to track their investment portfolio. Authenticity of data is essential and availability of various tools to ensure auto upload of data with no human involvement will help in building an error-free portfolio tracker. Access to the investment portfolio through Internet login helps to have an independent check on the advice. Attracting and retaining clients, places an enormous demand on expertise, technology and product capabilities. A complex range of services needs to be provided on-line and off-line. Personalized advice covering a diverse range of investment alternatives and related services (at a minimum, tax and inheritance planning and extending to real estate, art and gems) needs to be matched with sophisticated financial advice. Most individual investors believe they have a better understanding of their assets than their relationship managers do. They value personalized, timesaving service and expert advice on a wide range of investments. The challenge lies in dynamic implementation of investor suggestions and feedback and building a proactive model. *(Ajay Mahajan, President, Financial Markets, Institutions & Private Banking, Yes Bank Limited, Mumbai.)*
Source: Chartered Financial Analyst, October 2005. © The Icfai University Press. All rights reserved.

Section II

Prospects and Performance

6

Private Sector Banks in India – A SWOT Analysis*

Chowdari Prasad and K S Srinivasa Rao

The financial reforms launched during the early 1990s have dramatically changed the banking scenario in the country. New prudential norms, such as capital adequacy prescriptions, identification of bad debts, provision requirements, etc., were enforced; and interest rates were deregulated. As a sequel to these reforms, new private sector banks were allowed entry into the market. Many of these new private sector banks have brought with them state-of-art technology for business processing and service delivery, besides being efficient in catering to the customers' demands. Yet, the failure of Global Trust Bank made Indian depositors to question the sustainability of private banks. Against this backdrop, this article attempts to undertake SWOT analysis and other appropriate statistical techniques, to rank 30 private sector banks from the financial data collected for the three years—2002, 2003 and 2004. The study has, using four parameters—efficiency, financial strength, profitability, and size and scale, ranked the banks independently for each year.

---

* Paper presented at the International Conference on "Business and Finance" held during December 27–28, 2004 at The Icfai Business School, Hyderabad.

Introduction

Private sector banks have existed for over a century in India. Formation of the State Bank Group in 1955/1957 and two nationalizations in 1969 and 1980 have led to the dominance of Public Sector Banks. Economic reforms in 1991 and banking sector reforms in 1997-98 have changed the banking scene totally. People generally rely on nationalized banks backed by the Government. Change in the mindset of the customers forced the Reserve Bank of India (RBI) allow new private banks to come into existence a decade back. The World Trade Organization (WTO) and globalization initiated more foreign banks to add to the competition and a proper, level playing field.

It is pertinent and appropriate to mention that the Imperial Bank of India was a large private sector bank that handled all the commercial banking business as well as treasury-related work of the Government until the Reserve Bank of India (RBI) was formed in 1934. It was in the post-independent era in 1948 that RBI itself converted it into a fully state-owned bank, followed by the formation of the State Bank of India in 1955. The debate about RBI being fully autonomous or not is inconclusive even today, as it operates as the country's central bank and also advises the Government on monetary and fiscal matters; and yet, implements welfare-oriented policies as far as regulating the commercial banks are concerned, irrespective of the fact whether these banks are in the public, private, cooperative or foreign sector.

Prior to the first major nationalization of 14 banks in July 1969, private capital called the shots in commercial banking. The Tatas owned the Central Bank of India, the Birlas—the United Commercial Bank (UCO Bank now) and so on. The policy of social control of banks in India in 1969, brought in a different turn, but in retrospect, it is evident that political motives dominated the decision about the two nationalizations. Large-scale branch expansion, mass recruitment of staff to take banking to grassroot levels, directed investments and credit programs, administered interest rate regime, credit dispensation towards poverty alleviation programs through loan melas, etc., ruled the roost in the Indian banking scene for over two decades.

Private Sector Banks: Current Position

During the mid 80s, the scenario changed both at the political front and the banking system in India. Productivity, profitability, professionalism, introduction to technology, competition from private sector, innovation of new products and services, etc., have set in and necessitated dramatic changes, beginning with the Financial Sector Reforms in 1991. Public sector banks started declaring losses and experiencing the need for total change in their working, and preparing to face stiff competition from the new generation banks (which permitted to start in mid 90s after introducing prudential norms for the banking system in 1993). PSBs and old private sector banks realized their new role and also welcomed the new generation banks—Bank of Punjab, HDFC Bank, IDBI Bank, ICICI Bank, Centurion Bank, UTI Bank, IndusInd Bank, Times Bank, etc. These new banks had the advantage of starting with a clean slate, adequate capital resources, well-trained and professional manpower, absence of non-performing loans in their books, computerization, lean organizational system, a handful of branches in chosen centers, a new variety of products and services, etc.

The formation of WTO in January 1995, and India's commitment to open up financial services to global players had also brought in many foreign banks to open their offices and expand branches, offering a new range of products and services through ATMs, electronic services, credit cards and portfolio management for high net worth individuals and corporate customers. An entirely new level playing field was created to accept perfect competition among all types of banks in the country, particularly in the metro and urban centers. Amidst the transition from the traditional and controlled banking system, the old private sector banks which were carrying on their business within limited areas of operation started feeling the heat, both from the recharged PSBs and new private sector banks, besides the foreign banks. The new private banks to enter the scene are Kotak Mahindra Bank in March 2003 and YES Bank in September 2004.

Among the 30 private sector banks in India today, we have 21 old and nine new banks which are able to sustain the competition. Stringent capital adequacy requirements, compliance to prudential, asset liability and risk management norms, huge investment in technology to move towards total computerization, etc., have put tremendous pressure on all the banks, including the old private banks. In the post-reforms era too there have been several changes in the banking system in India. Times Bank was merged with an efficient counterpart, i.e., HDFC Bank, in 2000 for strategic reasons. ICICI Ltd., (a private sector Development Financial Institution formed in 1955-56) was reverse merged with ICICI Bank. In the

S. No.	Financial Indicator	21 Old Private Banks	Nine New Private Banks	Total 30 Private Banks
01	Deposits	1,09,805.46	1,58,743.80	2,68,549.26
02	Investments	49,545.70	85,255.33	1,34,801.03
03	Advances (Credit)	58,232.66	1,12,666.53	1,70,899.19
04	Total Assets	1,26,093.19	2,41,183.13	3,67,276.32
05	Gross NPAs	4,609.63	5,771.17	10,380.80
06	Net NPAs	2,142.07	2,664.40	4,806.47
07	Interest Income	9,472.84	16,068.95	25,541.79
08	Other Income	2,519.31	5,092.23	7,611.54
09	Total Income	11,992.15	21,161.18	33,153.33
10	Interest Expended	6,238.68	11,291.32	17,530.00
11	Operating Expenses	2,503.52	4,911.07	7,414.59
12	Total Expenditure	8,742.20	16,202.39	24,944.59
13	Operating Profit	3,249.89	5,116.35	8,366.24
14	Provisions/Contingencies	1,786.06	2,941.14	4,727.20
15	Net Profit	1,463.83	2,017.63	3,481.46

Table 1: Performance Data of All Private Sector Banks in India as on March 31, 2004

(Rs. in cr)

Source: IBA Bulletin, October 2004.

previous year, it also took over the south-based Bank of Madura. Simultaneously, certain erring or inefficient old private banks like Benares State Bank Ltd. and Nedungadi Bank Ltd. were asked by RBI to merge with public sector banks in recent years. But one question that arises is how reliable some of the new private banks are, in spite of their efficiency. This doubt arises because of the recent experience of Global Trust Bank failure. Better professional management techniques adopted by the ICICI Bank made it number one, in spite of rumors, two years back ("Best Bank", *Business India*, 16-29, August, 2004).

From the data available in the RBI Annual Report for 2003-04, it is observed that private sector banks have been discharging their responsibilities and obligations in extending priority sector lending more than satisfactorily. Table 2 demonstrates the status *vis-à-vis* public sector and foreign banks.

Table 2: Priority Sector Advances by Banks in India

(Rs. in cr)

As on Last Reporting Friday of	(27) Public Sector Banks	(30) Private Sector Banks	(34) Foreign Banks	Total
March 1999	1,04,094 (39.2)	13,947 (41.3)	8,268 (36.5)	1,26,309
March 2000	1,27,478 (40.3)	18,368 (38.0)	9,934 (35.2)	1,55,780
March 2001	1,49,116 (43.7)	21,567 (36.7)	11,572 (33.5)	1,82,255
March 2002 P	1,71,185 (43.1)	25,709 (40.9)	13,414 (34.0)	2,10,308
March 2003 P	2,03,095 (42.5)	36,705 (44.4)	14,848 (33.9)	2,54,648
March 2004 P	2,45,501 (43.9)	52,629 (47.3)	17,651 (34.2)	3,15,781

Note: Figures for the three years 2002 to 2004 in the above table are provisional. Figures in parentheses are percentages to net bank credit in the respective group. The target for aggregate advances to the priority sector is 40% of net bank credit for domestic banks and 32% of net bank credit for foreign banks.

Source: RBI Annual Report, 2003-04.

Private sector banks, as a group, have extended priority sector loans at 47.3% in the year 2004; over and above the stipulated 40% of the total advances. In absolute terms too, there has been nearly a four-fold increase in a six-year period, while their counterparts, viz., public and foreign banks, have increased their exposure by about one and half times.

From Table 3, we observe that public sector banks have always been at the command of the RBI and Government of India to disburse more and more funds to the much needy agricultural sector. Either in absolute terms or a

Table 3: Outstanding Agricultural Advance

(Rs. in cr)

End March	Public Sector		Private Sector	
	Amt. O/S	% of NBC	Amt. O/S	% of NBC
1999	37,632	14.2	3,467	9.1
2000	45,296	14.3	4,023	8.3
2001	53,571	15.7	5,634	9.6
2002 P	63,082	15.9	8,022	8.5
2003 P	73,507	15.3	11,873	10.8
2004 P	86,127	15.4	17,594	12.3

Source: RBI Annual Report, 2003-04.

proportion to Net Bank Credit, the performance of PSBs has always been much ahead of their private counterparts. This is a clear indicator that the very purpose of nationalization of banks in India has been well served by the PSBs over the last three decades even though the much smaller old private sector banks are operating mostly in rural and semi-urban areas and could have fared well in this segment.

Mergers of Some Private Sector Banks in India

Prior to nationalization of banks in 1969, mostly Indian corporates owned the commercial banks. There were large-scale failures of banks and insurance companies during the 1950s and the early 1960s for various reasons, and thus the Government of India had to intervene and decide in favor of mergers and amalgamations of such entities. This was necessary to maintain public confidence in the financial system and protect the small investors. Gradually, the regulatory mechanism made its place in the corporate scene and stability was maintained. Table 4 furnishes a list of names of private sector banks which were merged with public sector banks during the period 1985 to 2000.

S. No.	Name of the Private Sector Bank	Name of Public Sector Bank Merged with
01	Bank of Cochin Ltd.	State Bank of India
02	Laxmi Commercial Bank Ltd.	Canara Bank
03	Hindustan Commercial Bank Ltd.	Punjab National Bank
04	Miraj State Bank Ltd.	Union Bank of India
05	The Traders Bank Ltd.	Bank of Baroda
06	The Bank of Tamil Nadu Ltd.	Indian Overseas Bank
07	Bank of Thanjavur Ltd.	Indian Bank
08	The Parur Central Bank Ltd.	Bank of India
09	The United Industrial Bank Ltd.	Allahabad Bank
10	The Purbanchal Bank Ltd.	Central Bank of India
11	Bank of Karad Ltd.	Bank of India
12	Bareily Corporation Bank Ltd.	Bank of Baroda
13	Sikkim Bank Ltd.	Union Bank of India

Table 4: Names of Banks Merged Between 1985 and 2000

Source: Privatization of Banks in India: Present Positions and Future Options, Mangalore University Publication, 2002.

Table 5: Mergers of Private Sector Banks Post-2000		
S.No.	Name of Private Sector Bank Merged	Name of the Bank Merged with
01	Times Bank	HDFC Bank
02	Bank of Madura	ICICI Bank Ltd.
03	Nedungadi Bank Ltd.	Punjab National Bank
04	Benares State Bank Ltd.	Bank of Baroda
05	Global Trust Bank Ltd.	Oriental Bank of Commerce
Source: Various reports in Financial Newspapers.		

Immediately after the Indian economy began resorting to reforms in the year 1991-92, there have been several structural, legal, organizational and other changes. As far as the banking industry is concerned, an interesting development was the merger of one public sector bank with another. New Bank of India was merged with Punjab National Bank during the year 1993-94. The former was nationalized in 1980, while Punjab National Bank was among the 14 banks that were taken over by the Government of India in 1969. Both these banks are based in New Delhi. It is the only merger within the public sector banks and the experience was not too pleasant for both. However, there have been some more mergers in the private sector even beyond the year 2000 as per the Table 5.

Two other private sector bank mergers/conversions worth mentioning here are (1) the ICICI Ltd. reverse merger with ICICI Bank Ltd., and (2) RBI granting permission for conversion of a highly successful non-banking financial company, viz., Kotak Mahindra Finance into Kotak Mahindra Bank in March 2003. Another interesting development in the recent years as regards private sector banks in India was permitting of Foreign Direct Investoment (FDI), and The Vysya Bank Ltd., promptly utilized the facility. ING of Netherlands has taken the stake of the erstwhile Bank of Brussels, Lambart and the bank was rechristened as ING Vysya Bank Ltd. Its management and functioning has changed dramatically in the recent years.

In the Foreign Banks sector too, there have been changes in Bank Paribas, Grindlays and Standard Chartered Bank. The proposal for merging the sick-giant DFI, viz., Industrial Finance Corporation of India (IFCI) has been on cards for the last two years and the victim may again be either the New Delhi-based Punjab National Bank or IDBI. The future consolidation of public sector banks in India is now worth watching, thanks to the current policy of the Government of India for a large-scale shake-up in the industry.

Efficiency Measures

It is interesting to note that of the 21 old private sector banks, six each have originated in Maharashtra and Tamil Nadu, while four are based in Kerala, and of the remaining, two are from Karnataka and one each from Rajasthan, Uttar Pradesh and Jammu and Kashmir. Among the new private sector banks, Global Trust Bank is based in Hyderabad (AP), Bank of Punjab in Punjab and seven others are headquartered in Mumbai, although their registered offices are elsewhere.

As regards working of old private sector banks, some of them are nearly a century old and register considerable business—both deposits and advances—with wider range of branches all over India. The nine new generation banks commenced their operations about a decade back and have booked substantial business levels with adequate presence in almost all the important locations in India.

The advent of technology and installation of a large number of ATMs have saved these banks from opening branches all over, thus saving on huge establishment expenses. More information on business and efficiency are discussed in the following pages, supported by data for three financial years, viz., 2001-02, 2002-03 and 2003-04.

Perhaps, the best indicator of the banking industry's health is the levels of Non-Performing Assets (NPAs). Indian banks seem to be quite healthy now. At least one bank—Oriental Bank of Commerce—is a zero-net NPA bank, while five other listed banks (Andhra Bank, HDFC Bank, IDBI Bank, Kotak Mahindra Bank and Vijaya Bank) have less than 1% net NPAs as on March 31, 2004. Table 6 gives us the gross NPAs of all private sector banks in India as on March 31, 2004.

It may be seen that the gross NPAs of 21 old private sector banks stood at Rs.4,615.48 cr and that of the nine new private banks are at Rs.5,443.89 cr. These levels are commensurate with the levels of business, in particular the advances of these banks. While among old banks, the Federal Bank and Karnataka Bank are carrying at the two highest levels, ICICI Bank Ltd., is the single private sector bank with as much as Rs.3,047.59 cr, due to the fact that the business of

S.No.	Name of the Bank	Gross NPAs
	**Table 6: Gross NPAs of Private Banks as on March 31, 2004**	*(Rs. in cr)*
A	**Old Private Sector Banks**	Amount
01	Bank of Rajasthan Ltd.	237.32
02	Bharat Overseas Bank Ltd.	71.00
03	Catholic Syrian Bank Ltd.	175.24
04	City Union Bank Ltd.	167.42
05	Development Credit Bank Ltd.	211.61
06	Dhanalakshmi Bank Ltd.	136.55
07	Federal Bank Ltd.	600.75
08	Ganesh Bank of Kurundwad	30.29
09	Jammu and Kashsmir Bank Ltd.	286.51
10	Karnataka Bank Ltd.	598.47
11	Karur Vysya Bank Ltd.	239.23
12	Lakshmi Vilas Bank Ltd.	216.83
13	Lord Krishna Bank Ltd.	95.29
14	Nainital Bank Ltd.	9.65
15	Ratnakar Bank Ltd.	38.84
16	Sangli Bank Ltd.	80.66
17	SBI Commercial and International Bank Ltd.	69.25
18	South Indian Bank Ltd.	328.25
19	Tamil Mercantile Bank Ltd.	319.38
20	United Western Bank Ltd.	516.34
21	ING Vysya Bank Ltd.	186.60
	Total Old Private Sector Banks	4,615.48
B	**New Private Sector Banks**	
22	Bank of Punjab Ltd.	148.30
23	Centurion Bank Ltd.	221.41
24	Global Trust Bank Ltd.@	1,021.02
25	HDFC Bank Ltd.	324.00
26	ICICI Bank Ltd.	3,047.59

Contd...

Contd...		
27	IDBI Bank Ltd.	127.53
28	Indus Ind Bank Ltd.	259.36
29	Kotak Mahindra Bank Ltd.	19.96
30	UTI Bank Ltd.	274.72
	Total New Private Sector Banks	**5,443.89**
	Total all Private Sector Banks	**10,059.37**
Note: @ – since amalgamated with OBC in September 04.		
Source: The Journal of Banking Studies, November, 2004.		

the erstwhile ICICI and Bank of Madura were merged with the bank more than two years back. Global Trust Bank was saddled with Rs.1,021.02 cr and the bank was amalgamated with a public sector bank—OBC in September 2004. At the same time, HDFC Bank is carrying a modest Rs.324 cr as gross NPAs despite having taken over another new generation bank—Times Bank—about four years back.

Capital Infusion by IFC

There are reports that the Washington-based International Finance Corporation (IFC) is likely to invest in more private banks in India, including Kotak Mahindra Bank, although it has cut exposure in Centurion Bank and Global Trust Bank. "India needs more private banks. We are looking at investment in more banks," said Dimitris Tsitsiragos, IFC South Asia Director, recently. He said IFC was looking at Kotak Mahindra Bank, the erstwhile Kotak Mahindra Finance that converted itself into a bank after getting RBI Licence. Although the IFC official declined to give details, banking sources said that the World Bank's private lending arm was eager to extend $22 mn as a three year loan.

Assistance of the IFC assumes importance in the wake of KMB's (Kotak Mahindra Bank) aggressive expansion drive targeting 20 more branches to expand its reach from the present 75 odd outlets. The bank has deposits worth over Rs.1,500 cr and advances to the tune of Rs.2,500 cr. While eyeing fresh exposure in the banking sector, IFC has cut its exposure in two other new private sector banks.

CAR in 2003-04

The average Capital Adequacy Ratio (CAR) of 16 private sector banks under study increased from 12.81% during 2002-03 to 12.85% during 2003-04. With this upturn, all the private sector banks attained the stipulated CAR of 9% during 2003-04. The top five private sector banks in terms of CAR were Karur Vysya Bank (17.11%), J and K Bank (16.88%), Bharat Overseas Bank (16.25%), Kotak Mahindra Bank (15.25%), and City Union Bank (13.96%).

The net worth of Karur Vysya Bank (KVB) increased by 27.4% to Rs.712 cr as on March 31, 2004 from the level of Rs.559 cr as on March 31, 2003. This has helped the bank to get the highest CAR during 2003-04. Similarly, the net worth of J and K Bank increased by 28.3% to Rs.1,594 cr during 2003-04 from the level of Rs.1,242 cr the previous year. The bank achieved the second highest CAR of 16.88% during 2003-04 among the 16 private sector banks.

Significant decline in CAR was also noticed among private sector banks this year. Kotak Mahindra Bank's CAR was 25.97% in 2002-03 and came down to 15.25% in 2003-04, while that of ICICI Bank moved from 11.1% to 10.36% and Bank of Rajasthan from 11.29% to 11.18%.

Fee Income Growth: Higher in Private Banks

The rate of growth in the fee income of private sector banks has been significantly higher in the last few years compared to their peers in the public sector. This may be attributed to the private banks' larger product offerings and their technology platforms, which are better geared to provide customized solutions to customers. Greater thrust on retaining business growth, leveraging of technology, strong focus on cash management activities and increase in non-fund-based exposures to corporate clients have also helped them, according to a report prepared by the rating agency, ICRA Ltd.

However, over the medium term, the private sector banks' margins may come under significant pressure given that they would be striving to increase their own fee-based income out of sheer necessity. They have already become proactive in exploring ways to raise their fee income, and the results of such endeavor may well show up in the medium term, the report added.

An analysis of the fee incomes of the top four public sector banks (Punjab National Bank, Canara Bank, Bank of Baroda and Bank of India) and four private sector banks (ICICI Bank, HDFC Bank, IDBI Bank and UTI Bank) has revealed that the absolute fee income of PSBs is expectedly higher than that of their private counterparts because of the higher scale of operations, while the proportion of exchange and brokerage, as a percentage of the total fee income, is higher for the private banks.

Indian banks are heavily reliant on interest income, which accounts for over 80% of their total income. As for the component of non-interest income, the share of trading profits in such income has assumed significant importance during the last few years, given the declining interest rates in the economy. At present, with the scope of further reduction in interest rates being rather limited, ICRA expects banks' income from trading profits to decline over the medium term. Table 7 gives information about the old and new private sector banks with regard to four financial ratios.

Table 7: Financial Ratios of All Private Sector Banks as on March 31, 2004				
S. No.	Financial Ratio	21 Old Private Banks	Nine New Private Banks	30 Private Banks
01	Credit Deposit Ratio	53.03	70.97	63.64
02	Investment Deposit Ratio	45.12	53.71	50.20
03	Spread as % of Assets	2.56	1.98	2.18
04	Operating Exp. to Total Exp.	28.64	30.31	29.72
Source: IBA Bulletin, October 2004.				

Profits of PSBs – Up 60%: FICCI Study

A comprehensive survey by FICCI brings out that the combined average net profits of the much maligned public sector banks registered a robust growth of 59.5% in 2003-04 over the previous year, way above the increase in profits of private and foreign banks. The profits of Indian private banks rose by 36.3% and that of foreign banks by 23.3%. The survey went into the reasons for higher profitability of the PSU banks as compared to private and foreign banks.

All the three categories of banks—public, private and foreign banks—reported higher advances over the previous year. The growth rate in advances in 2003-04 was higher in the case of 82% of the banks. This is on account of considerable reduction in Non-Performing Assets and increase in the interest rate spread, despite the falling deposit rates and many corporate houses opting for External Commercial

Borrowings (ECBs) to raise finance. The average growth in advances for all public sector banks was 19%, while that of private sector and foreign banks were 26 and 20% respectively. Profitability per employee has increased every year for the last three years for all banks.

An important reason for the higher profitability of public sector banks is because of the much larger sums parked by them in Government Securities. While, on an average, the public sector banks, G-Secs to Total Assets Ratio is about 33.2%, a comparative figure for new private sector and foreign banks is 24.3%. The soft interest regime has provided a bonanza to the PSU Banks. Gains from the sale of Government Securities have contributed between 50% to 200% in net profits of different banks. On an average, 'other income'—mainly profits on sale of investments—grew by 25% for all banks. "With Bond prices and interest rates displaying an inverse relationship, treasury gains in the regime of falling interest rates is no surprise," says the survey.

Income from the traditional business of lending has grown at a slow pace of 7%, which the survey says was a 'matter of concern'. More than 60% of the PSBs feel that the balance sheet would be eroded in the event of interest rate rise because of decline in treasury profits. Nearly 70% of the private and foreign sector banks say that they will be able to make up for this decline. On issues relating to retail banking, the survey found that 74% of the respondents felt that the retail banking boom was supply motivated as banks flooded the market with cheap finance.

Bankers have already started working to sustain this boom. While a majority of them plan to widen their customer base to diversify risk and increase their market share, others are tying up with loser companies (such as auto companies for car loans). Extending the tenure loan is also being planned.

Regarding new avenues for business, 77% favored exposure of banks to the capital markets, almost 60% respondents suggested that the limit on market exposure at present capped at 5% outstanding advances should be hiked. More and more banks are looking for selling insurance as a viable source of additional revenue. As many as 85% of the respondents voted for relaxation of the present rule, which limits tie-up of banks to a single life and non-life insurance company.

Forty-three per cent of the banks and financial institutions surveyed were of the view that after the adoption of 90-day norm, NPAs will be in the range of 0 to 5% of total balances. Around 47% said that the NPAs will be in the range of 5 to 10%. Ninety per cent of the entities surveyed said that SARFAESI Act, 2002 has been successful in increasing the recoveries of NPAs. The Act empowers banks to sidestep the courts and dispose of the defaulters' properties given as securities by giving due notice to the borrower. Nearly 60% of the respondents held the view that the Corporate Debt Restructuring (CDR) mechanism has been successful in the recovery of NPAs.

RBI as the Banking Regulator

Private sector banks are more closely scrutinized for any weakness by RBI. Going forward, stressed out banks will be absorbed by more profitable banks, reducing the number of banks operating in India. More banking related products will be available from a single source and greater accessibility to funds raised in the market can be achieved by such intervention.

RBI, as a central bank and regulator, has been handling the onerous task of monitoring and supervision of the ever-changing industry with a variety of players—public, old and new private, foreign, cooperative (urban and rural), Local Area and Regional Rural Banks in India. At times, it appears that there is tremendous overlap in the roles of these financial outfits—be it banks or financial institutions at the central or state level. Every time a financial scandal surfaces, the regulator's role and responsibility comes under discussion. Fast changes in technology and communications have come handy for close governance of all these players and RBI has been gearing up readily to handle all such testing and trying situations from time to time. Besides, to cope with competition and invite new products and services, several legal changes are also being made by the government, the last one being enactment of SARFAESI Act, 2002.

In January 2004, RBI issued guidelines/norms regarding shareholding in private banks. It liberalizes foreign investment in banking sector, raising the FDI to 74% under the automatic route, including investment by Foreign Institutional Investors (FIIs). In June 2004, an inter-regulatory working group of RBI, Sebi and IRDA proposed identifying 'Financial Conglomerates' (FCs) to put them under special composite regulatory watch. Private sector giants like ICICI Bank Ltd. and HDFC Bank, and foreign banks, such as Citibank and StanChart Bank, would also come under this purview besides public sector units like SBI, PNB or Bank of Baroda.

In July 2004, RBI put out what is called, "A Comprehensive Policy Framework for Ownership and Governance in Private Sector Banks", which, among several other things, proposed a series of fresh restrictions on how much foreign banks and Indian private sector banks could hold in other private banks. However, the Government of India, Ministry of Finance is nudging the Reserve Bank of India to scale down the proposed Rs.300 cr entry norm—the minimum capital requirement for private sector banks.

This made the authors think of using SWOT Analysis and other appropriate statistical techniques to establish the efficiency of private sector banks in India.

Methodology – Statistical Analysis

The authors have taken cross-sectional data on banks from the *IBA Bulletin* (October 2004) and compared the 30 private sector banks among themselves for the years 2002, 2003 and 2004.

The four factors that have been considered are—efficiency, financial strength, profitability, and size and scale, based on the financial and business indicators, for these private sector banks. Each of the factors is given an equal weightage of 25%. Each parameter within a factor is ranked by giving equal weightage across all the private sector banks.

- *Efficiency* – is a composite of (1) Cost of Funds (CF)* (2) Ratio of intermediation costs to total assets (Total Expenses/Assets) (TE/A*) (3) Burden – Total non-interest expenses minus total non-interest income divided by total assets (B*) (4) Business per Branch (BPB) and (5) Operating Profit Per Employee (OPPE). So, each sub-parameter was given 5% weightage aggregating to 25%.

- *Financial Strength* – is a composite of (1) Capital Adequacy Ratio (CAR) and (2) NPA level (net NPAs to net advances) (NPA to NA*). Both these sub-parameters were given 12.5% weightage aggregating to 25%.

- *Profitability* – is a composite of (1) Spread as Percentage of Assets (SA) and (2) Return on Assets. Both these sub-parameters were given 12.5% weightage aggregating to 25%.

- *Size and Scale* – is a composite of (1) Aggregate Deposits (AD), (2) Operating Profits (OP), (3) Net Profits (NP) and (4) (Credit + Investment)/Deposit Ratio ((C +I)/D). All these four sub-parameters were given 6.25% weightage aggregating to 25%.

Note: The parameters that are by virtue of nature "higher is better" have been ranked in descending order but the other parameters (marked with *) have been ranked in ascending order. While giving the score, these ranking numbers were taken in opposite sense without loss of generality.

The authors have carried out Analysis of Variance (ANOVA) for each of these four parameters using F-test as a parametric case. The authors have also done the overall ranking of four factors—Efficiency, Financial Strength, Profitability, Size and Scale and ranked the banks using the overall performance. They also identified the topmost/bottom banks each year (2002, 2003 and 2004) using the methodology.

Findings

In the financial year ending March 2002, based on the total score obtained from four parameters (already described in the methodology), HDFC Bank, J and K Bank and Karur Vysya Bank are on the top three positions. However, based on the four selected parameters, the position shown in Table 8 emerged for the year.

Table 8: Outcome of Analysis for the Year 2002		
Parameter	Bank at the Top Position	Bank at the Bottom
1. Efficiency	IndusInd Bank	Centurion Bank
2. Financial Strength	Nainital Bank	Ganesh Bank of Kurundwad
3. Profitability	Karur Vysya Bank Ltd.	ICICI Bank Ltd.
4. Size and Scale	ICICI Bank Ltd.	Ganesh Bank of Kurundwad
Overall	HDFC Bank	Ganesh Bank Kurundwad

Kotak Mahindra Bank was only a finance company and not existing as a bank during the year. Hence, it was not reckoned for the purpose of this analysis during 2002.

In the financial year ending March 2003, based on the total score obtained from four parameters, J and K Bank, HDFC Bank and Karur Vysya Bank are on the top three positions. However, based on the four selected parameters, the following position emerged for the year, as shown in Table 9.

Table 9: Outcome of Analysis for the Year 2003

Parameter	Bank at the Top Position	Bank at the Bottom
1. Efficiency	IndusInd Bank	Ganesh Bank of Kurundwad
2. Financial Strength	Nainital Bank	Global Trust Bank
3. Profitability	J and K Bank Ltd.	Global Trust Bank
4. Size and Scale	ICICI Bank Ltd.	Ganesh Bank of Kurundwad
Overall	**J and K Bank**	**Ganesh Bank of Kurundwad**

Kotak Mahindra Finance Company was converted into a bank in March 2003 only and data for the year will be representing its performance for one month and not the full year. Hence, it was not reckoned for ranking purposes even though in two parameters (Financial Strength and Profitability), it emerged at the top position.

In the financial year ending March 2004, based on the total score obtained from four parameters, J and K Bank, IndusInd Bank and HDFC Bank are on the top three positions. However, based on the four selected parameters, the following position emerged for the year, as shown in Table 10.

Table 10: Outcome of Analysis for the Year 2004

Parameter	Bank at the Top Position	Bank at the Bottom
1. Efficiency	a. IDBI Bank b. UTI Bank	Ganesh Bank of Kurundwad
2. Financial Strength	SBI Commercial and Inter-National Bank Ltd.	IDBI Bank
3. Profitability	Karur Vysya Bank Ltd.	Global Trust Bank
4. Size and Scale	ICICI Bank Ltd.	Ganesh Bank of Kurundwad
Overall	**J and K Bank**	**Centurion Bank Ltd.**

Global Trust Bank was deteriorating in its performance year after year during the above three years study. It was finally asked to merge with a public sector bank—OBC in the month of July 2004.

ANOVA

In addition to the analysis of data for the 30 private sector banks for the three years 2002, 2003 and 2004 individually, a statistical test—ANOVA (Analysis of

Variance) was carried out for each of the parameters including the overall performance. The results indicated that there is a significant difference in the average efficiency at 5% level. Interestingly, a similar trend was observed in the performance of the 21 old private sector banks tested separately.

SWOT Analysis

A. Strengths

- All these private banks have professional, dedicated and well-trained manpower.

- In contrast to their public sector counterparts, efficiency is maintained at the highest level.

- The new private banks have commenced with strong financials and with a clean slate, i.e., without having to pursue NPAs.

- Almost all these banks have complied with capital adequacy requirements and prudential norms.

- Most of these banks are fully computerized and techno-savvy.

B. Weaknesses

- Both old and new private banks are operating in a limited area, confined to a region.

- Although highly networked, the number of branches is limited.

- The employee turnover appears to be on the higher side.

- There is dissimilarity between old and new private banks by virtue of their age, functional area, products and services, etc.

C. Opportunities

- Being in the private sector, these banks enjoy a high level of autonomy, facilitating them for faster decision-making.

- To face the stiff competition, they can innovate new products and services and achieve high customer satisfaction.

- With full computerization, they can offer cost-effective services like ATMs, Electronic Fund Transfer, etc.

D. Threats

- Expansion of foreign banks in the post-WTO era poses severe competition.

- Dominant PSBs which are recharged with a high market share will overshadow the private sector banks.

- Frequent announcements of takeover/mergers and acquisitions by PSBs as well as new private sector banks disturb the very functioning of old private sector banks.

- RBI/GOI relaxation of SBI investment norms cause worry among the managements.

Conclusion

In the post-reforms era, with a promise to maintain perfect competition and a level paying field for all types of banks in the Indian banking scenario, both old and new private sector banks will continue to strive, to offer cost-effective, efficient products and services to their customers. Increased usage of technology, best utilization of the manpower resources, along with professional management adopting corporate governance principles, these private banks will continue to give their best and evolve in the Indian financial system. This is possible in view of the "not so dominant" presence of the foreign banks and consolidation of public sector banks envisaged by the Government of India.

(Chowdari Prasad, Associate Professor (Finance Area) TA Pai Management Institute (TAPMI), Manipal-576104, Karnataka. (Tel Office): 0820-2571358/2573162 and K S Srinivasa Rao, Associate Professor (QM Area) TA Pai Management Institute (TAPMI), Manipal-576104, Karnataka. They can be reached at chowdarip@mail. tapmi.org and srinivas@mail.tapmi.org respectively.)

References

1. "Best Bank-2004", *Business India*, August 16-29, 2004.

2. "Banking Annual", *Business Standard*, October 2004.

3. "India's Best Banks-2004", *Banking and Finance*, July-August 2004.

4. *Business World*, November 15, 2004.

5. *The Icfai Journal of Bank Management*, February 2004, The Icfai University Press.

6. *Professional Banker*, October, 2004, The Icfai University Press.

7. *www.financialexpress.com*

8. *www.hinduonnet.com*

9. *www.thehindubusinessline.com*

10. *www.ficci.com*

11. *www.domain-b.com*

12. *www.karvy.com*

13. *www.rbi.org.in*

14. *www.finance.indiamart.com/investment_in_india/banks.html*

15. *www.highbeam.com/library/search.asp?q =private +banks +in +India&FN*

16. *www.indianbanksassociation.org/home/kbp1/pvt/income.asp*

17. Cris Infac, *Banking Annual Review*, August, 2002.

18. Bishwajit Bhattacharyya, "Don't Bank on it: The RBI Mustn't Doze Off on Duty", *The Times of India*, November 06, 2004.

19. Sarbajeet K Sen, "Ministry Wants RBI to Review Ownership Norms for Private Sector Banks", *Business Line*, November 08, 2004.

20. A M Sadre, "Competency Building for Improving Customer Service in Banks", *Banking Finance*, August 2004.

21. "Private Banks Seek RBI Nod for Foreign Branches and Gross NPAs of Private Sector Banks as on March 31, 2004", *The Journal of Banking Studies*, November 2004.

22. K P Padmakumar, "Old Private Sector Banks: Relevance in New Milieu", *The Hindu*, Survey of Indian Industry, 2003.

23. A Brief Note by Jayasree Menon, *Economist*, October 2004, "Performance Highlights of Private Sector Banks 2003-2004", IBA: *IBA Bulletin*, pp. 35-44.

24. Rajeev Kumar and R K Mittal, "Trust and its Determinants in Internet Banking: A Study of Private Sector Banks in India", *Decision*, Vol. 31, No. 1, January-June, 2004.

25. John Vietz, "Indian Banking: History of Reform and Personal Observations from Recent India Trip", Special Seminar in International Management, India, April 18, 2003.

26. *Privatization of Banks in India: Present Positions and Future Options,* Mangalore University Publication, 2002.

27. K S Srinivasa Rao and Chowdari Prasad, "Can Public Sector Banks Compete with Foreign/ Private Banks? A Statistical Analysis", *The Icfai Journal of Bank Management,* Vol. III (1), pp. 07-52, February 2004.

28. Chowdari Prasad, "Functioning of Foreign Banks in India", *WTO and the Banking Sector in India,* Mangalore University Publication, pp. 133-188, 2004.

29. RBI Annual Report, 2004.

7

Performance of the New Indian Private Sector Banks: A Comparative Study

Sanjay J Bhayani

The broad objective of the banking sector reforms in India has been to increase efficiency and profitability of the banks. For this purpose, the banking sector has been opened for new private sector banks. As a result, various new private sector banks have started their banking business. In this paper, the author analyzes the performance of new private sector banks through the help of the CAMEL model. For the purpose, four leading private sector banks—ICICI, HDFC, UTI and IDBI—have been taken as sample. After making an analysis of the CAMEL parameters, the author, first of all, assigns ranks to all the banks according to their performance in various parameters of CAMEL, and then assigns them overall ranking. The data of five years, i.e., from 2000-01 to 2004-05, has been used for the analysis. The findings of the study reveal that the aggregate performance of IDBI is the best among all the banks, followed by UTI.

Source: The Icfaian Journal of Management Research, Vol. V, No. 11, 2006. © The Icfai University Press. All rights reserved.

Introduction

Among the world's top 1000 banks, there are more large and medium-sized domestic banks from developed countries than from emerging economies. According to *The Banker* (2005), out of the top 1000 banks globally, over 200 are located in USA, just above 100 in Japan, over 80 in Germany, over 40 in Spain and around 40 in the UK. Even China has as many as 16 banks within the top 1000, out of which, as many as 14 are in the top 500. India, on the other hand, has 20 banks in the top 1000, out of which only 6 are in the top 500 banks. This is perhaps reflective of the differences in the size of economies and the financial sectors.

In most of the emerging markets, the assets of the banking sector comprise over 80 percent of total financial sector assets, whereas these figures are much lower in developed economies. Furthermore, deposits, as a share of the total banks' liabilities, have declined since 1990 in many developed countries; while in developing countries, public deposits continue to be dominant in banks. In India, the share of banking assets in the total financial sector assets is around 75 percent, as of end-March, 2005. No doubt, there is merit in recognizing the importance of diversification in the institutional and instrument-specific aspects of financial intermediation in the interests of wide choice, competition, and stability. However, the dominant role of banks in financial intermediation in emerging economies in general and India in particular will continue in the medium term and banks will continue to be special for a long time. In this regard, it is useful to emphasize on the dominance of banks in developing countries for promoting non-banking financial intermediaries and services, and for development of debt markets. Even where the role of banks is apparently diminishing in emerging markets substantively, they continue to play a leading role in non-banking financial activities including development of financial markets.

The global rating agency, Standard & Poor's, has studied the changes in the Indian banking sector. In September, it raised the outlook of Indian banks from negative to stable. The agency said that the key structural reforms had improved the asset quality, profitability and capital adequacy ratio of banks, besides raising transparency and efficiency in the system. Gross NPAs, as a percentage of the entire banking system's advances, have improved from 15.7 percent in March 1997 to around 9 percent in March 2003.

Review of Literature

After the liberalization of the Indian economy, many private sector banks have started their business in India. The issue that is addressed in this study is, how effectively these banks have performed? In the past, various studies relating to the financial performance of banks have been conducted by researchers. In his paper, Das (2002) has attempted to develop an objective method for ranking the nationalized banks, by analyzing the performance of 17 public sector banks. Swami and Subrahmanyam (1994) have tried to study the interbank differences in the performance of public sector banks in India with the help of the "Taxonomic method". It was found that many banks had wide disparities in their measures of performance. Noulas and Ketkar (1996) conducted a study to examine the technical and scale efficiency of banks. Bhattacharya *et al.* (1997) and Sathye (2005) have studied the impact of privatization on the performance of banks. The results of the studies were, however, contradictory. While Bhattacharya found that performance of the public sector banks were sound as compared to the private sector banks, Sathye found the opposite results in his study. Saha and Ravisanker (2000) rated 25 public sector banks using the data envelopment analysis (DEA). A study on technical efficiency and benchmark performance of 68 commercial banks has been conducted by Mukherjee *et al.* (2002), which revealed that, in India, public sector banks are more efficient than both private and foreign banks. Amandeep (1993), in her study on profitability of commercial banks, has examined the profits and profitability of 20 nationalized banks. She concluded that efficient management is a dominant factor of profitability. Swamy (2001) studied the comparative performance of different bank groups. Das (2002) has studied the interrelationship among capital, non-performing loans and productivity of public sector banks. Uppal (2004) conducted a comparative study of the business, efficiency, soundness and productivity of the new private sector banks. He concluded that private sector banks are sound in urban area and he has ranked the banks as per the parameters. Qamar (2003) has studied the profitability and resource use efficiency in scheduled commercial banks in India. He found that new private sector banks and foreign banks are marginally more efficient than the old private sector and public sector banks.

This study is an addition to the literature by using the CAMEL method for the assessment of performance of new private sector banks.

Methodology of the Study

Objectives of the Study

The basic objective of the study is to analyze the performance of the selected banks—ICICI, HDFC, UTI and IDBI—through the CAMEL model and to rank them according to their performance.

The Universe and Sample of the Study

For the present study, the universe is all private banks irrespective of their size. From this, a sample is selected which is based on the awareness of the general public regarding different private banks. In order to meet this requirement, a formal public research was carried out, from which it is understood that the four banks are the more popular banks. Initially, the study was confined to three banks; but after the analysis, IDBI was taken into consideration, owing to its popularity or familiarity with the general public.

Sources of Data

The study is based mainly on secondary data. The relevant information in this regard is collected from various sources like *the PROWESS* Software of CMIE (Center for Monitoring Indian Economy), Stock Exchanges, magazines like *Analyst* and *Business Today*, and *RBI and IBA Bulletins*.

Tools and Techniques of Analysis and the Period of Study

The CAMEL technique is used for financial analysis of the selected banks. The period of study for financial analysis of these banks covers five years—from 2000-01 to 2004-05. After CAMEL analysis, the author attempted to rank the banks by overall comparison and the individual parameters of CAMEL. For this purpose, the following steps have been taken:

- All the banks are ranked on the basis of CAMEL parameters (see Appendix Table 1). On the basis of ranks in various aspects, the frequency distribution of ranks is presented in Table 2 of Appendix. For the purpose of ranking, the average ratio of all the banks for the five years have been considered.

- First of all, ranks are given to each bank and then weights are assigned to each rank in descending order. The bank which has the highest rank will also get the highest weight. Since the study has been conducted on four banks, the weight pattern is as follows: The bank which gets 1st rank will get the highest weight, i.e., equal to 4 (because there are four banks); similarly 2nd rank will get equal to 3, and so on. These weights are presented in the Appendix (Table 3).

- The sum of the number of times a bank appeared in the four ranks as weighted by the above-mentioned weights is also calculated. These sums are presented in Appendix (Table 4) in respect of all the five aspects studied. Aspect-wise ranks and their frequency distribution are given in Tables 5 and 6 of the Appendix.

- On the basis of the values presented in Table 4 of the Appendix, the four banks were ranked from 1st to 4th in respect of five aspects. These are presented in Table 7 of the Appendix.

What is CAMEL?

Prior to 1992, there were financial inspections once in four years and annual financial reviews for the public sector banks. In case of private sector banks and foreign banks, financial inspections were carried out once in 18 to 24 months. In order to obviate the long interval between the two actual inspections, the two streams of inspections were synthesized into one Annual Financial Inspection (AFI) applicable to all banks, which was implemented in 1992. The scope of AFI was broadened and the CAMEL model was introduced for inspection of banks. CAMEL stands for:

C = Capital Adequacy

A = Asset Quality

M = Management

E = Earning Quality

L = Liquidity

Capital Adequacy Analysis of Selected Banks

Capital adequacy reflects the overall financial condition of the banks and also the ability of the management to meet the need for additional capital.

Capital Adequacy Ratio (CAR)

$$\text{Capital Adequacy} = \frac{\text{Tier-I Capital} + \text{Tier-II Capital}}{\text{Risk Weighted Assets}}$$

As per the latest RBI norms, banks in India should have a CAR of 9 percent. It is computed by dividing Tier-I and Tier-II capital by the weighted assets (CRAR). Simply stated, this is each bank's leverage calculated after assigning different risk, generally announced by RBI, i.e., credit risk, market risk, technology risk, liquidity risk, and contingent risk, to assets lying with bank.

Tier-I Capital: Otherwise known as core capital, it provides the most permanent and·readily available support to a bank against unexpected losses. It includes the aggregate paid-up capital, statutory reserves and other disclosed free reserves including share premium and capital reserves arising out of surplus on sale of assets.

Tier-II Capital: It contains elements that are less permanent in nature or less readily available, than those comprising Tier-I. It comprises:

- Undisclosed reserves and cumulative perpetual preference assets.

- Revaluation reserves, which arise from revaluation of assets, are undervalued in the bank's books.

- General provision and loss reserves.

- Subordinated debt of 5-7 years tenure.

Capital to Risk-weighted Assets Ratio (CRAR)

This ratio shows that the owned fund in proportion to the risk-weighted assets of the bank. The weight to the assets is prescribed by the RBI for calculating the risk-weighted assets of banks and to maintain the minimum level at 9 percent.

Table 1 indicates that, as prescribed by the capital adequacy norm, all banks are capable enough to maintain the CRAR of 9 percent. And, ICICI Bank has well maintained its capital adequacy ratio for the first three years, which then decreased in 2003-04 and showed 10.36. But in the next year, it raised to 11.78%

Table 1: Capital to Risk-weighted Assets Ratio of Selected Banks						
Bank	2000-01	2001-02	2002-03	2003-04	2004-05	Average
ICICI	11.57	11.44	11.1	10.36	11.78	11.25
HDFC	11.09	13.93	11.12	11.66	12.16	11.99
UTI	9.00	10.65	10.90	11.21	12.66	10.88
IDBI	11.72	9.59	9.56	10.38	15.51	11.35

which is a healthy sign. On the other hand, HDFC Bank, UTI Bank, and IDBI Bank have shown fluctuation in maintaining it, but all have a better margin than required. And in 2004-05, IDBI has highest capital adequacy, i.e., 15.51 percent. Thus, it can be interpreted that all the banks enjoy good financial position and the ability to meet the need of additional capital.

Debt-Equity Ratio (Times)

Debt-Equity Ratio is computed by dividing the total borrowing and deposits by net worth. Net worth is the addition of equity capital, preference capital, reserves and surplus and deducting revaluation reserves miscellaneous expenses not written off.

The Debt-Equity and deductions indicates the proportion of debt fund in relation to equity. This ratio is very often referred in capital structure decision as well as in the legislation dealing with the capital structure decision. Internationally, a debt-equity ratio of 50 times is considered to be healthy for the banking sector.

Table 2 shows that the Debt-Equity Ratio of all the banks is below 50. This indicates that all banks are not over-leveraged, and have scope to increase the debt component of their capital structure. UTI Bank is the only one subject in this study that has the highest debt equity ratio since the beginning in all the years than others. It shows that it is the most well-levered bank than the other banks.

Table 2: Debt-Equity Ratio (Times) of Selected Banks						
Bank	2000-01	2001-02	2002-03	2003-04	2004-05	Average
ICICI	13.50	13.81	12.66	12.91	10.33	12.64
HDFC	14.17	10.08	10.95	12.37	9.10	11.33
UTI	34.09	22.01	19.78	19.44	13.90	21.84
IDBI	16.54	20.37	20.45	19.14	10.98	17.05

Advances to Assets Ratio

An advance to Assets Ratio is computed by dividing total advances by total assets. This ratio shows the proportion of loan and advances to the total deployment of funds. This shows a bank's aggressiveness in improving its credit deposits ratio by higher advances, which determines the profitability of the banks.

Table 3: Advances to Assets Ratio (%) of Selected Banks						
Bank	2000-01	2001-02	2002-03	2003-04	2004-05	Average
ICICI	35.63	44.81	49.44	49.22	54.51	46.72
HDFC	29.70	28.61	38.56	41.87	49.71	37.69
UTI	44.60	38.00	36.58	38.73	41.34	39.85
IDBI	35.16	46.51	54.33	56.74	55.81	49.70

From Table 3, it can be interpreted that, initially UTI Bank and IDBI Bank were ahead in advances, which started fluctuating gradually. On the other hand, the other three show an increasing trend in advances. ICICI Bank stood second, while IDBI Bank is more efficient in advances than others.

G-sec to Total Investment Ratio (Percent)

This ratio is calculated by dividing the amount invested in government securities (G-sec) by total investment. G-sec to investments ratio indicates the percentage of risk-free investment in bank's investment portfolio. Since government securities are risk-free, the higher the G-sec to investment ratio, the lower is the risk involved in a bank's investments. However, there is also an inherent trade-off in the yield on investment in opting to park funds in G-sec.

The data in Table 4 indicates that all the banks are conservative, i.e., they have a decided preference towards risk-free securities than other investment avenue. ICICI has shown the highest investment in G-sec than others and along with

Table 4: G-sec to Total Investment Ratio (%) of Selected Banks						
Bank	2000-01	2001-02	2002-03	2003-04	2004-05	Average
ICICI	49.72	63.31	72.04	69.96	70.34	65.07
HDFC	47.76	44.11	47.48	59.85	58.06	51.45
UTI	57.82	64.16	59.16	64.70	52.81	59.73
IDBI	47.63	63.31	75.83	77.41	59.46	64.73

IDBI Bank, both report an increasing trend while others are fluctuating gradually. UTI Bank has always stood at third position, since the beginning.

Assets Quality Analysis of Selected Banks

Assets quality is also another important aspect of the evaluation of banks. The prime motto behind measuring the asset quality is to ascertain the quality of assets and majority of the segments are related with non-performing assets. The quality of loans is one of the most crucial aspects that decides the financial health of the banks.

Net NPAs to Total Assets (Percent)

Net NPAs are Gross NPAs' net of provisions on NPAs and interest in suspense account. Total Assets are considered as the net of revaluation reserves.

The Net NPAs for ICICI Bank have been to be around 0.78 percent of total assets during the year 2000-01, and have come down to an average 0.12 percent in 2004-05.

A conscious effort is being made by the banks to minimize their NPA level. The data in Table 5 reveals that in the year 2000-01, IDBI has the highest NPA, followed by UTI, and ICICI. HDFC has only lower NPA since the beginning. But ICICI Bank reflects much fluctuation in the performance of reducing their NPAs gradually. In the year 2003-04, ICICI, followed by IDBI Bank, shows the highest NPAs and the HDFC Bank the lowest. In short, HDFC Bank is well aware of its assets and is utilizing them effectively.

Table 5: Net NPAs to Total Assets (%) of Selected Banks						
Bank	2000-01	2001-02	2002-03	2003-04	2004-05	Average
ICICI	0.78	2.48	2.60	1.10	0.12	1.42
HDFC	0.13	0.14	0.14	0.07	0.18	0.13
UTI	1.68	1.29	0.83	0.46	0.80	1.01
IDBI	1.83	1.03	0.65	0.48	1.04	1.00

Net NPAs to Total Advances (Percent)

Net NPAs are the net of bills rediscounted and specific loan loss provision. They show the resources deployed as advances. A conscious effort is being made by the banks to minimize their NPA level.

Table 6: Net NPAs to Total Advances (%) of Selected Banks						
Bank	2000-01	2001-02	2002-03	2003-04	2004-05	Average
ICICI	2.19	5.48	5.21	2.21	1.65	3.35
HDFC	0.45	0.50	0.37	0.16	0.24	0.34
UTI	3.43	3.48	0.11	0.17	1.39	1.72
IDBI	5.25	2.21	1.20	0.84	1.74	2.25

Net NPAs, as percentage of Net Advances, is the most standard measure of asset quality. As per international norms, a ratio of 1 percent is considered to be tolerable and desirable. Going by this norm, ICICI shows (Table 6) the highest NPA since 2000. It was reduced to 1.65 in 2004-05, which does not conform to the international standards. On the other hand, in 2000, IDBI also has the 5.25 percent NPA, which it successfully reduced to 1.74 percent. Although the improvement was a marked one, yet it did not conform to the international norms. UTI Bank had initially 3.43 percent NPA, which has been going up very fast and in 2004-05, it was 1.39 percent. It is interesting to know that since from the beginning, HDFC Bank has recorded the NPAs below the required 1 percent. It shows its awareness, efficiency, and effectiveness in the proper utilization of available assets.

Total Investment to Total Assets (Percent)

This ratio is used as a tool to measure the percentage of total assets locked up in investment. In other words, it indicates the extent of deployment of assets in investments as against advances. A higher level of investment indicates the lack of credit off-take in the market.

Table 7 reveals that HDFC Bank has the higher ratio since beginning followed by IDBI. ICICI and UTI have been fluctuating gradually. In the year 2004-05, ICICI shows the lowest ratio. It means that, ICICI indicates the opportunity of credit off-take in the market.

Table 7: Total Investment to Total Assets (%) of Selected Banks						
Bank	2000-01	2001-02	2002-03	2003-04	2004-05	Average
ICICI	41.48	34.20	32.90	33.88	29.21	34.33
HDFC	45.75	50.40	43.91	45.46	37.62	44.63
UTI	38.83	39.02	40.02	32.32	37.82	37.60
IDBI	50.04	36.28	30.61	30.26	30.79	35.60

Management Analysis of the Selected Banks

The ratios in this segment measure the efficiency and effectiveness of management. Management is the most important ingredient that ensures the sound functioning of banks. With increased competition in the Indian banking sector, efficiency and effectiveness have become the rule as banks constantly strive to improve the productivity of their employees. Presently, it is common to see branches of private banks maintaining extended working hours, flexible time schedules, outsourcing marketing, etc., to attract customers. Another development over the years has been the deployment of technology. Almost all banks have upgraded to computerized systems. RBI's efforts to ensure Total Branch Automation in a phased manner have led banks to speed up the computerization process. Internet banking and telephone banking have become widespread, with most banks offering these services quite comfortably. These parameters are used to assess the quality of management.

Credit Deposit Ratio/Advance to Deposit Ratio

This ratio measures the efficiency of the management in converting deposit into advances. Total deposits include demand deposits, savings deposits, term deposits and deposits of other banks. Total advances also include the receivables.

Table 8 shows that in 2000-01, UTI is ahead of all banks in converting deposits into advances, followed by IDBI, ICICI and HDFC. But it is interesting to know that the ICICI Bank has very efficiently improved the performance and stood out in 2003-04. The ICICI Bank was followed by IDBI Bank, HDFC, and UTI in performance. This shows that the efficiency of ICICI Bank's management to pursue the competition and march towards the end results. And, in 2004-05, IDBI Bank registered an increasing trend, followed by ICICI Bank. On the other hand, UTI has a decreasing trend, but in 2003-05, it shows good improvement.

Table 8: Credit Deposit Ratio/Advance to Deposit Ratio (%) of Selected Banks						
Bank	2000-01	2001-02	2002-03	2003-04	2004-05	Average
ICICI	42.93	146.59	110.61	91.17	91.57	96.57
HDFC	39.77	38.60	52.53	58.35	70.33	51.92
UTI	53.02	43.56	42.32	44.68	49.20	46.55
IDBI	48.35	59.21	71.70	73.63	300.0	110.58

Table 9: Profit per Employee (Rs. Lakhs) of Selected Banks						
Bank	2000-01	2001-02	2002-03	2003-04	2004-05	Average
ICICI	10.45	5.33	11.00	12.00	11.00	11.52
HDFC	8.61	9.75	10.09	9.39	8.80	11.24
UTI	7.27	7.79	8.22	8.07	7.03	9.06
IDBI	2.50	4.34	4.89	8.20	6.85	7.59

Profit per Employee

It is computed by dividing the PAT earned by the bank by the total number of employees. A higher ratio indicates higher efficiency of management.

Table 9 shows that since 2000-01, the ICICI Bank has been following high profit per employee. The reason behind this is the small number of employees than other banks, which increase the profit per employee. And, in 2004-05, ICICI Bank is a top bank, which has the highest profit per employee, i.e., Rs.12 lakh. It shows the efficiency of the management.

Business per Employee

It is computed by dividing total business by the total number of employees. Business includes the sum of total advances and deposits in a particular year.

From Table 10, it can be interpreted that ICICI stands third in business per employee ratio, because of its larger employee base. On the other front, it shows greater efficiency than other banks in this study. It recorded its achievement by securing first position in 2002-03; and IDBI, which stood at fourth position in 2002-03, secured the first position in 2004-05. HDFC and UTI show fluctuation in the study.

Table 10: Business per Employee (Rs. Lakhs) of Selected Banks						
Bank	2000-01	2001-02	2002-03	2003-04	2004-05	Average
ICICI	815.22	486.49	1120.00	1010.00	880.00	862.34
HDFC	643.00	778.00	865.00	866.00	806.00	791.60
UTI	959.00	896.00	926.00	808.00	895.00	896.80
IDBI	684.67	689.88	712.84	1080.30	1349.60	903.46

Return on Net Worth

It is a measure of the profitability of a company. Profit After Tax (PAT) is expressed as a percentage of Average Net Worth.

Table 11: Return on Net Worth (%) of Selected Banks						
Bank	2000-01	2001-02	2002-03	2003-04	2004-05	Average
ICICI	12.37	3.92	16.56	19.58	15.54	13.59
HDFC	22.75	15.55	17.21	18.92	14.73	17.83
UTI	28.57	22.21	20.91	24.45	13.89	22.01
IDBI	7.22	17.42	20.07	21.42	5.18	14.26

From Table 11, it is clear that ICICI secured the fourth position in 2001-02; in 2004-05, it outdid all others in terms of profitability. On the other hand, UTI stood first in 2001-02, but in 2004-05, its profitability reduced and it stood at number three. IDBI Bank was number four in 2000-01, which fluctuated gradually and was placed second in 2003-04; but in 2004-05, it gained the fourth position. HDFC Bank has variation throughout the last five years. On the whole, IDBI Bank and UTI Bank show the good record in terms of profitability. In this context, ICICI shows a low level of performance.

Earning Quality Analysis of Selected Banks

This section assesses the quality of income in terms of income generated by core activities, i.e., income from lending operations. Investing additional funds forms an important part of the banking function along with lending. In the recent past, banks have been criticized for making most of their money from treasury operation and other investments rather than from core lending operations. Even as fee-based operations still account for a minority of bank's revenues, the share of non-interest income is higher. The ratios in this segment assess the quality and the source of earning of the banks. The risk and return having direct proportion in banking industry means you take higher risk and generate higher return. There are various parameters, which have been used for measuring the earning quality. They are:

Operating Profit by Average Working Funds

This ratio gives returns on total assets employed on the daily basis. Working fund is the daily average of the total assets during the year.

Table 12: Operating Profit by Average Working Funds (%) of Selected Banks						
Bank	2000-01	2001-02	2002-03	2003-04	2004-05	Average
ICICI	2.35	2.14	2.49	2.09	2.18	2.25
HDFC	2.83	2.61	2.58	2.56	2.56	2.63
UTI	1.50	3.43	2.55	3.49	2.04	2.60
IDBI	1.39	2.16	2.33	2.80	0.46	1.82

The average operating profit as percentage of average working funds of ICICI is 2.25 percent (average) for the last five years. On the other hand, where the average of other banks is concerned, they recorded an average ratio of more than 2 percent individually. HDFC Bank was at the first position in average operating profit, followed by UTI Bank, ICICI Bank and IDBI Bank. HDFC Bank secured the first position in 2000, but showed variation afterwards. ICICI has not stood first in any year, but shows fluctuation. Overall, ICICI shows average performance in this context.

Spread as Percentage of Total Assets/Net Interest Income to Total Assets (Percent)

It is the difference between the interest income and interest expenditure as a percentage of total assets. Interest income includes dividend income. Interest expended includes interest paid on deposits, loans from RBI, and other short-term and long-term loans.

Spread indicates a bank's ability to withstand pressure on margins, where a higher spread, considered better. From the information available in Table 13, ICICI has an average 1.43 percent spread over the last five years. On the other hand, HDFC Bank recorded the number one position. ICICI stands at number four since a long time, following IDBI Bank and UTI Bank. It shows that the interest income of HDFC Bank is higher than others. Thus, while most of the income is fund-based, it comes from investments rather than advances.

Table 13: Spread as Percentage of Total Assets/Net Interest Income to Total Assets (%) of Selected Banks						
Bank	2000-01	2001-02	2002-03	2003-04	2004-05	Average
ICICI	2.05	0.57	1.33	1.50	1.69	1.43
HDFC	3.24	2.65	2.70	3.16	3.45	3.04
UTI	0.91	1.38	1.64	2.34	1.93	1.64
IDBI	2.06	2.16	2.54	2.55	0.23	1.91

Return on Assets

This is arrived at by PAT divided by Average Assets, which is the average of total assets in the current year and previous year. This ratio measures return on assets employed or the efficiency in the utilization of the assets.

Table 14: Return on Assets (%) of Selected Banks

Bank	2000-01	2001-02	2002-03	2003-04	2004-05	Average
ICICI	1.01	0.41	1.13	1.40	1.36	1.06
HDFC	1.54	1.51	1.43	1.40	1.42	1.18
UTI	0.99	1.08	1.12	1.27	1.08	1.11
IDBI	0.41	0.90	0.97	1.26	0.78	0.90

The average performance of ICICI in terms of utilization of assets is lower as compared to other banks (Table 14). On the other hand, from the beginning, HDFC Bank shows the higher performance in utilization of assets in a very effective and efficient way, followed by IDBI Bank, and UTI.

Percentage Growth in Net Profit

It is a percentage change in net profit from the last year. It indicated growth in profit after tax in terms of percentage.

Table 15: Percentage Growth in Net Profit (%) of Selected Banks

Bank	2000-01	2001-02	2002-03	2003-04	2004-05	Average
ICICI	1.53	1.60	4.67	1.36	1.22	2.08
HDFC	1.75	1.41	1.30	1.31	1.31	1.41
UTI	1.69	1.57	1.41	1.45	1.20	1.46
IDBI	0.32	2.71	1.36	1.86	1.10	1.47

Table 15 reveals that in 2000-01 HDFC Bank has shown good performance, followed by UTI, ICICI and IDBI in PAT. It is interesting to know that in the year 2002-03, PAT of ICICI Bank moved up from 1.6 percent to 4.67 percent and then went down to 1.36 percent in 2003-04 due to the merger of ICICI and ICICI Bank in 2002. The average of last five years shows that ICICI Bank occupies the number one position, i.e., 2.08 percent, followed by IDBI Bank (1.47 percent), UTI Bank (1.46 percent), and HDFC Bank (1.41 percent).

Non-Interest Income to Total Income (Percent)

This measures the income from operation, other than lending as a percentage of total income. Non-interest income is the interest income earned by banks excluding income on advances and deposits with RBI.

Table 16: Non-Interest Income to Total Income (%) of Selected Banks

Bank	2000-01	2001-02	2002-03	2003-04	2004-05	Average
ICICI	52.41	66.30	40.05	43.85	45.54	49.63
HDFC	56.82	58.77	63.65	59.59	35.14	54.79
UTI	15.32	59.81	52.62	55.29	56.80	47.97
IDBI	61.89	55.83	48.48	45.29	31.28	48.55

Table 16 indicates that all the banks show the fluctuation. Hence, it is not easy to rank any bank. But on the basis of average, HDFC Bank has greater portion of non-interest income than others (54.79 percent). ICICI Bank (49.63 percent) is at the second position, followed by IDBI Bank (48.55 percent) and UTI Bank (47.97 percent). In short, it should be said that all the banks have almost more than 50 percent interest income.

Interest Income to Total Income

This ratio measures the income from lending operation as a percentage of the total income generated by a bank in a year. Interest income includes income on advances and interest on deposits with RBI.

Table 17: Interest Income to Total Income (%) of Selected Banks

Bank	2000-01	2001-02	2002-03	2003-04	2004-05	Average
ICICI	47.59	33.70	59.95	56.15	54.46	50.37
HDFC	43.18	41.23	36.35	40.41	47.47	41.73
UTI	84.68	40.19	47.38	44.71	43.20	52.03
IDBI	38.11	44.17	51.52	54.71	68.72	51.44

Table 17 shows that a major portion of the income came from fund-based income, that is, from investment rather than advances. This table shows an average performance of banks in earning quality segment. In this segment, it can be said, all the banks have performed well. Taking an average of the last five years' performance, UTI Bank stood first.

Liquidity Analysis of Selected Banks

Liquidity refers to the existence of the cash or near cash form. This ratio indicates the ability of the banks to discharge the liability as and when they mature. In other words, liquidity means the ability of banks to convert non-cash items into cash as and when needed.

The business of banking is all about borrowing and lending money. Timely repayment of deposits is of crucial importance to avoid a run on a bank. With cooperative banks going down frequently and with the recent collapse of Global Trust Bank, investors have become extremely sensitive. They are alert; they rush to the bank to withdraw money at the slightest hint of trouble. In such a scenario, even false rumors could wreck havoc with a bank. Hence, banks have to ensure that they always maintain enough liquidity. Through mandatory SLR and CRR, RBI ensures that banks maintain ample liquidity. In fact, over the last few years, banks have been washing with liquidity.

Liquidity Assets to Demand Deposit (Percent)

Liquid assets as a percentage of demand deposits are one of the most important measures of the liquidity position of a bank. This ratio measures the ability of a bank to meet the demand from demand deposits in a particular year. Liquid assets include cash in hand, balance with RBI, balance with other banks (both in India and abroad), and money at call and short notice.

Table 18: Liquidity Assets to Demand Deposit (%) of Selected Banks						
Bank	2000-01	2001-02	2002-03	2003-04	2004-05	Average
ICICI	137.07	467.31	176.00	116.69	100.73	199.54
HDFC	107.13	91.55	70.00	42.29	42.08	70.60
UTI	150.79	234.77	144.00	105.00	73.74	141.58
IDBI	86.28	38.63	56.10	37.51	145.45	72.79

Table 18 shows that ICICI Bank has good efficiency in converting the non-cash item into cash item, i.e., liquidity to meet the demand in a particular year. IDBI holds the second position compared to other banks in this study, followed by UTI Bank and HDFC Bank. UTI Bank holds average second position in all, and HDFC holds average last position in all.

Liquidity to Total Deposits (Percent)

Liquid assets are measured as a percentage of Total Deposits. Liquid assets include cash in hand, balance with RBI, balance with other banks (both in India and abroad), and money at call and short notice. Total Deposits include demand deposits, savings deposits, term deposits, and deposits of other financial institutions.

Table 19: Liquidity to Total Deposits (%) of Selected Banks

Bank	2000-01	2001-02	2002-03	2003-04	2004-05	Average
ICICI	21.94	39.9	13.47	12.44	12.95	20.13
HDFC	26.24	21.9	15.48	12.29	12.31	17.64
UTI	13.75	22.00	21.04	27.03	16.64	20.04
IDBI	11.15	13.70	11.64	11.34	37.65	17.01

From Table 19, it is found that ICICI Bank shows high liquid asset as percentage of total deposits, which shows ability of ICICI Bank in terms of maintaining liquidity. The average ratio of ICICI Bank for the last five year is 20.13 percent, which is higher than other banks, followed by UTI Bank (20.04 percent), HDFC Bank (17.64 percent), and IDBI Bank (17.01 percent).

Liquid Assets to Total Assets

Liquid assets are measured as a percentage of total assets.

Table 20: Liquid Assets to Total Assets (%) of Selected Banks

Bank	2000-01	2001-02	2002-03	2003-04	2004-05	Average
ICICI	18.21	12.18	6.02	6.71	7.71	10.17
HDFC	19.59	16.22	11.36	8.82	8.07	12.94
UTI	11.57	18.55	18.19	23.43	13.98	17.14
IDBI	7.98	10.78	8.82	8.74	6.95	8.65

Table 20 shows that ICICI has higher average liquid assets than all the other banks, followed by HDFC Bank, ICICI Bank and IDBI Bank. It shows that ICICI is behind other banks in terms of efficiency and effectiveness.

Approved Securities to Total Assets

Approved securities are investments made in state-associated bodies like electricity boards, housing boards, corporation bonds and share of regional rural banks.

Table 21: Approved Securities to Total Assets (%) of Selected Banks						
Bank	2000-01	2001-02	2002-03	2003-04	2004-05	Average
ICICI	0.21	0.07	0.03	0.02	0.02	0.07
HDFC	0.08	0.05	0.04	0.02	0.01	0.04
UTI	0	0	0	0	0	0
IDBI	0	0	0	0	0	0

From Table 21, it is clear that ICICI has recorded the highest investment in approved securities than other banks. Further, it is going downward year-by-year. It shows that ICICI has more liquidity than the other selected banks. It can be said that it has risk-free investment because of conservative approach.

Performance Analysis of Banks by Ranking Methods

- The result of overall ranks of the selected banks indicates that IDBI was the topmost bank, followed by UTI, HDFC, and ICICI Bank.

- The coefficient of variation gives the information about the extent of competition among banks. As greater competition would lead to the convergence of the value observed in respect of banks, a lower CV would indicate that the competition is higher and vice versa. The CV of study is 153 percent, which indicates lower competition among banks under study.

- According to different aspects of CAMEL, the IDBI was the topmost bank in capital adequacy, followed by ICICI and UTI. In assets quality, ICICI was the topper, followed by UTI and IDBI. IDBI was ranked first in the management aspects of CAMEL. Earning efficiency of HDFC is the best among all the four banks, followed by UTI. The liquidity management of UTI is the best among all these banks.

Conclusion

From the analysis, it can be concluded that the competition among banks is tough and consumers benefit from it. As a result, Indian customers enjoy better service quality, innovative products, and better bargains. The fact that an increasing size of the banking pie itself indicates that there is a lot of untapped potential in the market for banking. Given the low interest rate environment and economic recovery, banks have been able to increase credit off-take. Growth has been tremendous, particularly in the retail segment including housing loans, vehicle loans and credit cards. On the other hand, low interest rate means good treasury income. In fact, treasury income has occupied a major chunk of the 'other income' for banks. The loss in interest rates is a thing of the past; interest rates are all set to harden in the future. This could mean a loss in the treasury income for banks. But experts contend that the loss in treasury income would be more than offset by the interest income on advances, assuming that credit off-take will be as good as in the earlier years. The coming fiscal will prove to be a transition phase for Indian banks, as they will have to align their strategic focus to increasing interest rates.

(Sanjay J Bhayani, Associate Professor, Department of Business Management (MBA Program), Saurashtra University, Rajkot, Gujarat, India. He can be reached at sanjaybhayani@yahoo.com).

References

1. Altman E, Avery R, Eisenbeis R, and Sinkey J (1981), *Application of Classification Techniques in Business Banking and Finance,* JAI Press Greenwhich Connecticut.

2. Baruch L (1974), *Financial Statement Analysis: A New Approach,* Prentice Hall, Englewood Cliffs, New Jersey.

3. Bhattacharya A, Lovell C A K and Pankaj Sahay (1997), "The Impact of Liberalization on the Productive Efficiency of Indian Commercial Banks", *European Journal of Operational Research,* Vol. 98, pp. 175-212.

4. Das Abhiman (2002), "Risk and Productivity Change of Public Sector Banks", *EPW,* Vol. 37, No. 5, pp. 437-448.

5. Das M R (2002), "An Objective Method for Ranking Nationalized Banks", *Prajan,* Vol. 31, No. 2, pp. 111-136.

6. Maimbo S M (1996), "Interpretation of Financial Statements Using Key Performance Ratios", Financial System Supervision Department Discussion Paper, Bank of Zambia, Lusaka.

7. Mukherjee A, Nath P and Pal M N (2002), "Performance Benchmarking and Strategic Homogeneity of Indian Banks", *International Journal of Bank Marketing,* Vol. 20, No. 3, pp. 122-139.

8. Noulas A G and Ketkar K W (1996), "Technical and Scale Efficiency in the Indian Banking Sector", *International Journal of Development Banking,* Vol. 14, No. 2, pp. 19-27.

9. Qamar F (2003), "Profitability and Resource Use Efficiency in Scheduled Commercial Banks in India: A Comparative Analysis of Foreign, New Private Sector, Old Private Sector and Public Sector Banks", *Synthesis,* Vol. 1, No. 1, pp. 1-16.

10. Saha Asish and Ravisanker T S (2000), "Rating of Indian Commercial Banks: A DEA Approach", *European Journal of Operational Research,* Vol. 124, pp. 187-203.

11. Sathye M (2005), "Privatization, Performance, and Efficiency: A Study of Indian Banks", *Vikalpa,* Vol. 30, No. 1, pp. 7-16.

12. Swami B G and Subrahmanyam G (1994), "Comparative Performance of Public Sector Banks in India", *Prajnan,* Vol. 21, No. 2, pp. 185-195.

13. Swamy B N A (2001), "New Competition, Deregulation and Emerging Changes in Indian Bankings: An Analysis of Different Banks-Groups", *The Journal of the Indian Institute of Bankers,* Vol. 72, No. 3, July-September, pp. 3-22.

14. Uppal R K (2004), "A Comparative Study of Business, Efficiency, Soundness and Productivity of New Private Sector Banks (An Objective Method for Ranking of NPSBs)", *Journal of Indian Management Studies,* Vol. 8, No. 1, pp. 99-115.

APPENDIX

Table 1: Indicator-wise Ranking of Banks					
Sr. No.	Indicator	ICICI	HDFC	UTI	IDBI
Capital Adequacy					
1	Capital to Risk Weighted Asset Ratio	3	1	4	2
2	Debt Equity Ratio	3	4	1	2
3	Advances to Assets Ratio	2	4	3	1
4	G-sec to Total Investment	1	4	3	2
Asset Quality					
1	Net NPA to Total Assets	1	4	2	3
2	Net NPA to Total Advances	1	4	3	2
3	Total Investment to Total Assets	4	1	2	3
Management					
1	Credit Deposit Ratio/Advance to Deposit Ratio	2	3	4	1
2	Profit Per Employee	1	2	3	4
3	Business Per Employee	3	4	2	1
4	Return on Net Worth	4	2	1	3
Earning Quality					
1	Operating Profit by Average Working Fund	3	1	2	4
2	Spread as Percentage of Total Assets/ Net Interest Income to Total Assets	4	1	3	2
3	Return on Assets	3	1	2	4
4	Percentage Growth in Net Profit	1	4	3	2
5	Non-Interest Income to Total Income	2	1	4	3
6	Interest Income to Total Income	3	4	1	2
Liquidity					
1	Liquidity Asset to Demand Deposit	1	4	2	3
2	Liquidity to Total Deposits	2	3	1	4
3	Liquid Assets to Total Assets	3	2	1	4
4	Approved Securities to Total Assets	2	1	3.5	3.5

Table 2: Frequency Distribution of Ranks				
Capital Adequacy				
Bank	**1st**	**2nd**	**3rd**	**4th**
ICICI	1	1	2	0
HDFC	1	0	0	3
UTI	1	0	2	1
IDBI	1	3	0	0
Asset Quality				
Bank	**1st**	**2nd**	**3rd**	**4th**
ICICI	2	0	0	1
HDFC	1	0	0	2
UTI	0	2	1	0
IDBI	0	1	2	0
Management				
Bank	**1st**	**2nd**	**3rd**	**4th**
ICICI	1	1	1	1
HDFC	0	2	1	1
UTI	1	1	1	1
IDBI	2	0	1	1
Earning Quality				
Bank	**1st**	**2nd**	**3rd**	**4th**
ICICI	1	1	3	1
HDFC	4	0	0	2
UTI	1	2	2	1
IDBI	0	3	1	2
Liquidity				
Bank	**1st**	**2nd**	**3rd**	**4th**
ICICI	1	2	1	0
HDFC	1	1	1	1
UTI	2	1	1	0
IDBI	0	0	2	2

Table 3: Weight Pattern	
Rank (Best to Worst)	**Weight**
1	4
2	3
3	2
4	1
Total	10

Table 4: Weighted Sums					
Bank	**C**	**A**	**M**	**E**	**L**
ICICI	1.10	0.90	1.00	1.27	1.10
HDFC	0.70	0.60	0.90	1.80	1.00
UTI	0.90	0.80	1.00	1.50	1.20
IDBI	1.30	0.70	1.10	1.30	0.60
Mean	1.00	0.75	1.00	1.47	0.98
S.D.	0.258	0.129	0.082	0.244	0.263
CV (%)	25.820	17.213	8.165	16.630	26.974

Table 5: Aspect-wise Rank					
Bank	**C**	**A**	**M**	**E**	**L**
ICICI	2	1	2	4	2
HDFC	4	4	4	1	3
UTI	3	3	3	2	1
IDBI	1	2	1	3	4

Table 6: Frequency Distribution of Ranks – All Five Aspects				
Bank	**1st**	**2nd**	**3rd**	**4th**
ICICI	1	3	0	1
HDFC	1	0	1	3
UTI	1	1	3	0
IDBI	2	1	1	1

Table 7: Overall Ranks		
Bank	Points	Ranks
ICICI	1	4
HDFC	1.1	3
UTI	1.3	2
IDBI	16	1
Mean	4.85	-
S.D.	7.43	-
CV (%)	153.29	-

8

A Comparative Study on the Service Quality and Customer Satisfaction among Private, Public and Foreign Banks

Rengasamy Elango and Vijaya Kumar Gudep

The paper focuses on the service quality and customer satisfaction among the private, public and foreign banks in India. An analysis is carried out to examine the level of awareness among customers and to identify the best sector which provides qualitative customer service. This becomes relevant in the context of recommendations of various committees constituted by the Government of India and the RBI, from time to time, to suggest measures to improve customer service systems of the public sector commercial banks of India. A well-structured questionnaire is used to collect the views of respondents across the three banking sectors. The survey instrument includes various dimensions, pertaining to the quality of customer services in terms of banking personnel, convenient working hours, Web-based services, error free value-added services and efficient grievance redressal mechanism etc. Apart from the basic statistical tools such as measures of central tendency, the

Source: The Icfai Journal of Marketing Management, Vol. V, No. 3, 2006. © *The Icfai University Press. All rights reserved.*

authors also use 'factor analysis' and the 'One-way ANOVA' classification. The idea behind this is to extract the relevant factors and analyze whether there is any significant difference with respect to service quality within the three banking sectors. The results indicate that the level of awareness among the customers improved significantly during the study period. It is interesting to note that the results are consistent with the previous studies conducted on customer service aspects, and it has been observed that the foreign and the new generation private sector banks are serving the customers better. This has larger implications on the public sector commercial banks in India with respect to customer service delivery aspects. It is high time the public sector commercial banks made efforts to revamp their approach towards customers, so as to perform better and derive competitive advantage in the long run.

Introduction

Global banking scenario is currently undergoing radical transformation owing to the liberalization, privatization and globalization measures, introduced by the various economies of the world and Indian banking industry is no exception to the ongoing trend. Prior to liberalization of the economy, public sector commercial banks in India functioned in a protected environment and the banking transactions were simple characterized by less competition and customer orientation. The phenomenon of globalization brought about significant changes in terms of products and services that are being offered to Indian customers and consequently the complexion of the banking sector in India too underwent a noteworthy change in the last decade.

The entry of information technology into the banking industry has created a revolution and it has prompted public sector commercial banks of India to design world-class customer service systems and practices, to meet the growing customer needs. Indian banks are realizing that their internal administrative systems have to be geared up to face the unprecedented changes that are taking place in the environment due to global forces. The emergence of new private sector and foreign banks is one of the major challenges before the public sector commercial banks in India and this prompted the Indian banking industry to reckon with the challenges posed by the competition while rendering services to the customers.

On account of the competitive customer services and spirit, unleashed by the above said banks, there is a change in the customer needs like access to deposits anywhere anytime, speedy transfer of funds, quick remittances and bill collections, and fast screening of credit proposals without undue paper work etc. This was hitherto unknown to the public sector commercial banks of India and it necessitated them to focus on service quality and customer satisfaction dimensions not only to retain the existing clientele but also to attract new customers to remain competitive. This has major implications on the public sector commercial banks of India and it is against this background that the studies on customer service and service quality are gaining importance. At the time of nationalization, primary focus was laid on the concept of "more banking" whereas the present competitive scenario has necessitated all the players, big and small, to accord top priority with "better banking".

Bankers' Fight Results in Customers' Delight

The Banking sector being a service-oriented industry has to sustain on the quality of customer service. Analytical results of research studies, conducted world-wide reveal that the survival and growth of a bank not only depend upon its ability to provide qualitative services to its customers on a sustained basis, but in building a long-term mutually beneficial and trust-worthy relationship with its customers. In the current scenario, the three major segments of the banking sector i.e., private, public and multi-national/foreign banks vie with each other to attract large clientele, both traditional and innovative modern value-added services. The operational and service aspects of the bankers have witnessed significant changes owing to the innovations of science & technology and computer revolution. So, when bankers fight among themselves with improved and value-added services, it is the customer who is at delight as he/she gets first-rated services in all aspects.

Need and Importance of the Study

The study is relevant in the light of the recommendations of several committees, constituted by Government of India and the Indian Parliament, which urged the public sector commercial banks of India to design effective customer service systems, so as to compete effectively in the liberalized market. The present study also becomes valid in the light of the observations made by different committees like Narasimhan Committee on financial sector reforms, Gopiora Committee on customer service, Rangarajan Committee on mechanization and Talwar Committee on customer service. All the above said committees also focus on the customer service aspects of banking sector.

The changing profile of bank employees with the influx of qualified and ambitious workforce, hurdles faced by banks while designing effective manpower planning in the light of the challenge thrown by the recently introduced VRS, lack of effective training programs for the employees, comments made by the banking service commission on the existing performance appraisal techniques and problems faced by the public sector banks, while transferring the employees to rural and semi urban areas also validate the present study. The competition, unleashed by the combination of three major segments of bankers i.e., private, public and a foreign banks, also necessitated the investigation into the level of awareness and satisfaction of banking customers.

Objectives of the Study

The broad objectives of the study are as follows:

- To understand and analyze the dimensions of the awareness and satisfaction level of customers with regard to the services provided by the selected branches of the three major banking segments i.e., private, public and foreign banks.

- To identify and differentiate the best banking sector among the above cited three banks.

- To offer suggestions, if needed, based on the analytical results of the current study.

- The study also aims at testing whether there is a significant difference in terms of the awareness and satisfaction level of the customers of the three banking sectors i.e., private, public and foreign banks.

Limitations of the Study

In spite of the constant effort and care taken while administering the questionnaire, some of the respondents were apprehending that this questionnaire was designed by the bank administration to gauge their responses and this marginally limited the study. The other limitations which have no major influence on the study include:

- The study has incorporated only some statistical tools among the various tools, available in this context. In particular the entire study adhered mainly to Factor Analysis and One-way Analysis of Variance (ANOVA-I WAY) classification.

- The study is confined only to the three sectors of commercial ·banks of India due to the paucity of time and resources.

- The data were collected between December, 2003 and July, 2004 i.e., over a period of eight months. Changes in the policies of the government and the RBI and its impact on customer satisfaction are not considered in this study.

Literature Review

Several studies are carried out by various researchers of India and abroad, to find out the dimensions and factors, which influenced effective service. There is a growing body of literature demonstrating that the quality of customer service on an ongoing basis has an impact on the effective functioning of the banks. Studies made by Chase[3], Levitt[5], Roth and Jackson[7], Sherman and Gold[10] highlight that the quality of customer service also depends on the human resources practices of the service organization.

A study, named as Profit Impact of Market Strategy (PIMS), conducted by the US-based Strategic Planning Institute, utilizing comprehensive data from over 3,000 firms over a period of 15-years , found that those firms which delivered best quality and products, always came out on the top. The study also revealed that the reason of the success, is the quality of the customer service of the firm and not the advertising slogans (B Uttal, 1987)[12]. The study also revealed that the major challenge for service providing organizations across the world is to induce their human resources (people) to deliver quality products.

According to Berry[1] the service components of any bank product have a number of unique characteristics, which distinguish them from the tangible aspects of the product. Swartz, Bowen and Brown[11] feel that these characteristics affect the nature and quality of service in the banks. According to them, the service components of the bank products are evidently dependent on human action and behavior for their delivery to the customer. According to them, this behavior in turn is a consequence of service climate surrounding the bank and the climate components are identified as:

- The degree and power of authority, which the employee has, to deliver as a service component in a bank.

- The systems and procedures, which facilitate the employee to deliver the service components of the bank product.

- The appropriateness of the training, which the employee has received.

- The service provider's attitude towards his/her work and employer, which are a reflection of the reward system.

- The values of the organization for which the service provider works, is reflected in terms of the goals of the organization and its structure.

Bowen and Lawler[2] identify two broad quality-based service approaches, which can be instrumental in creating service excellence. They are "production line approach" and "empowerment approach". The authors suggest a combination of these strategies for a service-oriented organization. The "production line" approach recommends the implementation of standardized procedurally-driven operations. They are characterized by

- Simplification of tasks.

- Clear division of work.

- Substitution of equipment and systems for employees.

- Decision-making discretion to employees.

The "empowerment approach" aims at getting the best from employees by making them understand that the interests of the customer, interests of the organization and their own interests are similar. This is achieved by sharing the following four aspects with front line employees.

1. Information about the organization's performance.

2. Rewards based on the organization's performance.

3. Knowledge that enables employees to understand and contribute to the organizational performance.

4. Power to make decisions that influence an organization's overall performance.

In another landmark research on the dimensions of the customer service aspects, V A Zenithal, A Parasuraman and Berry L L[13] identify 10 criteria for judging servicing quality. These dimensions are directly dependent on the service provider (bank employee) and they arise out of the organizational policies of the bank. The 10 factors are:

1. *Tangibility:* Appearance of physical facilities, equipments, personnel and communication materials.

2. *Reliability:* Ability to perform the promised service dependably and accurately.

3. *Responsiveness:* Willingness to help the customers and provide prompt service.

4. *Competence:* Possession of the required skills and knowledge to perform the service.

5. *Courtesy:* Politeness, respect, consideration and friendliness of the contact personnel.

6. *Credibility:* Trustworthiness, believability, and honesty of the service provider.

7. *Security:* Safety from dangers, risks and doubts.

8. *Access:* Approachability and ease to contact.

9. *Communication:* Keeping customers informed in a language they understand and start listening to them in a continuous basis.

10. *Understanding the Customer:* Making efforts to analyze the customers and their needs.

Schneider and Bowen[8] observed that service-oriented firms in their pursuit of service quality, need to create two types of customer service climates, which are related to each other and not mutually exclusive. They are the climate for service and the climate for employee well-being. They define service climate in terms of managerial behavior, systems support, customer attention and logistics support. They present evidence to demonstrate that the service climate is strong when the standard of service delivered is high. They conducted an empirical study within a banking environment and they concluded that the key to manage efficient customer service with quality is to manage employee's experiences within the organization. The customer service dimensions identified in Schneider and Bowen's study are:

- *Work Facilitation:* Organization and job related aspects that facilitate task performance.

- *Supervision:* Supervisory behaviors such as providing feedback, establishing reward contingencies and sharing information.

- *Organization Career Facilitation:* Organization practices concerning career growth and development.

- *Organization Status:* The status and image, employee believes the organization has in the eyes of the outsiders.

- *New Employee Socialization:* Organization practices regarding the orientation/training/socialization of newcomers.

In 1983, the National Institute of Bank Management, Pune[4] conducted a large scale survey (by three banking experts) on the customer service climate of banking sector in India by collecting the opinions of the bank employees from 15 public sector banks from all the regions of India covering about 7,000 employees (which includes officers, clerks and allied staff) from about 1500 branches. The study revealed that those banks, which were low on the performance were perceived by their employees as low in customer service. The study also revealed that banks which were low on profitability and productivity were also lacking in customer service focus and personnel systems like job rotation, training and confidential reporting systems.

Several efforts were also made in the past by the Reserve Bank of India, the Government of India, the Ministry of Finance, and the Parliament of India to set up various committees from time to time to find out the customer service challenges and suggested ways and means to overcome them. The report of the working group on customer service in banks popularly known as RT Talwar Committee made recommendations to improve customer service in banks. Most of the recommendations of this committee focused on the human dimension of the employees in the bank and the RBI asked the banks to implement them. These recommendations highlighted areas like quality of customer service, customer oriented induction policies and promotional policies.

Shainesh and Tanuja Sharma[9] attempted to analyze the linkages between service climate and service quality. Contacting 271 employees, and 300 customers of 48 banks in India, they among others, tested whether employees' and customers' perception of service climate would differ across foreign, private and public banks. They found out that the employers' perception of foreign and private banks were similar. They also found that significant differences existed across bank types. Among the three set of banks, public sector banks scored low on three dimensions of service climate.

The present research aims at analyzing the level of awareness and satisfaction among the three different segments of banks. This study is different from others owing to the fact that it not only makes an attempt to examine the level of awareness and satisfaction of the customers applying the Principal Components and Factor Analysis, but also attempts to identify the bank that offers the best service among the three. Of course, the study offers suitable suggestions wherever necessary. Since urban centers are the only places where all the three types of banking segments function, a study in major metropolitan centers of India would enable the bankers and their think-tank to re-orient their level of operations, which would result in improved, modern, value-added and satisfactory customer services in the Indian commercial banking network.

Sources of Primary Data

The Questionnaire

A well-structured questionnaire was prepared and distributed to the selected bank customers in urban centers of India. The questionnaire was divided into three sections. Section A was designed to obtain demographic information about customers and the questions focused on age, sex, educational qualifications, occupation, average monthly income, marital status, nature of bank, where the customer transacts, nature of account and frequency of transactions etc. Section B had 39 questions which were intended to analyze the awareness and satisfaction of the customers contacted for this study.

In Section B, the questions were on the basis of Likert's five-point scale with the following numerical values; Strongly Agree (2), Agree (1), Neutral (0), Disagree (-1), and Strongly Disagree (-2). Section C, captioned 'Suggestions' had a blank space, which was aimed at eliciting the views, opinions and suggestions of the respondents.

Pre-testing of the Questionnaire

The questionnaire was pre-tested with the response obtained from 40 respondents. Results of the reliability tests resulted in an overall Cronbach alpha value 0.8435. The feed back of the respondents was useful in carrying out a few corrections/ modifications in the items included earlier in the questionnaire. The final questionnaire was again subjected to reliability test and the same resulted in an improvement in the alpha value 0.9464, thus further confirming that the instrument is fully reliable and internally consistent.

Since the preliminary questionnaire had an overall Cronbach alpha value, which is much higher than the benchmark (Cronbach alpha > 0.70 as suggested by Nunnally (1978)), the items included in the interval scale were considered reliable and internally consistent thus paving the way for designing the final questionnaire.

Data Collection

The final questionnaire was prepared and distributed to the selected bank customers in major urban centers of India. The researchers or their friends personally visited the bank premises and distributed them with a request to return the filled-in questionnaire on the same day. In other cases, the researchers personally visited the residences of bank customers; initial visit was followed up and the questionnaires were collected in a phased manner.

Table 1 gives the response rate of the distributed questionnaires. Out of 190 questionnaires distributed to the customers of public sector banks, only 166 completed questionnaires were received, thus registering a response rate of 87.36%. Out of 80 questionnaires distributed to the customers of private sector banks, 66 (response rate 82.5%) completed questionnaires were received. Again, out of 100 questionnaires distributed to the foreign multinational bank customers, only 48 completed questionnaires were found to be fit thus registering a response rate of 48%.

The survey was conducted among 280 (completed questionnaires) geographically dispersed banking customers. Both male and female customers were personally contacted. The demographic profile of respondents is given in Table 1.

Table 1: Response Rate of the Questionnaire				
Sampling	Public Sector Bank	Private Bank	Foreign Bank	Total
No. of questionnaires distributed	190	80	100	370
No. of questionnaires returned	166	66	48	280
Response Rate	87.36%	82.5%	48%	75.67%

The unit of observation and analysis of this study is the individual banking customer, either in private or public or foreign/multinational banks. Our definition of banking customer is "an individual who has had (during the study period) savings bank account in anyone of the above three banking sectors in the urban centers".

Only savings bank and current account holders are included in the framework of analysis due to the fact that only these customers have contacts with the bankers on a regular basis and visit the bank premises. The number of respondents in each sector of the banks is given in Table 1. Stratified random sampling method was adopted in this study. Customers of eight nationalized banks, four private sector banks and three foreign bank branches were contacted for this analytical study.

Analytical Results

To identify and analyze the level of awareness and satisfaction, 39 variables were identified based on the pilot study conducted at the time of initial finalization of the questionnaire. These 39 items in Section B of the questionnaire included every facility offered to the clients in the bank, like modern services, web-based services, including credit card facilities, payment of telephone bills and taxes through the bank etc. The rationale behind choosing only 39 variables is that these are the services and internal atmosphere, advertised prominently by the banks. These 39 variables were analyzed applying suitable multivariate tests. First, a Principal Component Analysis was applied to get a preliminary view of the major factors in the variables. This resulted in the extraction of eight major factors explaining 60.976% of the total variance in the components. In order to ensure meaningful alignment and extraction of the factors (with Kaiser's criterion of eigen value greater than 1) the variables were rotated applying Rotated Factor Matrix. The rotation method applied was Varimax with Kaiser Normalization. The rotation converged in 16 iterations.

Major Findings

Analytical Results of Awareness and Satisfaction

In order to test whether Factor Analysis was appropriate in this situation, Barlett's test of spheridty and Kaiser-Meyer Olkin (KMO) measure of sampling adequacy was applied. The approximate chi-square statistic is 4055.419 with 741 degrees of freedom, which is significant at 0.001 level. The KMO statistic (0.906) is also very large (>0.5).

Hence Factor Analysis is considered as an appropriate technique for further analysis of data.

Results of Principal Axis Factoring for Awareness and Satisfaction Section are presented in Table 2.

Retaining only such of those factors which have eigen values greater than 1 (as suggested by Kaiser), we can infer that totally eight factors have emerged. These eight factors put together have explained 51.228% of total variance. The variance explained by each of the eight factors is presented in Table 2.

Out of the eight factors which have eigen value greater than one, barring the Factor 8, all the seven factors have constituted of all those variables that have factor loadings greater than or equal to 0.5 (Refer Table 3). Thus, B47, B46, B38, B36, B48 and B37 constituted Factor 1.

Table 2: Results of Principal Axis Factoring			
Barlett's Test of Sphericity Approximate Chi-square 4055.419 Degrees of Freedom = 741 Significance = 0.000 Kaiser Meyer-Olkin Measure of Sampling Adequacy = 0.906			
Rotation Sums of Squared Loadings			
Factor	Eigen Value	Percentage of Variance	Cumulative Variance (%)
1	4.025	10.320	10.320
2	3.371	8.644	18.964
3	2.897	7.427	26.391
4	2.716	6.964	33.356
5	2.523	6.469	39.825
6	1.834	4.703	44.528
7	1.467	3.762	48.290
8	1.146	2.939	51.228

A close look at all the variables in the Factor 1 prompted us to identify a common name and we conceptualize this factor as "Awareness Regarding Modern And Value-Added Services". Similarly, items B20, B21, B18 and B19 constituted the Factor 2. We conceptualized this factor as "Satisfaction Regarding Services and Internal Environment". In the same way, items B26 and B27 formed a factor. Factor 3 could be named as "Satisfaction Regarding Helpful Bank Personnel". Factor 4 is related to the officers and second level executives working in the branches. Contents of this factor prompted us to conceptualize this factor as, "Satisfaction Regarding Humane And Accessible Officers". Factor 5 is pertaining to the equal treatment and interest rates. This factor was conceptualized as "Satisfaction Regarding Equal Treatment and Competitive Interest Rates". Similarly Factor 6 which had three items highly correlated, was conceptualized as "Accuracy In Billing And Convenience". Factor 7 had only one statement B11, i.e., services helped cordial banker-customer relationship with a loading 0.550. This Factor was conceptualised as "Satisfying Relationship" related factor. The Factor 8 had eigen value > 1, but had a loading of 0.384.

Analytical Results of Best and Satisfactory Services

This section makes an attempt to identify that a particular banking sector, which provides the best and satisfactory services and tries to examine whether the services of the three sectors of banks significantly differed. To serve this, all the factors related to "Awareness and Satisfaction" totaling eight factors were included for analysis. Since the number of banks considered for analysis were three, involving multiple comparisons, One-Way Anova was considered appropriate. Out of the eight factors, compared, it is interesting to note that highly significant differences were noticed with regard to three factors i.e., Factor 1 (Significance (Sig.) 0.000 < 0.01 at 1% level of significance), Factor 6 (Asymptomatic significance (Asymp) 0.000 < 0.01 at 1% level of significance) and significant differences were noticed in the case of Factor 2 (Asymp 0.027 < 0.05 at 5% level of significance) and mildly significant differences were noticed in the case of two factors—Factor 4 (Sig 0.057 < 0.10 at 10% level of significance), and Factor 8 (Asymp 0.067 < 0.10 at 10% level of significance). This means that out of eight factors significant differences were noticed in the case of five factors.

Summary of Findings

- The analytical results reveal that the customers in all the three sectors of banks are by and large aware of the various facilities offered by their respective bank branches.

- The customers, it is noticed, are also satisfied in terms of various services offered, the personnel, the internal environment, interest rates and the cordial relationship. This is evident from the fact that the factor analysis has given an idea of the various dimensions of awareness and satisfaction of the customers.

- The one-way Anova test, applied to analyze whether the awareness and satisfaction and problems encountered by the customers, gave the following results.

  - It is interesting to note that foreign banks have secured the first position in four out of eight factors in terms of mean scores obtained on all the eight factors—Factor 1 (0.63), Factor 2 (0.24), Factor 4(0.18) and Factor 7 (0.19). In the same way, private sectors banks have also secured first position in all the remaining four factors—Factor 3 (0.15),

Factor 5 (1.5), Factor 6 (8.99) and Factor 8 (5.42). So, public sector banks could not secure first place in any of the eight factors compared. This shows that the services of foreign banks and the new generation private sector banks are not only moving in tandem with each other

Table 3: Identification of Awareness and Satisfaction Related Factors

Factor Name	Item No.	Variables	Factor Loadings
Factor 1: Awareness regarding Modern and Value-Added Services	B47	My banker has a highly automated environment	0.743
	B46	My banker has cash counting machines	0.680
	B38	My banker offers credit card facilities	0.640
	B36	My banker offers web-based banking services	0.612
	B48	My bank has enough parking facilities	0.584
	B37	My banker answers queries made over telephone	0.552
Factor 2: Satisfaction Regarding Services and Internal Environment	B20	The waiting area is very comfortable	0.691
	B21	My banker readily attends to my needs	0.593
	B18	The equipments in the bank are the latest	0.589
	B19	The physical facilities are very appealing and pleasant	0.533
Factor 3: Satisfaction Regarding Helpful Bank Personnel	B26	Accurate and timely updating of pass books takes place	0.641
	B27	Lost/damaged cards/books get replaced on time	0.612
Factor 4: Satisfaction Regarding Accessible Officers	B33	My grievances are redressed immediately	0.671
	B35	Managers/Heads have a genuine concern to redress my grievances	0.638
Factor 5: Satisfaction Regarding Equal Treatment and Competitive Interest Rates	B14	My bank accords equal treatment to all customers	0.654
	B41	Interest rates are cheaper	0.576
Factor 6: Accuracy in Billing and Competitive Interest Rates	B29	There is clarity in statements and billings	0.645
	B28	Receive statements of accounts regularly	0.566
	B16	Convenient working hours	0.515
Factor 7: Satisfactory Relationship	B11	Services helped cordial banker customer relationship	0.550
Factor 8: New Services	B23	My banker introduces new services	0.384

but also they are far more superior when compared with the public sector banks in providing satisfactory services to customers. It is noticed that they not only continue to enjoy the confidence and support of the customers, but introduce umpteen number of innovative modern value-added services to their clientele. So this qualitative and satisfying services of these two banking sectors are consistent with the research findings of G Shainesh and Tanuja Sharma, referred to earlier.

– Public sector banks lag behind in all the eight factors compared. This shows that the services of public sector banks when compared with the foreign and private sector banks are far from satisfactory. This requires drastic change in outlook and the way in which public sector banks are functioning in this highly volatile and competitive environment.

• The Null hypotheses H_o that the awareness and satisfaction level of the customers of the three banking sectors do not significantly differ, has been rejected in five out of eight factors. Significant differences are noticed in Factor 1, "Awareness Regarding Modern And Value Added Services" (Asymp Sig 0.000 < 0.01 at *1%* level), Factor 2, "Satisfaction Regarding Services and Internal Environment" (Asymp Sig 0.015 at *1%* level), and Factor 6, "Accuracy in Billing and Convenience" (Asymp Sig 0.000 < 0.01 at *1%* level).

Summary and Conclusion

Our analytical study made an attempt to analyze the level of awareness and customer satisfaction of the three major banking sectors of India, i.e., public, private and foreign banks. Our results revealed that the awareness and satisfaction level of the public, private, and foreign banks in India is high which is consistent with the previous studies carried out by a few other researchers. This indeed has implications for all the commercial banks of India. The comparative analysis of the services among the three major segments has revealed that the foreign banks have topped the list in delivering qualitative customer service. The results also revealed that the private sector banks are also competing successfully with the foreign banks and are making efforts to provide better banking services in tune with the changing global competitive scenario. However, it is also observed from the analytical results that the public sector commercial banks are lagging behind the above two sectors in providing satisfactory services as per the expectations of the clients.

Although public sector commercial banks played a vital role in reaching every segment of the society in the past, the performance in the current scenario is not encouraging. So, efforts should be made to ensure that public sector commercial banks compete effectively with the above cited banks by delivering qualitative customer service in the days ahead so as to move in tandem with the current transformations in the global banking system.

(Rengasamy Elango, Faculty Member, Department of Business, Majan College, Muscat, Sultanate of Oman. He can be reached at drelan63@yahoo.com

Vijaya Kumar Gudep, Consultant and Faculty Member, Business and Management Studies, Skyline College, Sharjah, UAE. He can be reached at vijayakumargudep@gmail.com, vijjuband@yahoo.com).

References

1. Berry L L (1980), "Service Marketing is different", *Business,* May-June, pp. 24.

2. Bowen D E and E E Lawler (1992), "The Empowerment of Service Workers: What, Why, How and When", *Sloan Management Review,* Spring, pp. 1-20.

3. Chase R B (1981), "The Customer Contact Approach to Services: Theoretical Bases and Practical Extensions", *Operations Research,* Vol. 29, pp. 698-706.

4. Kulakarni S S, Prakasam R and Nangia (1983), *Personnel Policies in Banks: An Employee Opinion Surveys,* National Institute of Bank Management (NIBM), Mumbai.

5. Levitt T (1972), "Production Line Approach to Service", *Harvard Business Review,* Vol. 50, pp. 41-52.

6. Pemmaraju S K and Gudep Vijaya Kumar (2005), "Issues and Challenges in the New Generation Customer Relationship Management (CRM): Coping with the Unreliable Data", *Skyline Business Journal,* Vol. 1, No. 2, Spring, Sharjah.

7. Roth A V and Jackson W E (1995), "Strategic Determinants of Service Quality and Performance: Evidence from the Banking Industry", *Management Science,* Vol. 41, pp. 1720-1733.

8. Schneider B and Bowen D E (1993), "The Service Organization: Human Resources Management is Critical", *Organizational Dynamics,* Spring, pp. 39-52.

9. Shainesh G and Sharma Tanuja (2003), "Linkages between Service Climate and Service Quality", A Study of Banks in India, IIMB, *Management Review,* Vol. 5, No. 3, September, pp. 74-81.

10. Sherman H and Gold F (1985), "Bank Branch Operating Efficiency", *Journal of Banking and Finance*, Vol. 9, pp. 297-315.

11. Swartz T, Bowen D and Brown S (1992), *Advances in Service Marketing and Management*, Greenwich, JAI Press.

12. Uttal B (1987), "Companies that Serve you the Best", *Fortune,* December 7, p. 72.

13. Zenithal V A, Parsuraman A and Berry L L (1990), "Delivering Quality Service", *The Free Press,* pp. 9-10.

9

Sustainability of Foreign Banks in India
A Statistical Analysis

Chowdari Prasad and K S Srinivasa Rao

It is interesting that some foreign banks were operating in India for over a century. But, greater awareness among Indian customers about them came only after economic reforms in India (1991). There were certain regulations on foreign banks operating in India. They were allowed to operate only through branches till 2000-01 subject to reciprocity and other considerations. Foreign banks had only 5% of total deposits and 7% of total loans. Larger foreign banks can be increasingly expected to record greater market share.

In Union Budget 2003-04, Government of India permitted foreign banks to either operate as branches of their overseas parent bank or corporatise as domestic companies. With a view to reducing disparity between domestic and foreign banks, with regard to priority sector obligations, their minimum lending was fixed at 32% (against 40% for domestic banks) of their total advances. Customers dealing with foreign banks derive higher satisfaction for sophisticated service rendered. Being global players, foreign banks may not have any obligation to extend finance to priority sector. After over a decade since WTO, Indian banks are able to overcome competition from foreign banks by improving their products and services, professionalism, ambience of offices, technology usage, change in employee attitude and by downsizing their staff strength and unviable branches. This made the authors to work on foreign banks to study their functioning in India by using closed model of only those foreign banks which existed throughout their study period and an open model of studying all such foreign banks that entered sometime or left the country during the period of study. The period of study considered is five years (1997-1999 and 2000-2003), and the authors made an effort to analyze each of the foreign banks and its development on various parameters/sub-parameters under CRAMEL.

Introduction

Indian banking system is transforming very fast in recent years in tune with changes taking place world over. Legal, Technical, Organisational and Market changes are occurring in India, facilitating an evolution of a highly competitive banking field. Liberalisation, Privatisation and Globalisation principles adopted by Government of India in the early nineties with Financial Sector Reforms are having direct bearing on all the types of banks in India since the year 1993. Indian banking industry comprises a good blend of 27 Public (including 8 of State Bank Group), 30 Private (21 old and 9 new), 32 Foreign, a large number of Cooperative, 196 Regional Rural Banks (RRBs) and 4 Local Area Banks (LABs). There are also other players like (a) Development Finance Institutions (DFIs), (b) Non-Banking Financial Companies (NBFCs) and (c) Post Office/Small Savings Schemes in the four-pillared Financial System.

Commercial Banking in India has undergone dramatic changes in the last three decades. Some experts divided the working of the banks into three phases— viz., (1) pre-nationalisation period up to July 1969, (2) post-nationalisation and up to Financial Sector Reforms in June 1991 and (3) post-reforms era and onwards. Opening of new Private Sector and inviting of more Foreign Banks (FBs) did impact the working of the entire banking industry. Several remedial steps like deregulation of interest rates were taken to bring back profitability and productivity in the system. Balance Sheets of banks are more transparent now. Introduction of new products and services including Credit Cards, ATMs, Electronic Clearing System, Electronic Funds Transfers, Bancassurance, Mutual Funds, Dematerialisation, Retail Banking, Venture Capital Funding, Securitisation, Asset Management/Asset Reconstruction Companies, Portfolio Management Services, Private Banking, Internet Banking, etc., by FBs is adopted simultaneously by Public and Private Sector Banks too in a highly competitive environment. While there was a conscious policy of branch expansion of RBI for Public and Private Sector Banks, FBs enlarged their operations in a moderate way. FBs had their origin from countries like USA, UK, France, Belgium, Germany, Netherlands, Scotland, UAE, Bangladesh, Ceylon, Japan, Malaysia, Indonesia, Singapore, Hong Kong, Bahrain, Muscat, Oman, Mauritius, etc.

World Trade Organization (WTO) came into existence on January 01, 1995. WTO regime opened up business opportunities among member countries and moving towards competition and globalization. With certain relaxations to the member countries, after the Financial Services Agreement in 1997, the share of FBs in All Scheduled Commercial Banks (ASCBs) in India has increased substantially under all the parameters.

The year 2005 is witnessing celebration of bi-centenary year (200 years) by SBI with its long history while two other Public Sector Banks viz., Corporation Bank and Canara Bank have declared completion of one hundred years of their service. Others like Punjab National Bank, Allahabad Bank, Central Bank, etc., in public sector as well as Federal Bank, Vysya Bank and others in private sector have also been in existence for long. Equally interesting is the functioning of FBs in India for over one hundred sixty years (since the year 1842) conforming to rigid business standards and complying with various regulations. In February 2005, RBI announced a *'Roadmap for presence of Foreign Banks in India and Guidelines on Ownership and Governance in Private Banks'.* FBs can now enter India via a branch or set up a wholly owned subsidiary (WOS). The minimum start-up capital requirement for a WOS would be Rs.3 billion (US$68 million). The WOS would also be required to maintain a Capital Adequacy Ratio of 10 percent or as may be prescribed from time to time on a continuous basis, from the commencement of its operations. FBs applying to RBI for license of WOS must satisfy the RBI that they are subject to adequate prudential supervision in their home country. Other factors that will be taken into account while considering such application include economic and political relations between India and country of the FB as well as its ownership pattern. Looking at the above developments and the moderate market shares in deposits and advances the FBs had in India as well as their varying numbers due to entry and exit in the last decade (post WTO era), a question arises about their sustainability in Indian banking scenario.

Objectives of Study

During late sixties and the next two decades, banking system in India underwent stressful and testing times. In fact sustainability of some of the PSBs was at stake in mid-nineties. It was only during the post-reforms era that with several changes and with the competition emerging in the banking scene, FBs are able to perform independently now. In the mean time, Public and Private Sector Banks faced stringent treatment through reforms to stand on their own amidst favourable circumstances for FBs. The recent guidelines from RBI gave rise to this study because even after Financial Services Agreement with WTO, several FBs have been moving in and out of the Indian banking scene. In contrast, barring a few, domestic banks have been proving themselves successful and accepting challenges in the new environment.

The authors have taken up the study to find out the 'Sustainability of Foreign Banks in India', in view of long history of some of them in the Indian scene—before and after Independence, and some others before and after the economic reforms/WTO era. The total number of FBs had risen to 43 by the year 1997-98 but came down to 32 by 2005. Accordingly, the paper attempts to examine the following aspects in which FBs in India were functioning during the five year period viz., 1997-98 to 2002-03 (except 1999-2000) and the aspects as under:

1. To study the sustainability of FBs that are existing in India throughout the study period;

2. To study and identify the FBs which are vulnerable and the reasons for their vulnerability;

3. To study the working of FBs newly entered during the study period; and

4. To forecast the levels of various parameters of the FBs for the year 2005-06.

Literature Survey

Historical Development: Multilateral Banking originated in the country in the second quarter of 19th century. In the year 1842, the Oriental Banking Corporation established the first Anglo-Indian Commercial Bank at Bombay through a Royal Charter. Within three years of its establishment at Bombay, its Head Office was shifted to London in 1845 to provide a real multinational character. After some time, two other banks appeared on Indian scene, they were: (1) The Chartered Bank of India, Australia & China, and (2) The Chartered Bank of Asia, later known as Mercantile Bank of India, England & China, which were registered under Royal Charters in England. These banks commenced business in Calcutta in the year 1857. By 1870, only three multinational banks operated in India with their deposits of Rs.52.31 lakhs. The number of banks increased to eight towards the close of the 19th century.

FBs of real multinational character appeared on Indian scene in the first quarter of 20th century. Four banks, namely: (1) The Mercantile Bank Ltd., (2) Grindlays Bank Ltd., (3) The Chartered Bank and (4) The Hong Kong and Shanghai Banking Corporation were established in 1914. The Mercantile Bank Ltd., and the Hong Kong and Shanghai Banking Corporation were registered in Hong Kong whereas Grindlays Bank Ltd., and the Chartered Bank were registered in London. Two more banks, namely the American Express International Banking Corporation and the Algemene Bank of Netherlands N.V. were established in 1920. The former was registered in United States of America and the latter in Netherlands.

The rate of increase of such multinational banks was quite stable. About three to four banks were added in each decade up to the beginning of the Second World War. The number of such banks rose to 19 in 1939 with an average deposit of Rs.390 lakhs per bank which was much lower than the corresponding deposit of Rs.500 lakhs in 1920. In 1961, though the number remained the same, the average deposits made further improvement to Rs.1,362 lakhs. The years 1936, 1948, 1952, 1953, 1954, 1956, 1964 and 1966 made the addition of one bank each in these years. Five more banks were established between 1979 and 1981.

In 1979, a German Bank known as European Asian Bank was established at Bombay. In 1980, Bank of Oman Ltd., of United Emirates with Head Office at Dubai was established at Bombay. Similarly, another Gulf Bank from Abu Dhabi known as Emirates Commercial Bank Ltd., was allowed to function in 1981. The government allowed a Sri Lankan Bank known as Bank of Ceylon and French Bank known as Banque de L'Indochine et de Suez (Indosuez), but they could not start the operations till 1981. (Dr. R D Sharma)

There are 32 Foreign Banks (FBs) currently operating through 220 branches/offices in India. The larger FBs enjoy strong franchises, both in corporate as well as in retail savings products, among High Net-worth Individuals (HNIs). They have an increasing market share in retail lending like auto loans, credit cards and personal loans. Growing acceptance of FBs is partly as a result of the high 'aspirational value' attached by consumers to banking and associating with a foreign brand. Robust systems, well-defined processes of their global network and an attractive market have enabled these banks to move from a 'dipping the toe' strategy to establishing and cementing their foothold in the Indian market.

Whereas the state and private banks are locally incorporated, it is important to note that most of the FBs operate as branches of the parent bank as regulatory consideration puts a constraint on the number of branches they can open. Although the central bank has been meeting its WTO commitments with regard to allowing the branches of Foreign Banks to be set up, they may have to wait for some time before they have flexibility on their distribution network. This presents an interesting conundrum for the FBs that recognize the need to establish a distribution network but is limited due to their current structure and by the Government's ceiling on foreign ownership of private banks.

An alternative that FBs are increasingly pursuing is the creation of NBFCs. Although there are various restrictions on resource mobilization and certain foreclosure rights otherwise available to banks, NBFCs are subject to relatively less stringent regulatory requirements than banking subsidiaries. For example, NBFCs are not required to comply with certain prudential measures such as Cash Reserve Ratio (CRR) or provide, at RBI's behest, priority sector lending (NBFCs are, however, subject to higher Capital Adequacy Ratio requirements than banks). Although many internationally active banks have an 'India strategy' in order to succeed, it is imperative that FBs understand the culture within each state they wish to operate in. This alone is a significant challenge that should not be underestimated. (PwC)

The compounded growth rate of operational productivity of FBs in terms of the interest income/working funds in the pre-liberalization period was 5.08 percent. It declined in the post-liberalization period to –2.27 percent. As far as the growth rate of the non-interest income/working funds was concerned, in the pre-liberalization period, it was –1.83 percent. In the post-liberalization period, though it was still negative i.e., –0.18 but compared to the pre-liberalization period, it has improved. The compounded growth rate of operational expenses/operational income was negative before liberalization i.e., –1.04 percent but in the post-liberalization period, it was positive i.e., 0.89 percent. The compounded growth rate in terms of cost of deposits improved in the post-liberalization period. It decreased from 1.29 percent before to 0.78 percent after liberalization. The decline in the growth rate of spread/working funds could also be noticed in the post-liberalization period as compared to pre-liberalization period. The performance of FBs was better before liberalization, but surprisingly during post-liberalization, deteriorated in terms of the interest income/working funds, operational expenses/operational income, spread/working funds. They were concentrating on the non-fund based activities, but they should also try to concentrate on their fund based activities and should improve their spread. (Dr. Monika Aggrawal)

Although FBs have been present in India for a long time, there have been several limitations on their operations. In line with the economic liberalization policy, the regulator is gradually relaxing the norms for these banks. Since banking is a sensitive area, sudden opening up of the sector is not desirable. Hence, to prepare the banking sector for future, regulator has charted a roadmap for FBs on their entry strategy. The RBI roadmap has been divided into two phases. During the first phase, between March 2005 and March 2009, FBs can establish their presence by way of setting up a wholly owned subsidiary (WOS) or conversion of existing branches into a WOS. The second phase commences from April 2009 after a review of the experience gained and after due consultation with all the stakeholders in the banking sector.

In response to a recent survey conducted by FICCI, New Delhi it was expressed that FBs should be allowed to enhance their stake in private sector banks in line with FDI norms. Some of the respondents enlightened the related norms prevalent in other countries. In other Asian countries like China, Taiwan, etc., ceilings for foreign ownership are less stringent. In USA, mergers and acquisitions within banks are freely permitted subject to applicable anti-trust laws. Also, in countries like UK, USA, France, Germany, Italy, there is no automatic limitation of shareholdings for FBs. An approval or prior notification from the respective Central Bank is required if the proposed holdings in the share capital rise or increase beyond certain threshold limits. In India, initially FBs can hope to acquire about 15% in a private sector bank and a prior approval of RBI is required to acquire any larger stake. (FICCI)

We have compared efficiency and productivity of PSBs relative to private sector banks, both domestic and foreign. This comparison is attempted over a nine-year period (1992-2000), out of which eight years belong to what might be called the post-deregulation period, if we use the generally accepted year of 1992-93 as the cut off date for the big push in bank deregulation. The findings of this study thus reinforce those of Ram Mohan (2002) and Ram Mohan (2003) that failed to uncover any significant differences between PSBs and other categories of banks using financial measures of performance or returns to stocks. One explanation could be that there has been a change in orientation in PSBs from social objectives towards an accent on profitability, especially given that some of these have come to be listed on the exchanges and have private investors. (T T Ram Mohan and Subhash C Ray)

In the year 1999, British Bank of Middle East (BBME) was merged with HSBC Bank. During the year 2002-2003, four Foreign Banks viz., (1) Commerze Bank (2) Dresdener Bank AG (3) KBC Bank and (4) The Siam Commercial Bank PCL, closed their Indian operations. Further, Indian branches of Standard Chartered Grindlays Bank Ltd., were merged with the Indian branches of Standard Chartered Bank while The Development Bank of Singapore Ltd., changed its name to DBS Bank Ltd. *(IBA Bulletin Special Issue*, January 2004). Similarly, during the year 2003-04, another three FBs in India were closed down. These are Overseas-Chinese Banking Corporation Bank Ltd. (OCBC), and The Toronto Dominion

Bank Ltd. while Bank Muscat SAOG was taken over by the Centurion Bank (since being merged with Bank of Punjab in 2005). Same year, Credit Agricole Indo Suez Bank, however, changed its name to CALYON Bank.

IBA Bulletin of December 2004 carried a detailed annual review on Performance Highlights of FBs in 2003-04. Under Total Assets, it said that 10 banks reported higher growth than the group average with Antwerp Diamond Bank N.V. (entered India in 2002-03) occupying the top position with a growth of 102.8 percent while 12 others showed decline in asset growth. Societe Generale recorded highest growth in deposits with 222.4 percent closely followed by Development Bank of Singapore (DBS) with 202.7 percent and JP Morgan Chase Bank with 111.0 percent. 13 FBs recorded negative growth in deposits than the previous year.

Credit disbursement by FBs during 2003-04 was impressive with figures of Rs.60,507 crores compared to Rs.52,018 crores in previous year. Societe Generale topped the position with a growth of 97 percent followed by Antwerp Diamond Bank (69.2 percent). 19 FBs recorded negative growth in advances which was compensated by the 14 other banks during the year. Gross NPAs of FBs increased from Rs.2,820 crores in 2003 to Rs.2,893 crores in 2004 with growth rate of 2.6 percent. Unlike FBs, the Public and Private Sector Banks showed decline in growth of gross and net NPAs during 2003-04 as compared to 2002-03.

Overall, FBs repeated their good performance during 2003-04. Though the number of banks in India reduced from 36 in 2002-03 to 32 in 2003-04, the performance of the group was good. Deposit mobilization of the FBs was lower as compared to previous year. However, profitability ratios like Business per Employee and Profit per Employee showed considerable improvement during 2003-04. (*IBA Bulletin*, December 2004).

The Government of India and Reserve Bank are considering a proposal to expand FBs' share to around 20 percent from the present 15 percent. On the basis of funded assets, FBs' market share is only about 7-8 percent. If, however, one takes into consideration non-funded assets, such as derivatives and fee-based businesses as well, their share could be around 15 percent. The Government is now said to be contemplating a change in the formula for calculating the total share of FBs in India. The proposal has gained steam following the bilateral agreement signed with Government of Singapore in June 2005 which signaled better treatment to their banks to operate in India *vis-à-vis* other FBs. As per the agreement, three Singaporean banks will get to start with three branch banking licenses each and will also be allowed to enter the insurance industry. Normally, a Foreign Bank gets license to set up a representative office and depending on its performance, it converts the representative office into a branch. If the Government decides to raise FBs' share, it will lead to more relaxation in branch licensing policy for FBs in India.

Under the World Trade Organization (WTO) Treaty, India is committed to increase the number of foreign banking licenses from 12 a year to 15-18. The RBI is, however, in favour of inserting a clause of reciprocity with respective nations who get licenses to operate banks in India. This will pave the path for Indian banks setting shops overseas. The RBI is believed to have pointed out to GOI that FBs do not serve un-banked areas and normally focus on metros which are heavily banked. Therefore, the new branching licenses may have some riders on areas to serve or kind of services to focus on. Once this is done, the formula for arriving a banks' share in the market is likely to change to take into account to include non-fund business which for FBs is too large. This will prop up FBs' share in the total banking pie substantially.

A slew of FBs from Japan, China and the Middle East have evinced interest in opening branches in India. Recently, Commonwealth Bank of Australia got the license to set up a Representative Office. Union Bank of Switzerland had applied for a bank license but the application has hit the roadblock after Securities & Exchange Board of India (SEBI) found fault with UBS Securities of the Group in its stock market activities. General Electric (GE) also wants to set up a bank in India through the acquisition route. (*Business Standard,* July 05, 2005)

The Institute of Chartered Financial Analysts of India (ICFAI), Hyderabad in its Special issue of Chartered Financial Analyst, October 2005, contained a comprehensive study and ranking of the performance of banks in India, based on the CAMEL model. The study covers 55 banks (including 15 FBs) whose annual results for 2004-05 were available. These banks were divided into three categories— 21 large sized banks, 15 medium and 19 small banks. While one Foreign Bank each found place in 21 large (Citibank with 4th rank) and 15 medium banks (American Express Bank Ltd., with 12th rank) categories, 13 others occupied different ranks in the third category of the 19 Small Banks. With Indian banks going global and many global banks setting up shops in India, the Indian banking system is set to evolve into a totally new level. International banks like Deutsche Bank are planning to re-open retail operations in India. GE is also showing signs to start banking operations in India. Merrill Lynch is looking to get a banking license in India. The Credit Suisse Group is also looking at augmenting its Indian operations. UBS, the world's seventh largest bank has also applied for banking license from RBI. All this could well mark the beginning of a trend of big financial service conglomerates looking at India. (*CFA*, October 2005)

Review of Working of Foreign Banks in India

The starting point of studying the Foreign Banks in India is the number of banks and branches over the study period. Between the years 1997 and 2005, the total number of FBs has come down from 43 to 32 despite entry of several new FBs while number of their branches increased from 188 to 215. The details can be observed from the Table 1.

Table 1: Number of Foreign Banks and Branches During 1997-2005		
		(Data as on June every year)
Year	No. of Foreign Banks	No. of Branches
1997-1998	43	188
1998-1999	42	178
1999-2000	42	186
2000-2001	42	192
2001-2002	40	246
2002-2003	36	204
2003-2004	33	213
2004-2005	32	215
Source: Trend and Progress of Banking in India: RBI various reports.		

FBs in India trailed the revitalized Indian banks in 2004-2005. The growth in credit as well as deposits of FBs during the year was lower compared to that for the public sector and the private sector banks. FBs' annual credit growth was

24.6 percent, as on March 31, 2005 against the highest growth of 33.5 percent for nationalized banks, 31.9 percent for private sector banks and 26 percent for State Bank of India (SBI) and its Associates. FBs lagged behind in credit disbursements even though their loan books swelled much more than they had done in 2003-2004. And FBs fell behind despite the fact that their credit growth in 2004-2005 was much higher than the 15.3 percent rise in 2003-2004.

The growth in deposits for FBs in 2004-2005 was scanty—only 5.2 percent compared to 15.7 percent for SBI group, 15.9 percent for nationalized banks and 17.8 percent for private sector banks. This is in contrast with FBs' deposits growth in 2003-2004—the highest at 28.6 percent against 19.7 percent for the SBI group, 16.2 percent for nationalized banks and 23 percent for private sector banks. In 2004-2005, the banking sector's aggressive credit jumped 30.6 percent to Rs.11,57,807 crores, while total deposits grew 15.6 percent to Rs.17,53,174 crores.

Table 2: Growth of Banks' Business in 2004-2005		
Growth in Percentage	Credit	Deposits
SBI and Associates	26.0	15.7
Nationalized Banks	33.6	15.9
Private Sector Banks	31.9	17.8
Foreign Banks (FBs)	24.6	5.2
Source: Business Standard, August 20, 2005.		

One major cause of concern was the reduction in number of FBs even in the post-reforms and WTO era. After having reached a high number of 43 in 1997-1998, the position today is that there are only 32 FBs in India. While the strong and long staying banks like Citibank, American Express, HSBC, Standard Chartered, Bank of America, etc., are going steady with their operations in metros and big cities, new entrants are moving in and out with short periods of stay. Surprisingly, with limited and focused operations too, these FBs are not able to catch up in growth of deposits or advances like their counterparts in public and private sectors. Table 2 gives a comparative position of growth in the year 2004-2005.

Total outstanding credit of SBI and Associates at the end of March 2005 stood at Rs.2,57,668 crores. Private sector banks' loan books, as on March 31, 2005 were Rs.2,32,232 crores, while those of nationalized banks were at Rs.5,48,236 crores and FBs at Rs.77,113 crores. Similarly while aggregate deposits of FBs were a five-digit Rs.77,160 crores, those of the SBI group were Rs.4,24,750 crores, nationalized banks Rs.8,72,585 crores and private sector banks—Rs.3,17,253 crores—all higher.

Data on Capital Adequacy Ratio (CAR) of all types of banks in India for seven years between 1998 and 2004 is given in Table 3.

Table 3: Bank Groupwise CAR as at the End of March							
Bank Group	1998	1999	2000	2001	2002	2003	2004
Scheduled Comml. Banks	11.5	11.3	11.1	11.4	12.0	12.7	12.9
Public Sector Banks	11.6	11.3	10.7	11.2	11.8	12.6	13.2
Nationalized Banks	10.3	10.6	10.1	10.2	10.9	12.2	13.1
State Bank Group	14.0	12.3	11.6	12.7	13.3	13.4	13.4
Old Private Sector Banks	12.3	12.1	12.4	11.9	12.5	12.8	13.7
New Private Sector Banks	13.2	11.8	13.4	11.5	12.3	11.3	10.2
Foreign Banks (FBs)	10.3	10.8	11.9	12.6	12.9	15.2	15.0
Source: RBI/IBA.							

It may be noted that while all the types of banks in India complied with RBI stipulation of CAR of 9%, FBs have strengthened with a higher percentage between 10.3 and 15 percent in the last seven years. ASCBs have had an average between 11.5 and 12.9 (with a marginal increase by 1.4 percent) of CAR during the same period.

Table 4: Movements in Prime Lending Rates, 2002-2004				
Types of Banks/Year	2001-2002	2002-2003	2003-2004	June-04
1. Public Sector Banks	10.00-12.50	9.00-12.25	10.25-11.50	10.25-11.50
2. Private Sector Banks	10.00-15.50	7.00-15.50	10.50-13.00	9.75-13.00
3. Foreign Banks	9.00-17.50	6.75-17.50	11.00-14.85	11.00-14.85
Source: RBI T&P of Banking India. 2003-4/IBA Year Book 2004.				

Table 4 indicates the movement of (Prime) Lending Rates of all types of banks in India during the previous three years 2002 to 2004. In a falling interest rates regime, there has been stiff competition among all the players to accept deposits at around 5-7 percent per annum and lend at about 11-12 percent with an exception of retail loans like housing finance, auto loans, etc., which are offered on liberal terms at 7-8 percent (sub-PLR rates) interest rates per annum by even the Public Sector Banks. However, for reasons best known to them, FBs are not able to offer such low-priced lending and this is evident from the range of PLRs.

Further, the Table 5 below indicates that post-reforms and WTO era, the performance and market shares of FBs have been coming down as the other two sectors viz., Public and Private have been gearing up their efficiency. Addition of new FBs does not seem to have any major impact on the system when compared to new Private Sector Banks. In fact, all the indicators viz., Income, Expenditure, Total Assets, Net Profit and Gross Profit have gone down drastically between the years 1995-96 and 2002-03 *vis-à-vis* the other two types of players.

Table 5: Bank Groupwise Shares, Select Indicators			
			(Percent)
Types of Banks/Select Indicators	1995-96	2000-01	2002-03
Public Sector Banks			
Income	82.5	78.4	74.5
Expenditure	84.2	78.9	74.8
Total Assets	84.4	79.5	75.7
Net Profit	-39.1	67.4	64.8
Gross Profit	74.3	69.9	76.6
Private Sector Banks			
Income	8.2	12.6	18.5
Expenditure	7.4	12.3	18.6
Total Assets	7.7	12.6	17.5
Net Profit	59.3	17.8	15.6
Gross Profit	10.1	14.4	18.7
Foreign Banks			
Income	9.4	9.1	7.0
Expenditure	8.3	8.8	6.6
Total Assets	7.9	7.9	6.9
Net Profit	79.8	14.8	19.6
Gross Profit	15.6	15.7	4.7
Source: Rakesh Mohan (2004): EPW, March 19, 2005 'Financial Sector Reforms in India'.			

Further data on FBs in India given in the Table 6 for seven-year period between 1997-98 and 2003-04 indicates that in general, their market share of certain business parameters as percentage terms is either very low or on the decreasing trend although in absolute terms they are increasing. This, again, shows that the other categories of banks viz., Public and Private are growing at a better rate with regard to deposits, advances, assets/liabilities, etc.

Table 6: Aggregate Deposits, Assets/Liabilities of Foreign Banks in India

(Rs. in Crore)

Particulars	2003-04	2002-03	2001-02	2000-01	1999-00	1998-99	1997-98
Deposits	79,745 (5.2)	69,095 (5.2)	56,129 (4.8)	59,228 (5.8)	49,377 (5.7)	46,476 (6.3)	42,824 (7.0)
Assets/Liabilities	1,36,316 (6.9)	1,16,314 (6.8)	1,01,064 (6.6)	1,11,657 (8.2)	89,770 (7.8)	81,367 (8.2)	70,099 (8.3)
Advances	60,507 (7.4)	52,018 (7.4)	47,048 (7.7)	43,051 (8.7)	35,857 (8.6)	29,300 (8.8)	29,317 (9.8)
Priority Sector	14,058 (5.1)	11,417 (5.2)	10,446 (5.9)	9,222 (6.0)	7,624 (5.9)	6,475 (5.8)	5,490 (5.7)
No. of Branches	217 (0.4)	180 (0.3)	184 (0.3)	189 (0.4)	181 (0.4)	175 (0.3)	182 (0.4)
Staff in Numbers	14,662 (1.7)	11,751 (1.4)	11,083 (1.3)	14,143 (1.6)	13,509 (1.4)	14,910 (1.6)	14,893 (1.5)

Note: Figures in brackets are percentage to total for all banks in India.

Source: EPW, March 19, 2005.

Research Methodology

Business India, one of the country's leading fortnightly magazines, collects annual data of all types of banks in India every year and carries out the exercise of ranking of banks. They adopt CRAMEL method to analyse the annual financial data and assign ranks on the overall performance of each bank.

CRAMEL stands for Capital Adequacy, Resources Deployed, Asset Quality, Management, Earnings Quality and Liquidity which is a well known and accepted method. The authors have worked on the above data, pertaining to FBs for a five-year period for the years 1997-98, 1998-1999, 2000-2001, 2001-02 and 2002-03. Data with CRAMEL analysis for one year in the middle i.e., 1999-2000 was not available. The number of FBs in each of these years was 38, 40, 33, 32 and 26 respectively but the gross list of names of FBs during the study period was at 50.

Wherever there was merger and/or change of name, the data was not reckoned and hence the list was condensed to 45 banks. There have been both entry and exit of FBs during the study period of mergers and changes of names of banks like 1. Antwerp Diamond Bank, 2. BBME, 3. Bank Nova Scotia, 4. Commerz Bank, 5. Dresdner Bank, 6. Fuji Bank, 7. JP Morgan Bank, 8. Mizuho Bank, 9. Standard Chartered Bank, 10. Grindlays Bank, 11. BNP Paribas, 12. ING Bank, 13. DBS, 14. OCBC, 15. KBC, 16. Credit Agricole, 17. Sanwa Bank, 18. Sakura Bank, 19. Siam Commercial Bank, 20. Bank Muscat International, 21. Chase Manhattan Bank, 22. UFJ Bank, etc.

We have considered the 17 foreign banks whose data is available throughout the study period i.e., 1997 to 2003 (except 1999-2000) under Closed Model. For each of the six parameters under CRAMEL, equal weightage of 16.66% was given aggregating to 100%. These parameters were divided into sub-parameters which were given appropriate weightages. For example, in respect of the first letter/parameter C—Capital Adequacy, the sub-parameters are CAR, D/E, A/A, GS/I, GS/A with a further weightage of 3.33 each. Similar exercise was carried out in respect of other parameters and the respective sub-parameters for each parameter too (like R, A, M, E and L) as explained in the Table 7.

Table 7: Parameters and Weightages for Study				
Parameter	Weightage	No. of Sub-Parameters	Sub-Parameters	Weightage of Sub-Parameter
Capital Adequacy	16.67	5	CAR, D/E, ADV/AST, G-SEC/INV, G-SEC/AST	3.33
Resources Deployed	16.67	6	TOTAL AST, LIQ.AST, INV, ADV, FIX. AST, OTHER AST	2.78
Asset Quality	16.67	7	NNPA/NADV, ADV/AST, ADV/GTH, INV/AST, A/YLD, I/YLD, I/GTH	2.38
Management	16.67	4	CRED/DEP, NP/EMP, BUS/EMP, ROANW	4.17
Earnings Quality	16.66	5	NP, NP/GTH, SPREAD, OI/NII, NP/TAA	3.33
Liquidity	16.66	3	LIQ/TOT AST, G-SEC/T. AST, A-SEC/T. AST	5.56
Total	100.00	30		

Note: Please see List of Abbreviations furnished at the end of Paper.

For each of the five years under study i.e., 1997-98, 1998-99, 2000-01, 2001-02 and 2002-03, the actual financial figures for the six parameters of CRAMEL were considered by taking secondary data from *Business India.* These parameters were already divided into sub-parameters. These data in each sub-parameters were given ranking based on their nature/type. For example, CAR being the first sub-parameter under Capital Adequacy, the bank with highest value was given the highest ranking. Then, the rank number was multiplied with corresponding weightage of the sub-parameter (in this case 3.33) to arrive at the weighted scores. Thereafter, the cumulative weighted scores were calculated by adding up all the weighted scores of all the sub-parameters for each of the six parameters viz., CRAMEL.

Using the cumulative weighted scores for each year, we have forcasted cumulative weighted scores for the next three time points i.e., years 2003-04, 2004-05 and 2005-06. Since there was no published data available for the years 2004-05 and 2005-06, we have given ranks again to the cumulative weighted scores for each of the 17 banks. Based on our observations, we have identified these banks as: (a) performing well (b) average and (c) weak banks.

CRAMEL being an established method of evaluating the performance of banks of all types, the same was adopted for our study. All the parameters and sub-parameters in this method focus on compliance to prescribed regulations like CAR etc., efficiency ratios like D/E, liquidity and profitability ratios as also the quality of management. Banks which maintain consistency and compliance, registering growth and continue to operate over the years amidst stiff competition, offer excellent customer service, etc., can be treated as meeting the sustainability standards. Instead, those whose results show declining trend or close their business within short period of operations leaving the customers—both depositors and borrowers—in lurch can be deemed to be unsustainable, particularly in view of the banking reforms that have taken place.

Findings

We can observe that from the list of 17 FBs operating throughout the period of study, 10 banks were declared as performing well, five as average performers and the remaining two as weak performers in view of the scores obtained at the end of the exercise. These are furnished in the Table 8.

Table 8: Categorization of 17 FBs under Closed Model		
Ranking for 2005-06	Category of Banks	Names of Banks
1 to 10	Performing Well	1. Bank of Tokyo-Mitsubhishi 2. HSBC Holdings 3. Citibank 4. Deutsche Bank 5. Credit Loynnais 6. ABN Amro Bank 7. Credit Agricole Indosuez (Calyon Bank) 8. Bank of America 9. Mashreq Bank 10. Bank of Bahrain and Kuwait
11 to 15	Average Performance	1. Barclays Bank 2. Scotia Bank 3. DBS 4. Krung Thai Bank 5. Sonali Bank
16 and 17	Weak Performance	1. BNP Paribas 2. Sumitomo Bank

Out of the 35 FBs considered under Open Model, 17 have already been categorized into three types as per table given above. Two more banks viz., OCBC and Toronto Dominion Bank have closed their business in the year 2003-04. The remaining 16 banks have obtained forecasted cumulative weighted scores for the year 2005-06 ranging between –150.3 and 1688.8 based on past performance trends and interpolations. Once again based on the criteria of cumulative weighted scores for 2005-06, (above 1000, 501 to 1000 and up to 500 score) these 16 FBs were categorised as: (a) performing well, (b) average and (c) weak performers.

The individual scores are shown in Table 9.

Table 9: Categorization of 16 FBs under Open Model		
Range of Cumulative Weighted Scores	Category of Banks	Names of Banks (with Cumulative Weighted Scores)
1000 and above	Performing Well	1. JP Morgan Chase Bank (1,688.8) 2. Abu Dhabi Commercial Bank (1,532.1) 3. Antwerp Diamond Bank (1,501) 4. Mizuho Corporate Bank (1,500.1)

Contd...

Contd...		
		5. State Bank of Mauritius (1,402.1) 6. China Trust Commercial Bank (1,280.6) 7. Standard Chartered Grindlays (1,194.1)
501 to 1000	Average Performance	1. UFJ Bank (848.3) 2. Oman International Bank (757.6) 3. Societe Generale (686.1) 4. Cho Hung Bank (680.2) 5. Bank of Ceylon (664.9)
Up to 500	Weak Performance	1. Arab Bangladesh Bank (364) 2. American Express Bank (217) 3. Bank International Indonesia (26.9) 4. ING Bank (-150.3)

Conclusions

As already stated in the beginning, foreign banks have been functioning in India as part of the banking system side by side with Public, Private, Regional, Rural and Cooperative Banks for over one hundred sixty years. For obvious reasons, they have been operating in Urban and Metropolitan cities only with limited number of branches; catering to elite clientele. These banks have been complying with the 32% requirement under Priority Sector Lending but mostly concentrate on Retail Banking. The low Debt to Equity ratio of FBs indicates that more than lending to business and industry, they resort to investment operations. Globalization or Financial Service Agreement under WTO have encouraged more frequent traffic of moving in and out of Indian banking scene by some FBs with short standing.

However, banks like ABN Amro, American Express, Bank of America, Bank of Bahrain and Kuwait, Barclays, Bank of Tokyo-Mitsubishi, Citibank, Deutsche Bank, HSBC and Standard Chartered Bank have been in long and successful business in India retaining the confidence of the customers and regulators. Liberalization by RBI to invite more branches has not been utilized by some FBs efficiently calling for close supervision and policy changes. Banking is a financial service where tremendous trust is essential. Else, RBI has to nominate its representatives on the Boards of management of these banks to monitor their performance at quarterly intervals to the best advantage of the customers—both depositors and borrowers.

Table 10 gives a glance view of the 33 FBs now in India and their functioning. While 17 of them are performing well as indicated by the research findings, 10 are in the average category and the remaining 6 need to be closely monitored. Otherwise, there is a threat that their poor performance will lead to unwanted repercussions and stringent corrective steps to be taken for remedial action.

Table 10: Summary of Findings from Closed & Open Models				
Category	No. of FBs under Closed Model	No. of FBs under Open Model	Total No. of FBs	Remarks
Performing Well	10	7	17	Progress to be maintained
Average	5	5	10	Performance to be watched/improved
Weak Performance	2	4	6	Progress to be closely monitored and corrective steps taken immediately
Total	17	16	33	2 FBs already closed in 2003-04

Accordingly, the first two categories of FBs (17 plus 10) can be considered as sustainable while the remaining six FBs of third category can be treated as not sustainable.

Limitations

- The study period covered five years between 1997 and 2003 with secondary data taken from *Business India* magazine. Data for the year 1999-2000 was not available.

- Two more financial years viz., 2003-05 have already been over and several developments have taken place. Forecasting of data for these two years does not convey proper meaning but helps in projecting further for 2005-2006.

- Data for the year 2003-04 is available in RBI website and *Indiastat.com* but is not in the form of CRAMEL format for a comparative study.

- Data for the year 2004-05 is yet to be released so as to study the performance in real terms and arrive at realistic conclusions and offering better recommendations.

- Best Banker and other Surveys carried out by business magazines are readily available to the general/investing public and carry stronger impressions in the absence of authentic data from RBI well in time.

Scope for Further Research

The present work done was based on the secondary data available from the business magazines. It is more than two and half years old and many changes have occurred in the interregnum. RBI announced its new policy in February 2005 and there has been overwhelming response from a fresh bunch of six leading banks from Singapore, Switzerland, etc. Further research can be taken up with regard to identifying the specific reasons for frequent moving in and out by some FBs to and from India so that meaningful solutions can be offered with regard to branch licensing policy, taxation policy, repatriation of foreign exchange policy, priority sector lending by FBs and relaxations to encourage more and more banks to set up offices in India.

List of Abbreviations

1. ADV   Advances
2. ADV/GTH   Advances/Growth
3. ASCB   All Scheduled Commercial Banks
4. ASEC/AST   Approved Securities/Assets
5. AST   Assets
6. ADV/AST   Advances to Assets
7. ATMs   Automated Teller Machines
8. BBME   British Bank of Middle East
9. B/E   Business per Employee
10. CAR   Capital Adequacy Ratio
11. C/D   Credit Deposit Ratio
12. CRAR   Capital to Risk Adjusted Ratio
13. CRR   Cash Reserve Ratio
14. D/E   Debt to Equity Ratio
15. DFI   Development Finance Institutions
16. FBs   Foreign Banks

17. FICCI   Federation of Indian Chambers of Commerce and Industry

18. FDI   Foreign Direct Investment

19. FIX/AST   Fixed Assets to Total Assets

20. GOI   Government of India

21. G-SEC   Government Securities

22. HNI   High Net-worth Individuals

23. IBA   Indian Banks Association

24. INV   Investment

25. I/YLD   Investment to Yield

26. LABs   Local Area Banks

27. LIQ/A   Liquidity to Assets

28. NADV   Net Advances

29. NBFC   Non Banking Finance Company

30. NII   Net Interest Income

31. NP/EMP   Net Profit per Employee

32. NP/GTH   Net Profit to Growth

33. NPA   Non-Performing Assets

34. NNPA   Net Non-Performing Assets

35. OCBC   Overseas China Banking Corporation

36. OI   Other Income

37. OTH/AST   Other Assets to Total Assets

38. PSBs   Public Sector Banks

39. PLR   Prime Lending Rate

40. RBI   Reserve Bank of India

41. ROANW   Return on Average Net Worth

42. SBI	State Bank of India
43. TA	Total Assets
44. WOS	Wholly Owned Subsidary
45. WTO	World Trade Organization

(Chowdari Prasad, Associate Professor (Finance Area) TA Pai Management Institute (TAPMI), Manipal-576104, Karnataka. (Tel Office): 0820-2571358/2573162 and K S Srinivasa Rao, Associate Professor (QM Area) TA Pai Management Institute (TAPMI), Manipal-576104, Karnataka. They can be reached at chowdarip@mail. tapmi.org and srinivas@mail.tapmi.org respectively.)

References

1.   *Best Banks Surveys, Business India,* January 11-24, 1999; February 7-20, 2000; November 25 – December 08, 2002; November 24 – December 07, 2003; August 16-29, 2004.

2.   *Business Line:* (1) Credit concentration of foreign banks high: RBI, November 15, 2002; (2) Foreign banks may be allowed controlling stake in private banks – Chidambaram moots 10 pc acquisition a year, October 30, 2004.

3.   *Business Standard:* (1) Foreign banks may increase domestic spread, says Fitch, November 07, 2003; (2) Mint Road makes foreign ventures easier for banks, March 02, 2005; (3) Foreign banks to get more leeway, July 05, 2005 and (4) Foreign Banks trail Indian banks, August 20, 2005.

4.   Uday Bhasin, *Challenges in India's Banking Sector,* PricewaterhouseCoopers, October 18, 2005.

5.   Dr. K S Srinivasa Rao and Chowdari Prasad, "Can Public Sector Banks compete with Foreign/ Private Banks? A Statistical Analysis", Vol. III, Number 1, February 2004 of *The Icfai Journal of Bank Management.*

6.   "Data Base on Indian Banking 2000-03", *IBA Bulletin,* January 2004.

7.   Dr. R D Sharma, *Financial Working of Foreign Multinational Banks in India,* Mittal Publications, Delhi, 1987.

8.   "Foreign banks permitted fully owned arms in India", February 28, 2005, *http://news.web india.123.com/news/showdetails.asp?id=69927&cat=Business.*

9.   Chowdari Prasad, "Functioning of Foreign Banks in India", Paper presented at Seminar and Chapter included in the book, *WTO and the Banking Sector in India,* ed. Dr. G V Joshi and published by Corporation Bank Chair in Bank Management, Department of Economics, Mangalore University, Mangalore, 2004.

10. *IBA Bulletin,* Special Issue 2005 on "Consolidation in Banking Industry: Mergers and Acquisitions", January 2005.

11. *Indian Banking Year Book 2004,* IBA, Mumbai.

12. Indian Banking 2005 Special, *Chartered Financial Analyst,* October 2005.

13. "Indian banks ahead of foreign peers", August 20, 2005, *www.rediff.com*

14. Dr. Monika Aggrawal, "Liberalisation Effect on Operation Productivity of Commercial Banks in India", *IBA Bulletin,* June 2005.

15. "Middle path – The central bank opts for a safety-first approach", *Financial Express,* Edits & Columns, March 01, 2005.

16. "Money, Banking and Finance", *Economic and Political Weekly,* Special Issue, March 19-25, 2005.

17. "Performance Highlights of Foreign Banks 2003-04", *IBA Bulletin,* Indian Banks Association, Mumbai, December 2004.

18. T T Ram Mohan (IIM-A) and Subhash C Ray (University of Connecticut, Storrs), "Productivity Growth and Efficiency in Indian Banking – A Comparison of Public, Private and Foreign Banks", paper published in BANCON 2004 Bankers' Conference on Indian Banking: Realizing Global Aspirations.

19. RBI Annual Reports, 2003, 2004 and 2005.

20. Report on Trend and Progress of Banking in India 2003-04, RBI.

21. Survey on "Status of Indian Banking Industry – Progress & Agenda ahead", from website of FICCI, New Delhi, *www.ficci.com*

22. Foreign banks in India Resource, *www.greenwichmeantime.com/time-zone/asia/India/India-links/foreign-banks-in-india*

23. *www.indiaserver.com/biz/indian-banking-sector.html*

24. *www.indianslivingabroad.com/resources/bank-new.asp*

25. Census of India 2001, Foreign Banks, Figures at All India/State Level, *www.Indiastat.com/india/ShowData.asp?secid=104&ptid=3&level=2*

26. *www.ncrc.org/global/australAsia/India_Page.htm*

27. *www.rbi.org.in:* (1) Roadmap for Presence of Foreign Banks in India and Guidelines on Ownership and Governance in Private Banks; (2) Liberalised policy for overseas presence of Indian banks and foreign banks' presence in India: February 28, 2005.

10

HDFC Bank – Fostering Relationships through Private Banking

Sushuma G

From the time of its inception, HDFC Bank aims to satisfy the financial needs of the customer under one roof. High quality service, novel products and implementation of latest technologies has made HDFC Bank as the leader among the top three in almost all areas they deal with. HDFC Bank provides investment management and advisory services to high net worth individuals and to large companies. The article briefs about the HDFC Bank's private banking operations, their growth and future plans.

Liberalization in the banking sector in the 1990s has led the Reserve Bank of India (RBI) to grant permissions to set up banks in the private sector. HDFC Bank was the first private sector bank to receive approval from the RBI. The HDFC Bank promoted by Housing Development Finance Corporation was set up in 1994 with its registered office in Mumbai. The bank started to function as a Scheduled Commercial Bank in January 1995. In 2006, the HDFC Bank in India had a network of 535 branches in 228 cities across the country and had more than 1300 ATMs.

HDFC Bank, one of the leading private sector banks in India, offers various products like housing loans, insurance, mutual funds, securities and credit cards. In a short period, the bank began offering services like Net banking, Phone banking, Inter-branch banking, Private banking and NRI banking services to its customers. Due to its exceptional services provided to the customers the *Euromoney magazine* has rated HDFC Bank as *"Best Private Bank in the Super Affluent Category in India"*.

Wealth Management to Maximize Returns

Wealth management includes financial planning and guidance to investors. It helps the high net worth individuals to invest for maximum return and minimize risk and tax liability. The high net worth individuals to are occupied in generating wealth. Hence, they approach wealth managers to manage wealth on their behalf and maximize the returns. However, the wealth managers representing the banks have to take the consent of the investors and get a written permission before investing or entering into any deal. With the increase in the number of high net worth individuals in India, wealth management business of private banks is at its peak and the number of customers seeking them for advice is increasing.

Customized Service through Private Banking

Barron's Dictionary of Banking Terms defines Private Banking as "banking services, including lending and investment management, for wealthy individuals". HDFC Bank offers private banking services to high net worth individuals and institutions. Usually banks specify a threshold level for customers to avail private banking services. HDFC Bank does not specify explicitly any level to avail private banking services instead it charges the customers for the services they provide. To track a portfolio up to Rs.35 lakhs, the bank charges around Rs.35000 per annum[1].

The bank provides wealth management and advisory services to its customers. These private banking services are provided to the clients through an advisory team. The advisory team consists of experienced people in financial and investment services.

The Relationship Manager (RM) acts as a one-point contact for the customers for all their banking needs and portfolio management. The relationship manager,

---

[1]   Banking for the privileged, *http://inhome.rediff.com/money/2003/may/20spec.htm*

supported by a research team, provides guidance to the clients based on their requirements. Abhay Aima, HDFC Bank's Country head, equities and private banking, says, "The number of customers under one RM would depend on how profitable the client is. In the top end of private banking, the number of clients would be fewer, while customization of products and time spent by RM on individual clients would be much greater". The relationship manager acts as a family member of the client, whom the client can contact for any help.

The wealth management programme of HDFC Bank manages the clients' portfolio based on their investment objectives and optimizes the returns from investment. The bank provides advisory services on direct equity, mutual funds, insurance and bonds and helps the clients to manage their investments efficiently.

Advisory Services

HDFC Bank's advisory services to high net worth clients stresses on asset allocation based on their financial goals and risk profile. Asset allocation is the process of spreading the investment in different assets to reduce risk and maximize returns. The risk profile of the client also determines the investment pattern. The investment advisor assesses the clients' needs and their risk tolerance level and alters their existing portfolio based on their expectations and the financial market conditions. The advisor updates the client with the current investment opportunities suitable to the client's investment plans. The investor has to review his/her portfolio frequently and change the asset allocation based on the performance of the assets invested.

HDFC Bank provides advisory services on the following types of investments:

- *Mutual Funds:* Based on the investor's profile, the advisor helps to select, purchase and monitor the mutual fund investment. The advisor analyzes the investment strategy and the performance of various mutual funds available in the market and suggests an appropriate mutual fund for investment. They also give regular updates on those mutual funds invested based on which the clients can alter their investment plan.

- *Bonds:* Based on the risk profile and the tax planning needs of the investor the advisor would suggest the amount of investment to be made in bonds.

- *Insurance:* Based on the investment needs of the customer the advisor suggests an insurance plan which would provide sufficient risk cover.

- *Direct Equity:* Based on the risk profile the advisor suggests direct equity investment. With the help of the research reports generated by the research team of HDFC Bank, the advisor suggests on what type of stocks to invest and how much to invest in equity. The advisor also helps the clients in restructuring their investment pattern.

As part of the advisory services, HDFC Bank offers various research reports like Personal Finance Insight, Company Recommendations and AAG at a Glance to the investors. These reports give information on the latest market conditions based on which the investors can make or modify their investment. Apart from these periodical magazines, daily email updates are also provided to the investors regarding the market impulse and market trends.

Equi*All*

Equi*All* is a net based equity advice provided to the clients. If a customer opts for Equi*All* service, the advisor initially restructures the existing portfolio of the clients based on their profile. The designed portfolio will also consist of the recommended purchase price, the maximum purchase price and the sale price. Then frequent updates are provided for modifying their portfolio based on the market conditions to maximize the returns. Through e-mail, HDFC Bank provides this advisory service priced at Rs.10,000[2] irrespective of the size of the portfolio.

Preferred Banking – Makes the Customer Feel Special

HDFC Bank Preferred Programme is an extension of the advisory services provided by the bank. It takes care of all the banking and investment needs of the customer. It provides a relationship manager to take care of all the banking activities on behalf of the preferred customer. HDFC Bank has listed certain criteria like maintenance of an average monthly balance of Rs.15 lakhs to avail the preferred banking services.

For preferred customers, apart from advisory services, the bank provides customized investment solutions based on their profile. It also restructures the

---

[2]   *www.hdfcbank.com*

investment portfolio based on the financial market conditions and helps to achieve the customer's investment goals. Under preferred banking service, preferential rates are charged on various products and exclusive benefits are being provided. For preferred customers, charges up to Rs.2000 per annum are waived for services like stop payment, duplicate statements and demand draft charges. It also offers services like check pick up facility, opening Demat accounts free of charge, and reduction of the locker rent. Apart from providing services to the preferred customer and their families, the bank also provides working capital overdrafts, trade finance loans to their business.

Classic Banking – A Bid to Render True Value

Similar to preferred banking service, the HDFC Bank Classic Programme offers preferential prices for various products, waive service charges and investment solutions. To become a classic customer of HDFC Bank, maintenance of an average quarterly balance of Rs.1 lakh in a savings account or a monthly balance of Rs.5 lakhs in the savings account and term deposits is required. Special benefits like waiver of 25% of the locker rents, monthly statement of accounts, preferential forex rates and no service charge for not maintaining average quarterly balance are provided under this program.

Financial Planning – A Key for Long-Term Investors

Financial planning service is provided to long-term investors. This service includes asset allocation which is based on long-term investment, building cash flows and aims at achieving the investor's future goals. The financial plan designed by the dedicated advisor would indicate the amount of savings required to achieve the client's financial goals and the plan is reviewed by the advisor on a quarterly basis.

Corporate Banking – A One-stop Shop for Diverse Needs

The bank offers Corporate Banking services to large and blue chip companies. Services like commercial, transactional banking, cash management, supply chain management etc. are provided to these corporate clients. The bank assesses the client's profile, risk tolerance level and requirements and provides tailor-made solutions to achieve their goals. Innovative products, superior technology and services have led HDFC Bank to be recognized as a leading provider of cash management services. Table 1 shows the awards received by HDFC Bank for cash management service.

Table 1: Best Cash Management Awards		
Award	Magazine	Year
Best Local Cash Management Bank in Large and Medium segments	*Asiamoney*	2006
Best Cash Management Bank	*Asset*	2006
Best Cash Management Bank – India	*Asiamoney*	2005
Best Local Cash Management Bank in India	*Asiamoney*	2004

Customer Segmentation

HDFC Bank provides these different services to satisfy the customer needs. The private banking business varies in tune with the diverse needs of the customer. Hence, it is necessary to maintain a customer database with a clear distinction between different groups. Proper segmentation of the customers helps to understand the needs of the customers and customize the solutions based on their needs.

HDFC Bank has various other links with its co-subsidiary companies like HDFC Standard Life Insurance. So, the bank can easily build a customer database and yield good results. HDFC Bank has segmented its customer database into the following segments:

- *Resident Indian:* This segment is further divided into Upper Middle Class, Salaried Middle Class and High Net Worth individuals. The bank provides Personal Banking, Investment Banking, Loans and Credit Cards to this type of customers.

- *Non-Resident Indian:* Based on the services provided the bank has identified three sub segments – Rupee Account, Foreign Currency and Value Added Services.

- *Corporate:* HDFC Bank has identified a few companies who are performing well in their respective sectors and who would require financial services. This segment includes large companies, MNCs, Small-Medium Enterprises and Internet Communication and Entertainment (ICE) companies.

- *Financial Services Providers:* This segment includes Mutual Funds, Insurance Companies, Stock Brokers and Financial Institutions.

Customer Contact Management Program

In the process of understanding the needs of existing customers and expanding future business opportunities, HDFC Bank has carried on Customer Contact Management Program (CCMP). CCMP aims at contacting existing customers and finding new business opportunities. CCMP is based on the Management Information System where the details of the customers are stored. The relationship manager shortlists the customers to be contacted, contacts them and gathers information for new business. Once any opportunity is found, they meet the customer and necessary steps are taken to close the lead.

Customer Convenience – Motto of HDFC Bank

Since its inception, HDFC Bank's motto has been "Customer Convenience". To facilitate the customers, HDFC Bank has become a "one-stop financial supermarket". The customers can approach the bank for all their needs. The experience of a customer illustrates how HDFC Bank, through its representatives, helps its clients to accomplish their needs.

Minoo Dewan, an NRI customer of HDFC Bank, was not able to find a match for his daughter. While discussing an acquisition of a pharmaceutical company with his private banker, Mr. Dewan had told him that he was not finding a match for his daughter. The private banker had taken efforts to find a match for Mr. Dewan's daughter and Mr. Dewan was able to celebrate his daughter's marriage within a month.

This shows how private bankers at HDFC Bank go far beyond providing financial services. They also help the customers in satisfying their personal needs and they can be contacted at any time round the clock.

In the process of promoting one of the bank's strategy "one-stop financial supermarket", the marketing department had tied up with *Business Today* and sponsored 10,000 copies of the magazine in each metro. The sponsored magazine talked about HDFC bank being rated as the "Best Bank" and about the bank strategy. Mr. Ajay Kelkar, Vice-President and Head, Marketing, HDFC Bank, said, "These copies would be circulated among top corporates and our high-profile customers." This promotion was based on the results of the data mining and data analysis conducted by the bank. So it is expected to have a positive impact on the target audience.

Performance

Prompt and efficient service, implementation of latest technology, good network and maintenance of a proper customer base has increased the financial status of the bank. For example, the income received from fees and commission has increased by 44.2% in 2006. The investment management and advisory services provided to high net worth individuals and structure corporate banking services are one of the reasons for the increase in fee income.

In a short span of three years since the bank started its private banking business, the number of customers have increased by 100% every year. Similar to retail segment, wealth management business for the bank is profitable. Many international and domestic magazines have awarded HDFC Bank for its excellent performance and service provided.

Box 1 shows some of the awards received by HDFC Bank.

Box 1: List of Awards
• Best Bank in India for three consecutive years, *Business Today* – KPMG Survey
• Best Domestic Bank – 2006, *Asset Magazine*
• Best Listed Bank of India 2006, *BusinessWorld*
• "Company of the Year" award for corporate excellence 2004-05, *Economic Times*
• "One of India's Most Respected Companies" 2004, *BusinessWorld*
• Best IT User in Banking – 2003, IT User Awards
Compiled from www.hdfcbank.com

Building Relationships – The Hallmark of Private Banking

Efficient service and good performance has helped the bank to increase its customers. Private banking services provided by the bank helps to maintain a close relationship with the customers. The RM contacts the customers according to their convenience. It might be even during the odd hours. Abhay Aima, the HDFC Bank country head, equity and private banking group, says that "Doctors want their relationship managers to call on them late in the evening. Doctors are usually available only after 8 pm, and if they are out on house calls, relationship managers might end up waiting till 10 pm."

Over the years, the relationship between the RM and the client becomes more personal. One such instance was that a client had presented the RM with a diamond set. As the RM should not receive any gifts from the clients, the client was asked the reason for such an expensive gift. The client had said that the RM had wished him on his 40th wedding anniversary and had given him a bouquet of roses, which his wife liked. He added that he had two sons and they had forgotten about his wedding anniversary but the RM had remembered it and wished them on that day. The client said, "I was touched by the gesture."

By maintaining good relationships with the customers, satisfying all their needs through innovative products and proper management of client's funds, HDFC Bank is carrying on private banking business profitably. However, private banking in India is developing and has a long way to go. HDFC Bank has to strengthen their advisory team with experts from various fields to target, capture and retain customers.

(Sushuma G, Research Associate at Icfai Business School Research Center, Chennai. She can be reached at sushumag@gmail.com).

References

1. "Banking for the privileged", *Business Standard.*
2. "HDFC Bank – Setting new standards", *Equitymaster.com*
3. "HDFC Bank Investors Presentation", *hdfcbank.com*
4. "Private Banking: Friend, confidante and private banker", Business Standard Banking Annual Year 2003.
5. "Promotions to mark HDFC Bank strategy", *The Hindu Business Line.*
6. Wikipedia, the free encyclopedia.
7. *www.hdfcbank.com*

11

ABN-Amro's Private Banking in India

Nancy John

The article briefs about ABN-Amro's private banking operations in India, its growth and performance and tries to highlight the bank's strategies and plans for the future. ABN-Amro's private banking division handles assets worth $60 billion worldwide. The bank's private banking section provides a complete range of advisory services to HNIs to help them in financial planning.

The liberalization of banks and the introduction of various banking reforms in the 1990s led to the growth of the private sector banks in India. During the recent years, the increase in the percentage of worldwide wealth and also the growing Indian economy have led to an increase in the number of High Net Worth Individuals (HNIs) in India. This growth in the number of HNIs has paved way for domestic as well as foreign private banks in establishing and expanding their private banking operations in India.

ABN-Amro is one such bank that established its private banking operation in 1992 with the aim of providing personalized banking services under one roof. The private banking services offered by the bank are mostly aimed at High Net Worth Individuals along with non-individuals such as Trusts, NGOs, Clubs &

Associations, Corporates and Pension & Provident Funds of Companies of both resident and non-resident status[1]. This article gives a brief introduction about ABN-Amro private bank's operations in India, its growth and performance, and also highlights the bank's strategies and plans for the future.

ABN-Amro Private Banking in India

ABN-Amro, a Dutch bank that is headquartered in Netherlands, has an international presence in more than 76 countries. With more than $500 billion worth assets worldwide, ABN-Amro is fast spreading its business across the globe. According to Mr. Joster Avest, Executive Vice-President (Private Clients), the ABN-Amro Private Banking division handles assets worth $60 billion worldwide. In the Indian market, ABN-Amro has 8 decades of experience. In 1920, ABN-Amro set up its first Indian branch in Kolkata. The bank, which was traditionally known as the "diamond financing bank", has gradually emerged into a bank that provides a wide range of services to its clientele.

With the help of its parent bank, ABN-Amro Bank (India) has succeeded in establishing a stronghold on the consumer and commercial clients in India. As a result of its sectoral expansion and diversification strategy, the bank restructured its

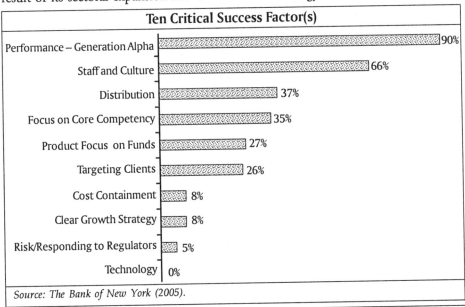

Ten Critical Success Factor(s)

Performance – Generation Alpha	90%
Staff and Culture	66%
Distribution	37%
Focus on Core Competency	35%
Product Focus on Funds	27%
Targeting Clients	26%
Cost Containment	8%
Clear Growth Strategy	8%
Risk/Responding to Regulators	5%
Technology	0%

Source: The Bank of New York (2005).

---

[1] *www.abnamro.com*

business into three Strategic Business Units (SBUs) that focused on different client groups. The Bank's three SBUs are Consumer Banking, Wholesale Banking Services and Private Banking. These units mainly concentrate on multinational corporations, small to medium-sized business enterprises and individuals and undertook activities such as asset gathering and fund management and other advisory services.

ABN-Amro started its private banking operations in India in 1992 and currently offers private banking services from its offices located in the four major cities in India, i.e., New Delhi, Mumbai, Bangalore and Chennai. The Private Banking Services offered by the bank are aimed at individuals such as Resident Individuals, Non-Resident Individuals (NRIs) and non-individuals such as Corporates, Trusts, and NGOs with additional funds looking for superior wealth management solutions under one roof. Majority of ABN-Amro's private banking clients are those customers that are drawn from corporate or retail banking divisions. Yet the bank draws other customers from the referrals provided by the existing customers.

Private Banking Services

Private banking means offering services such as investment management, advisory and wealth management services to the bank's wealthy clients, who want their assets to be managed. The services offered by the bank are on a personalized basis to individuals with a wealth of more than $100,000. The private banking division provides a one-stop shop service offering a broad series of financial solutions to non-resident as well as resident clientele. The aim of the bank in providing private banking is to manage the clients' wealth on a long-term basis. This is done with the objective of maintaining the rich clients' wealth not only for themselves but also for their family and future generations.

ABN-Amro's private banking division also offers a whole range of advisory services to High Net Worth Individuals (HNIs) to help them in financial planning. The advisory services comprise guiding the clientele on taxation issues and legal issues, investment in real estates etc. In an interview with *Business Line*, Executive Vice-President (Private Clients), ABN-Amro Private Banking Mr. Joster Avest, said, "We assess the risk profile of our clients and the investment horizon they are looking for, on the basis of which we create a financial plan for them."[2]

---

[2] "ABN-Amro keen to grow private banking biz", *www.thehindubusinessline.com*, March 2006.

ABN-Amro offers a seven day week service to its private banking clients, so that its clients are advised and are kept abreast with the day to day operations of global stock markets. The clients are offered online service to access their accounts and are also provided personalized services by a team of experienced relationship managers. Each individual customer/client is given a Private Banker, who, based on the client's exclusive financial circumstances, provides financial solutions to the individual. He also serves as a link in providing Investment Advisory Services, so that the client benefits from investment opportunities that arise in today's competitive and challenging investment environment.

ABN-Amro practices a 'true partnership' model with its Private Bank Clients. The Portfolio Advisory Service (PAS) provided by the bank to its rich clientele is a process, which begins with an understanding of the clients' requirements and preferences such as unique tax status and risk inclinations. Then, a distinct Financial Plan and portfolio of select securities is constructed. After the desired

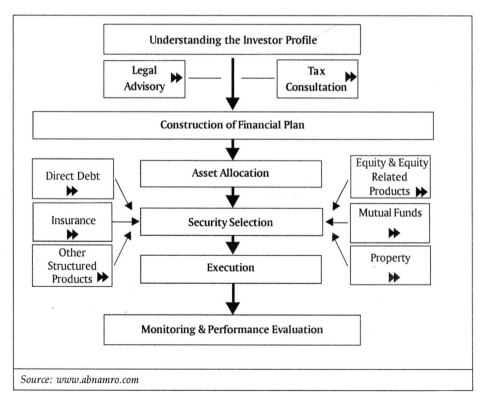

Source: *www.abnamro.com*

portfolio is constructed, the final part of the PAS involves performance evaluation. The main objective in providing this service is to optimize returns within the clients' pre-defined risk parameters.

ABN-Amro Private Banking also provides a wide range of value-added services to its clients. Apart from providing Portfolio Advisory Services, it also offers services such as the Transaction Execution platform. This service helps the clients in performing transactions such as equity, debt, mutual funds, insurance, property and foreign exchange. To further smoothen the progress of the above transactions, ABN-Amro makes use of its Institutional Equity Brokerage Firms in India along with other leading External Broking Houses, Brokers in Debt segment, and specialists at ABN-Amro Banks FX treasury unit.

Growth and Performance

Within a span of 15 years ABN-Amro private bank in India has spread itself, has made great progress and has carved a name for itself. ABN-Amro Bank has plans to increase its private banking business in India by at least 300 percent over the next five years. According to the bank's Vice-President and Head, Private Banking (India), Ms. Sutapa Banerjee, the current assets under management (AUM) for the private banking operations is about $800 million (Rs.3,445.3 crore) in the country. She also feels that in the next five years the AUM would increase to about $2 billion (Rs.9,186.9 crore).[3] The bank has also started to channelize its resources in a way that would further build the already strong position held by the bank in the Private Banking segment in the Indian market.

By the end of the current financial year, the bank hopes to expand its private banking service in at least eight to nine cities in the country. Ms. Sutapa Banerjee in an interview with *Business Line* expressed that in order to reach out to the customers the bank would utilize the hub and spoke arrangement. Thus, wherever the bank does not have branches, it would reach the customers through its neighboring branches. In order to build on the mass of customers, the bank has been strictly in conforming to the internationally accepted 'Know Your Customer' norms.

---

[3]   "ABN-Amro keen to grow private banking biz", *www.thehindubusinessline.com*, March 2006.

Presently, the private banking services in India cater to about 600 groups, which consist of families, proprietors and trusts. The total number of individual accounts within the 600 groups is about 2,500. On the consumer side, private banking services are offered to top private clients and private clients/mass affluent and mass retail. On the corporate side, services are offered to large corporates such as the multinationals to the small enterprises such as the mid market/financial institutions and the SMEs (Small and Medium Enterprises).

Keeping in view the increasing number of HNIs across the country, the bank has increased its staff strength to cater to their financial needs. However, the bank is looking out for high net worth individuals with assets more than Rs.2.5 crores.

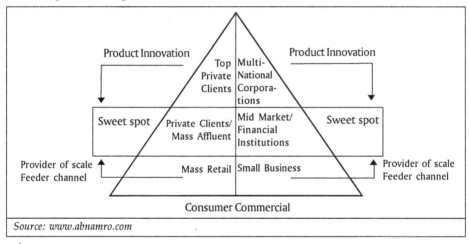

Source: *www.abnamro.com*

Thus, the bank is keen on moving from inclusive banking to exclusive banking. In the next two years the bank plans to heighten its private banking operation in India by doubling its assets under management. As a part of its expansion strategy in Asia, the bank has increased its private banking staff from 250 in 2005 to 400 at present. In India, the private banking staff has increased from 30 to 50. In India, ABN-Amro's private bank currently has roughly about $1 billion under management and expects it to increase to $2-3 billion in the next two years.

The Road Ahead

In Asia, ABM-Amro considers India to be an increasingly growing market for its private banking operations. It considers acquisition as an expansion strategy for foreign banks to increase their minority holdings in Indian private banks. It considers the above as the fastest road to future growth in India. Over the next two to three years ABN-Amro plans to increase its private banking business from four centers to at least 10-12 centers with focus on the Northern, Western and Southern parts of the country. It aims to look beyond the metros to class one cities such as Hyderabad, Mysore, Pune and Baroda. It has also plans to further expand its operations not only into class one cities but also into smaller towns and rural areas. This is to tap into India's dissimilar high net worth individuals, diamond merchants and also to focus on leaders of SMEs. It has been estimated that private banks have targeted less than 10 percent of India's HNIs.

The government's decision to hike the foreign direct investment capital to at least 74 percent in the banking sector has further given boost to the bank to increase its presence in India. According to the bank possible options are being looked at acquiring an Indian private bank and setting up of subsidiaries. According to Peter Schmittmann, ABN-Amro Bank NV senior executive vice-president, at least 51 percent stake and management control is preferable, if the bank plans to go for acquisition. He also said, "India is the fourth major 'home market' for us after the US, Netherlands and Brazil."[4]

Conclusion

ABN-Amro private banking division in India foresees a major growth in the private banking business in the years to come. Talking about the future growth of private banking, Mr. Joster Avest, Executive Vice-President (Private Clients), ABN-Amro Private Banking, expressed his views as follows, "We handle assets of around $800 million in India. It is possible to grow to $2-3 billion in the next couple of years."[5] According to him, the rising number of HNIs seems to pave way to increased private banking operations in India. He also expressed, "The Indian economy is creating more and more wealthy people, many of whom are our potential clients."[6]

(Nancy John is a Faculty Associate at Icfai Business School Research Center, Chennai. She can be reached at victor.nancy@gmail.com).

---

[4]   "Local Buyout on ABN Amro Radar", *www.business-standard.com*

[5]   "ABN-Amro seeks to expand pvt banking", *www.thehindubusinessline.com*, March 2006.

[6]   Ibid.

Section III

Lessons from Regional Trends

12

Private Banking in Asia: Wealth from Wealthy

Indu Prasad

The private banking market in Asia is growing more rapidly than in other parts of the world with the offshore bankers reaping the maximum rewards.

According to many independent studies, private wealth in the Asia-Pacific region will grow at a faster rate than in any other region at least in the next three to five years. This is being driven by improved economic conditions, further liberalization and deregulation of economies and markets, new wealth creation and demand for professional wealth management advice.

— Deepak Sharma.

Asia's high net worth individuals are getting rich quicker than those elsewhere in the world due to wealth management, which has never been so competitive in the region but is now providing good opportunities for bankers. A few years back private banking was synonymous with hiding money, but now this has completely changed. Private banking now is about making returns and finding solutions. Behind these new challenges and dramatic changes lies a fundamental shift in the private banking business model. From being of a peripheral importance to many wholesale and retail banking organizations, it has become a core strategic business unit.

The greatest opportunity for private banking in Asia lies in regions like China, Taiwan, Hong Kong and South Korea. Although China and Korea remain closed markets, their growth potential is too huge to be ignored. China is already the single biggest wealth market in Asia outside Japan, with assets of $500 bn, and Korea is not too far behind. Once these countries float their currencies and allow their citizens to hold assets in foreign currencies, growth will be tremendous. Even though growth potential is unlimited, reaping benefits is also not so easy. So, what are the challenges private bankers are facing to cater to the rich and how are they going about it?

Promising Potential

Over the past few years, growth in the Asia-Pacific private wealth market has been relatively flat because of sluggish economic conditions as well as many external and geopolitical factors such as the dotcom meltdown, the aftermath of the Asian financial crisis, 9/11 and the war on terror, the SARS crisis and the Iraq war. "Looking ahead, according to industry projections, the Asia-Pacific private wealth market is estimated to grow at about 10% per annum for the next three to five years," says Sharma. He adds, "We think this is a conservative estimate. Higher double-digit rates could be expected in light of improved economic conditions as well as new opportunities and markets for private wealth such as Korea, India and China."

According to Boston Consulting Group (BCG) Wealth Manager Performance Survey conducted in 2003, the number of wealthy Asian households grew by 200,000, reaching 2 million and their assets increased from $1.9 tn to $2 tn in the year 2002. On an average, revenues and profits for wealth managers in Asia-Pacific grew by more than 15% in 2002. Several factors contributed to the good performance results. The first factor is that Asia has the advantage of being a relatively immature wealth market. For years many Asian investors favored cash, direct investments and property, and often preferred to manage their own assets. As a result, while private banking boomed in North America and Europe, it remained relatively underdeveloped in Asia. Then the Asian financial crisis severely damaged the holdings of many investors in the region. The property market declined dramatically. Yields on cash accounts plummeted as interest rates declined to 40-year lows. Finally, equity markets crashed, undermining investors' faith in their own skills. To make their money work better for them, Asian investors began looking for other wealth management options, embracing sophisticated investments, such as structured products and hedge funds. These products demand professional expertise. Thus, in recent years, wealth managers in Asia have adopted the European offshore business model and have nurtured an emerging demand for professional advice. The approach is based on client relationship managers rather than sales-oriented brokers and has proved successful in turning skeptical Asian investors into clients.

The second factor is the strong performance of several of the region's economies. Growth in China and South Korea has remained high and savings rates in the region have continued at impressive levels, which is promising for sustained asset

---

Paradigm Shift in Private Banking

– Deepak Sharma
President, Asia-Pacific and Middle East,
The Citigroup Private Bank.

We emphasized KYC (Know Your Client), in all our business dealings, with great rigor (KYC is a client qualification process to ensure that the client's wealth being invested is genuine, not tainted).

We pushed a team-based approach rather than a single banker relationship. The private banker orchestrates the client relationship with the bank, involving a team of specialists—a portfolio manager, investment counselor, capital markets' specialist, and investment finance specialist. Additionally, experts in niche areas of wealth management may be involved depending on client needs. Expertise in family advisory, art investment and advisory, philanthropy, and real estate are some of these.

We leveraged the Power of ONE of Citigroup, bringing to the client the single largest platform of financial products and services that no other financial institution could match.

Yet, we offered an open architecture where we proactively offered our clients access to best-in-class products and services from third-party providers.

We practised a 'holistic approach' true to its meaning. In addition to our proprietary product platform with integrated open architecture capabilities, we brought to the client new dimensions in financial services such as art advisory, farm advisory, family practice, and whole net worth asset allocation.

accumulation among wealthy Asian investors. Asian economies are showing a lot of promise for growth and there has been a sharp increase in the surplus funds available for investment. N R Parasuraman, Professor, Finance, SDM Institute for Management Development, says, "We have witnessed great improvement in market-related activity and transparency. While market perfection may still be quite a distant dream, the surveillance mechanism has shown progress and these have contributed to increased investor confidence." He further adds, "Thanks to the better performance of the economies of a number of Asian countries, the surplus available for investment has gone up here. Avenues for value enhancement are emerging continuously and contributing to the progress."

But the concept of private banking has gone through dramatic changes in recent years. Sharma says, "I think the private banking world has traditionally had an air of mystery about it. The myths are of secretive figures placing money in offshore havens, protected by bank secrecy, possibly for tax reasons. The reality is that private banking is changing fast, and clients and institutions wedded to the old model are quickly being left behind." Performance, value-added advice, and global capability are replacing secrecy and execution efficiency as the driving business propositions. The old private banking model is being further hurried to its demise by anti-money laundering measures, which are helping to fight international crime and combat the abuse of secrecy rules. The other big driver of change is technology, and consequently information being more freely available. However, the challenge this poses is information overload. Clients don't want information especially in excessive amounts; they want information that has been harnessed into value-added advice.

Clients are seeking a private bank that is able to provide global access, offer long-term financial stability, extend a superior product platform and intellectual leadership in investment management, practice a holistic approach in wealth management and yet act independently, objectively and with trust and confidentiality. A private bank whose business model is able to cater to these demands will be popular with the clients and is most likely to succeed in the long-term. "The business model must also be adaptable to local regulations and local needs. In more regulated markets, where there are capital controls and/or where offshore banking services are prohibited or tightly controlled, the private banking model cannot be applied to its fullest extent. There may also be a need to develop a strong onshore platform to ensure adherence to local regulations," maintains Sharma.

More Asian clients are seeking private banking expertise because they are more astute about risk and return, and cognizant of the importance of diversification. The Asian financial crisis awakened many clients to diversification, and deepened their understanding of risk. They are certainly more sophisticated in their investment approach and more demanding in terms of increasing return and reducing risk. Prof. Parasuraman says, "The factors that drive wealthy Asian investors to seek private banking include the direct inaccessibility to international money and finance markets and to the use of sophisticated instruments. Most of these new instruments are traded on a 'over the counter' basis and have not found a regular place in the stock or money exchanges. Thus, financial intermediation becomes imperative. Besides, the investor will never be able to establish his credentials directly in the international market and herein comes the role of the banker."

Challenges

Private banking in Asia though performing well is still facing some challenges. "The industry is facing three particular challenges, which are not necessarily related to competition, these are: talent, awareness of private banking capabilities and complexity regarding markets and products," says Sharma. The industry is not opportunity-constrained but is resource-constrained. Talent supply needs to increase to meet the anticipated growth in demand. It is expected that private wealth in the Asia-Pacific region will grow at double-digit rates. Relationship managers and product specialists, highly skilled in wealth management, will be in great demand. There is a great need of generating awareness among Asian families about private banking. Many of the region's wealthy families are familiar with the importance of private banking in their wealth management, but many more are yet to discover the opportunities a private bank can provide in terms of financial peace of mind as well as growth in wealth and preservation for future generations. The third challenge is the complexity regarding managing wealth and lack of expertise. Structuring an appropriate portfolio from today's arsenal of financial tools is also not easy, and is more than most individuals can do on their own. At the same time, more and more Asian investors are touching other jurisdictions through their investments, businesses, or families and they need to understand different tax and legal frameworks. In these complex and volatile times when opportunity and uncertainty come in equal measure, managing wealth requires astute skills of experts.

Due to increasing competition, private banking has become more challenging and it's a challenge for both bankers and investors. Private banking has to clearly come to terms with the risk-return balance, with the investors willing to take a higher inherent risk of certain new instruments only if they are rewarded higher compared to the risk undertaken. Prof. Parasuraman says, "Of course, private bankers will vie with one another for developing new instruments which seek to outdo this balance. Herein lies the challenge of the private banker. Merely sticking on to the conventional methods might not attract customers in a large-scale and adding on new aspect is easier said than done, because it entails a 'presence' in the international markets and a network for safety of the returns and a clear measurement of the risk involved."

Unlike Western clients, Asians are seldom interested to invest in domestic markets, they rather prefer global service. The supposed reason for this could be the financial crisis of 1997-98 that taught them to spread their risks. This creates a major challenge for the bankers who have to constantly develop new products to keep the clients happy.

The other problem in front of bankers is prevalence of family businesses in Asia. The problem is due to the generation gap. The older people did not know when to let go and the younger were reluctant in getting into their parent's shoes. The Asian families did not know how to bridge the gap and proceed with the conversation. Whereas, the concept of the American style, which combines wealth management and transfer of estates, is widely spread.

Private banks in the region also have to spend a great deal of time on due diligence of potential new clients, since regulations on money laundering are becoming stricter and Asians are often secretive about the origin of their wealth. This is one more challenge private bankers are facing. Moreover, the markets with the biggest potential, China and India, remain closed. Foreign banks cannot offer their services there, while residents are not allowed to invest offshore. All these issues make private banking expensive and labor-intensive in Asia.

Future

The future of private banking is bright in Asia. Sharing his views on this, Prof. Parasuraman says, "The general progress in the economies resulting in the availability of more surplus funds for investment and secondly, the possibility of earning higher returns through a basket of instruments brought forth through the opening up of many economies promises a bright future." It is also expected that the development and acceptance of new derivative instruments will reduce risk in some cases and give rise to a potential for high speculative profit in other cases.

"We are very positive about the future of private banking in Asia because the region is the fastest growing in terms of wealth creation. Also, markets like Korea, India and China offer tremendous opportunities in the medium to long-term for local and international financial institutions as the countries benefit from improved economic conditions and undergo further market liberalization and deregulation," says Sharma.

The development of this sector would ultimately depend on the sustenance of customer faith. This will come about only through a good surveillance mechanism and the compulsion for transparency. "Regulatory measures need to be revised from time to time to suit the needs of changes in the scenario so that bad market practices do not spoil a potentially solid means of value enhancement," says Prof. Parasuraman.

(Indu Prasad is an Analyst with the Icfai University Press.)

13

Private Banking in Singapore: Riding on Asian Economic Boom

D Satish

The flourishing class of millionaires in emerging Asian economies offers enormous opportunities for private banking in the region. Will Singapore, which has congenial environment for the growth of wealth management companies, emulate Switzerland as the most favorable nation for private banking?

Asia's burgeoning class of millionaires backed by strong economy growth offers a vast market for the world's wealth managers. Against this milieu, private banking in Asia is growing faster than any other region in the world. Especially, Singapore is witnessing the boom backed by low taxes, political stability, banking confidentiality, strong legal system, professional workforce and more importantly better regulatory environment. Besides the growing Asian client base, most of big private banks have set up their branches to cater to Singapore-based Europeans, non-resident Indians, Chinese and the Middle East community. In fact, Asia is bundling more millionaires at a faster rate than any other region in the world. For instance, the number of millionaires in India and South Korea surged at a remarkable rate of 19.3% and 21.3%, respectively, while Indonesia and Hong Kong recorded double-digit growth. An interesting fact is that most of them are self-made millionaires or billionaires rather than inheritors of wealth. So, the ways of managing the money are entrepreneurial as well and they are no longer interested to invest in bonds and property. They are more interested to manage their wealth effectively and are expanding their investment bar from hedge funds and private equity to currencies and derivatives.

According to industry sources, private wealth in Singapore is at US$150-170 bn, with more than 10% made up of European money. Because Europeans are looking for diversification and believe that their Asian investment could be managed by the experts based in Singapore. The island-state's central bank, Monetary Authority of Singapore's (MAS) recent survey reveals that around US$150 bn of private wealth managed in the country with more than 30 private banks. UBS, the world largest private bank, declared that 'Asia-Pacific is the world's fastest-growing wealth management market.' It estimates that liquid assets held by individuals in the region, apart from Japan, will be 7.6% per annum against global rate of 6%. Marcel Kreis, Managing Director and Head of the UBS wealth management is very bullish about private banking in Singapore. He says, "...nowhere is the surge in the private banking more evident than in Singapore. This is testament to the successful transformation and active marketing of Singapore's financial industry by the government."

On the Growth Path

In Singapore, business is rolling because most of the Asians are keeping their wealth in the region. As the penetration of private banking is relatively low compared with the US and Europe, there is plenty of room for growth. In fact, the island has plenty of its own millionaires to service. Though Switzerland has been the banking wealth management hub, the majority of private bankers in Europe believe that Singapore will overtake Switzerland within two years as the world's most important growth center for offshore banking. Raymond A Mason, Chairman and CEO of Legg Mason, a US investment firm, says "I have been very impressed with Singapore's commitment to the financial sector, as supported by the high quality of its professional community and its overall infrastructure." On the other hand, going by booming banking activity in Singapore, Switzerland recently announced 35% tax concession to the European Union which opened the door to fast-growing Singapore.

A Leading Wealth Management Hub

Backed by the growth of High Net-worth Individuals (HNIs) at 7% a year, Asia's wealth is expected to reach US$10.6 tn by 2010 from about US$7.1 tn in 2004. These trends are favoring Singapore to emerge as a leading wealth management center, not just in Asia, but also in the world. The island is backed by strong fundamentals of high standards of regulation and supervision, and a robust legal and judicial framework as well as its ideal location to gain access to global and regional financial markets. Experts say that the soaring growth rates in the economies of China and India are behind the boom. They further say, "If you open up economies for two billion people in 10 years, multiplied by strong market performance and fewer capital controls, you get a phenomenal amount of wealth creation." As Asia's economic growth stories unfold, new opportunities will arise. Asian investors are becoming more sophisticated and demanding of their private banking relationships. Going by this, private banks are pursuing ambitious growth strategies by competing for new clients as well as positioning for a greater share of existing clients' wealth. According to the central bank's estimates, many of the major private banks have already established their force and are growing rapidly in Singapore and it is matched by more than 300 asset management firms investing throughout the region. Ong Chong Tee, Deputy Managing Director of MAS says, "Moving forward, we expect an enlargement of

Box: Fastest Growing Millionaires, 2005	
	(annual gain in percentage)
Country	Percentage
South Korea	21.3
India	19.3
Russia	17.4
Africa	15.9
Indonesia	14.7
Hong Kong	14.4
Saudi Arabia	13.4
Singapore	13.4
UAE	11.8
Brazil	11.3
Source: Merrill Lynch World Wealth Report, 2006.	

the wealth management eco-system. This will include trust companies, philanthropy, family offices and the ancillary service providers such as tax, legal advisors, consultants and technology platform providers. Together, these specialists will help deepen and broaden our offerings as a global wealth management centre."

Skilled Professionals – A Key Differentiator

As the wealth management is people-centric and the business is built on trusted advice and good relationships, financial sector needs skilled manpower. Against this, most of the top bankers in Singapore continue to invest in talent and in fact the most significant stumbling block for Asia's private bankers is finding enough qualified people to meet the demand and their key challenge lies in recruiting enough qualified people to support the growth.

Banking experts say, "Working with wealthy clients requires a passion to serve and to deliver with the utmost promising quality and there can be no shortcuts or compromise. This requires both a broad and deep knowledge of the spectrum of financial services or instruments at one's disposal." Besides, private banks should know and follow the ethical standards. More importantly, financial matters are part of clients' privacy and they have to handle with utmost discretion. Commenting on the initiatives, MAS Managing Director says, "As Singapore extends its financial catchment beyond the region, the competition we face in skills and talent *vis-à-vis* other major centers will sharpen. The quickening pace of innovation in global financial services will also demand a more rapid and continuous infusion and upgrading skills. What ultimately defines as a successful financial center will be the infrastructure or rules, networks and capabilities that encourage Singapore-based players to seize new business opportunities."

Outlook

The major global private banks are attaching a lot of importance to the Asia-Pacific region especially Singapore and it will be a focal point of their business in Asia. They view the island nation as a vibrant financial center with significant business opportunities and almost all top global banks that have not established their base, have announced their expansion plans in Singapore. Bank Experts predict, "With greater participation by international players, Singapore dollar capital markets grow in size, liquidity and sophistication." The island's excellent communications and transport links tribute its strategy as a financial hub. On the whole, Singapore has remarkably established the convergence of financial information and manufacturing hub, which benefits not just private banks but any company that recognizes these as competitive advantages.

(D Satish, Deputy Editor, the Icfai University Press. He can be reached at d_satish_2000@yahoo.com).

Singapore: A Private Banking Tiger

– Michel Benedetti

In the financial world Switzerland enjoys an unchallenged reputation as the world leader in private banking services. An extremely stable economy and many years of experience and expertise have helped Swiss banks attain their present status. In recent years, however, Singapore has been developing as a further centre of financial advisory and other services to high net worth individuals.

The offensives undertaken by major international banks often give the financial industry a major clue as to whether recent developments in the sector are here to stay. Credit Suisse, for example, is planning a strong presence in the Singapore market with the massive expansion of its "Center of Excellence". The new regional headquarters are designed as an international backoffice for the whole of South-East Asia, with a headcount that is expected to rise to around 3100 by 2007. Alongside Citigroup, the world's largest bank, and the British HSBC, Credit Suisse and UBS currently make up the top four private bankers in Singapore.

Success Factors in Private Banking

If a financial centre is to specialize in private banking, it must avoid concentrating too sharply on potential short-term returns. Rather, the success factors that are crucial here are those which have also been factors in Switzerland's status and success. It goes without saying that these include significant, visible growth in client assets. According to estimates from the financial community, private assets under management by banks in Singapore amount to 150-170 billion US-Dollars. One major international bank is estimating that private client assets in South-East Asia (excluding Japan) will grow by 7.6 percent per year up to 2007. One of the region's fastest-growing client groups are the NRIs, or non-resident Indians. According to Merrill Lynch/ Cap Gemini's "World Wealth Report", there are some 20 million NRIs around the world, 150 000 of whom are millionaires. Taken together, this client group has an investible surplus of 360 billion US-Dollars.

A Small-scale Economic Miracle

Just as vital to the development of a private banking centre is the stability of the host economy, because private banking clients often wish to invest their assets over the long-term, if not over generations. The positive effects that a liberal economic policy has had on Singapore are beyond dispute. Furthermore, the Singapore government is determined to compete with Hong Kong for the title of Asia's most important financial centre. Coming right after London, New York and Tokyo, Singapore is now the world's number four foreign exchange trading centre, while its stock exchange, Singapore Exchange Limited (SGX), is one of Asia's largest. Finally, it is worth mentioning Singapore's banking confidentiality laws. The tiger state ferociously defends this legislation, which was drafted for the financial sector along the same lines as its Swiss model.

Contd...

Contd...
The basic rule is that the banks are not allowed to pass any client information whatsoever to third parties although, just as in Switzerland, certain exceptions apply (under the 2001 Banking Act) to the judicial authorities. **Innovations in Financial Information** In addition to its economic strength, the financial market has displayed a degree of originality where financial information is concerned. Additionally, Singapore offers the technological framework required to support the availability and distribution of financial data. This is illustrated by two recent examples. Around a year ago, "Islamic Banking" came to the attention of the international financial world as an interesting growth segment. In 2005, Moody's Investor Services estimated that, globally, there were around 300 Islamic banks with more than 250 billion US-Dollars in assets under management. Moody's also estimates that this segment is growing at 10-15 percent a year. Islamic financial instruments must be structured in accordance with Islamic (or "Sharia") law. Sharia law forbids Muslims to charge interest or to gamble, and this is interpreted to cover many forms of derivatives, as well as conventional insurance policies. It means that lending, derivatives and bonds, as well as investments in companies which have high levels of borrowed capital, are all prohibited under Sharia law. Islamic banking is based on the creation of constructs which comply with Islamic law while also offering the same benefits as "forbidden" financial transactions. Singapore is actually something of a newcomer in this area, but makes up in ambition what it lacks in experience. For example, the financial sector is planning to establish a banking hub for Islamic investment funds, as well as an Islamic interbank money market.
Source: www.telekurs-realtime.com © Telekurs Financial Information Ltd. Reprinted with permission.

14

Private Banking in Europe – Getting Clients and Keeping Them!

Philip Molyneux and Anna Omarini

The paper examines the features of private banking business in Europe and focuses on the key roles of client segmentation, retention and acquisition. There has been substantial growth in private banking business over the last decade or so as commercial banks have targeted both the 'mass-affluent' and more upmarket high net worth individuals (HNWIs). The combined amount of investable assets at the disposal of these two groups amounts to around Euro 6 trillion and a wide range of banks, investment firms and other operators have focused on devising strategies aimed at grabbing a share of this potentially lucrative market. The private client wealth management industry in Europe remains relatively fragmented although a few major players have emerged and consolidation is an ongoing theme in the sector. Given the commercial opportunities afforded by this business area, the increased complexity of clients needs continues to be a critical strategic issue for industry participants. This paper illustrates important themes relating to the wealth management service proposition and focuses on client segmentation, retention and acquisition

> *strategies. Overall, we find that private banks will have to adopt a more systematic approach to these areas and in particular also have to pay greater qualitative and quantitative attention to client satisfaction, trust and loyalty issues if their client retention and acquisition strategies are to be a success.*

1. Introduction

Private banking concerns the high-quality provision of a range of financial and related services to wealthy clients, principally individuals and their families. Typically the services on offer combine retail banking products such as payment and account facilities plus a wide range of up-market investment related services.

Market segmentation and the offering of high quality service provision forms the essence of private banking and key components include:

- tailoring services to individual client requirements
- anticipation of client needs
- a long-term relationship orientation
- personal contact
- discretion
- investment performance.

The market for private banking services has been targeted by many large banks because of the growing wealth of individuals and the relative profitability of private banking business. The Capgemini Merrill Lynch Wealth Report (2005)[1] highlights various features of the market for high net-worth individuals (HNWIs):

- 8.3 million people globally each hold at least US$1 million in financial assets
- HNWI wealth totalled US$30.8 trillion, an 8.2% gain over 2003
- Wealth generation was driven by fast-paced GDP performance and moderate market capitalization growth

---

[1]   Capgemini Merrill Lynch Wealth Report (2005). *http://www.merrilllynch.com/media/48237.pdf*

- HNWI wealth and population growth in North America outpaced those in Europe for the first time since 2001

- Singapore, South Africa, Hong Kong, and Australia witnessed the highest growth in HNWI numbers

- HNWI financial wealth is expected to reach US$42.2 trillion by 2009, growing at an annual rate of 6.5%.

An important feature of the private banking market relates to client segmentation which will be discussed in more detail later in the paper. The bottom end of the market is referred to as the 'mass affluent' segment – typically individuals who have up to $300,000 of investable assets. The top-end of the market are often referred to as 'ultra HNWIs' with over $50 million in investable assets and in-between lie HNWIs ($300,000 to $5 million) and very high HNWIs ($5 million to $50 million). Note that these definitions are by no means precise and different banks and commentators use various definitions for their own market segmentation strategies. The level of service and the range of products on offer increases with the wealth of the respective client.

The number of HNWIs tends to fluctuate in line with developments in the economy and global stockmarkets. Since 2001/2 the growth in the number of HNWIs has been relatively slow in both the US and Europe. For instance, the population in Europe increased at a compound annual rate of 4.3% between 1998 and 2003, while the US growth has been only 1.7% over the same period. As noted by Datamonitor (2005)[2]:

> The worst year for these regions was 2002, when the population of high net worths in Europe fell by 6.7% to 3.3 million and in the US the population fell by a substantial 13.9% to 7.3 million. In the US however, the HNW population had been falling since 2000, while for Europe, this represented the only year of decline during the five year period. 2003 on the other hand has witnessed a great improvement in these markets. Over the course of the year the high net worth population in Europe reached 3.6 million individuals, representing an increase of 8.7% compared to 2002. In the US, the picture was also far more positive, with the high net worth population increasing 16.3% during the year to 8.5 million. (p.8)

---

[2]   Global Wealth Predictions 2005 – What's in Store for Wealth Next Year, *Datamonitor*, January 2005.

There are an estimated 3.5 million European HNWIs and these are believed to hold an estimated Euro trillion in 2003 (compared with the $7 trillion held by wealthy US individual) as shown in Table 1. You can see from the table that the mass affluent market in Europe (defined as individuals with up to Euro 300,000 in investable assets) constitutes an estimated 25.5 million individuals with a total of just under $3 trillion in assets to invest. It can also be seen that the size of the market has been growing somewhere in the region of 3 to 4% in recent years, and other forecasts suggest that this rate is likely to increase to around 5% up to 2008 leading to HNWI assets growing to just under $5 trillion by 2008. Germany has the largest market, followed by France, UK, Italy and Spain. During the 1990's the Spanish HNWI market has been growing at the fastest rate.

Table 1: Wealth Management Market in Europe, 1998-2003							
Individuals (000s)	**1998**	**1999**	**2000**	**2001**	**2002**	**2003**	**CAGR**
HNW	2,898	3,180	3,338	3,523	3,286	3,571	4.3%
MA	21,865	27,595	29,059	26,258	23,828	25,522	3.1%
Total	24,763	30,776	32,398	29,782	27,114	29,093	3.3%
Liquid Assets (EURbn)	**1998**	**1999**	**2000**	**2001**	**2002**	**2003**	**CAGR**
HNW	2,447	2,777	2,761	2,771	2,653	3,028	4.3%
MA	2,420	2,958	3,170	2,957	2,683	2,930	3.9%
Total	4,868	5,735	5,931	5,728	5,336	5,958	4.1%
Countries included Germany, Greece, under Europe: Austria, Belgium, Denmark, Finland, France Ireland, Italy, Netherlands, Norway, Spain, Sweden, UK.							
Note: MA = mass affluent defined as having investable assets of £30,000 and £200,000. (EUR 50,000 to 300,000). HNW = high-net worth individuals have investable assets of greater than £200,000 (Euro 300,000) CAGR = compound annual growth rates							
Source: Global Wealth Predictions 2005, Datamonitor, January.							

A wide range of different banks and other financial institutions offer private banking services to HNWI clients. Table 2 shows a listing of major private banks taken. It can be seen that major Swiss banks such as UBS and Credit Suisse are represented – and this is not surprising as Switzerland is the global capital of offshore private banking business (where HNWIs have there investments managed by banks outside their home country). In addition, other large commercial banks have substantial private banking operations including HSBC, Deutsche Bank and Barclays. The table also shows that the top US investment banks such as

Table 2: Top 25 Global Private Banks by Worldwide Assets under Management, Year End 2003

(Global AuM)

Rank	Company	Home Country	(€bn) 2003
1	UBS Wealth Management[1]	Switzerland	858.8
2	Credit Suisse Private Banking	Switzerland	329.2
3	Merrill Lynch Global Private Clients[2]	US	183.8
4	Deutsche Bank Private Wealth Management[1]	Germany	162.0
5	Citigroup Private Bank[3]	US	158.6
6	Barclays Private Clients[4]	UK	155.3
7	HSBC Private Banking Holdings	UK	1375
8	JP Morgan Private Banking	US	112.2
9	Morgan Stanley Private Wealth Management	US	105.7
10	ABN-AMRO Private Clients[5]	Benelux	102.0
11	Pictet & Cie	Switzerland	100.4
12	BNP Paribas Private Bank	France	96.0
13	Bank of America Private Bank	US	85.0
14	Northern Trust Personal Financial Services[6]	US	84.8
15	ZKB Private Bank	Switzerland	75.9
16	RBC Global Private Banking[5]	Canada	75.1
17	Lombard Odier Darier Hentsch	Switzerland	74.0
18	Sal. Oppanhelm	Germany	61.0
19	US Bancorp – Private Client Group[7]	US	55.5
20	Wachovia Wealth Management	US	52.7
21	Fortis Private Banking	Benelux	50.0
22	Credit Lyonnais Private Banking	France	46.5
23	Societe Generale Private Banking	France	45.1
24	National Australia Bank Wealth Management[8]	Australia	43.9
25	Union Bancaire Privee (UBP)	Switzerland	43.2

Note: [1] Invested assets; [2] Assets in asset priced accounts; [3] Client business volumes under management; [4] Total customer funds; [5] Assets under administration; [6] Managed assets; [7] Assets under custody; [8] Total funds under management.

Source: The Wealth Management Super League – Breaking Away from the Pack? Datamonitor, March 2005.

JP Morgan, Goldman Sachs and Merrill Lynch also rank highly in private banking as do some lesser known Swiss banks (such as Pictet & Cie and Lombard Odier Darier Hentsch – *'If you have not heard of the latter – you are probably not rich enough to avail of their services!!!!')*. It is important to note that the (mainly commercial and investment banks) shown in Table 1 all deal with HNWI clients whereas it is really only the commercial banks that focus on the mass affluent market – where the latter differentiate services for their upmarket retail banking customers.

A similar listing of the 'Best Global Private Banks' from a Euromoney Survey (in January 2005) is shown in Table 3 – this is based on a survey of market and other participants. It can be seen that many of the private banks that appear in Tables 2 and 3 are similar.

Table 3: Best Global Private Banks (Euromoney Survey, January 2005)			
1	UBS	14	Rothschild
2	Citigroup Private Bank	15	Morgan Stanley
3	Credit Suisse Private Banking	16	Societe Generale Private Banking
4	HSBC Private Bank	17	ING Private Banking
5	JPMorgan Private Bank	18	Lombard Odier Darier Hentsch
6	Goldman Sachs	19	Barclays
7	Pictet & Cie	20	Union Bancaire Privee
8	Deutsche Bank, Private Wealth Management	21	Julius Baer
9	Merrill Lynch	22	Nordea
10	ABN Amno Private Banking	23	Royal Bank of Canada
11	Coutts & Co	24=	Carnegie
12	BNP Paribas Private Bank	24=	LCF Edmond de Rothschild
13	MeesPierson		

Source: Euromoney (2005) January.

A key feature of the industry structure, however, is the general lack of concentration (especially compared with investment banking). For example, it has been estimated that the top 10 private banks in Europe manage around 20% of HNWI wealth, and within a country no player has more than 5% of the domestic private banking market. Note however that in Switzerland, UBS and Credit Suisse are major managers of offshore wealth – Switzerland being the capital of offshore private banking.

2. Relationships among Private Banking Institutions, Services and Clients

A precise definition of what constitutes private banking business is problematic as the product and service offering can vary considerably across national boundaries and also according to clients' needs. For instance, the state of the domestic economy, capital market performance, tax and inheritance laws can all have a strong influence on the types of services demanded by clients. In addition, the organizational structure (e.g. the set-up within a universal bank) of the institution that is offering private banking services can also determines the possible scope of services offered. In Switzerland, for instance, private banking services are provided through traditional private banks (like Pictet) and universal banks (such as UBS and Credit Suisse), whereas in the US and UK both commercial and investment banks are the main operators in the private banking market (although there are of course some specialist private banking firms although their role is as not as prominent as in Switzerland). In recent years various large European banks have emphasized the role of their private banking operations as major strategic units as an attempt to achieve a clearer segmentation of this line of business from other activities. However, there is still no clear cut way of defining the private banking offer for all banks as the products and services combine elements of both commercial banking and investment related business. As a result, the terminology "trust banking", "commercial banking" or "investment banking" are frequently applied to describe the business of private banking activities. Typically private banking forms a part of trust banking (in Japan, for instance, there are stand-alone trust banks that effectively do mass-affluent and HNWI business, and the main city banks all have trust divisions), and in many cases country-specific banking law determines in which division or part of the bank the "private banking" operations are to be located. (See Exhibit 1)

In Exhibit 1 it is best to think of "private banking" as organizationally positioned from a market oriented view where this type of business focuses strongly on personal relationships with the clients, in contrast to an institution-oriented structure where the banks' services are not tailored to the needs of an individual person. Obviously, private banking and retail banking both belong to the

Exhibit 1: Private and Retail Banking Overlaps

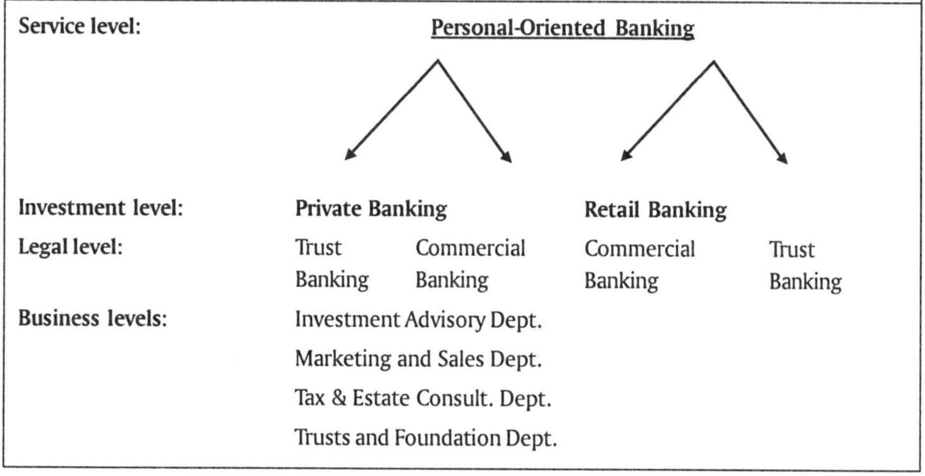
Service level:
Personal-Oriented Banking
Investment level:
Private Banking
Retail Banking
Legal level:
Trust Banking
Commercial Banking
Commercial Banking
Trust Banking
Business levels:
Investment Advisory Dept.
Marketing and Sales Dept.
Tax & Estate Consult. Dept.
Trusts and Foundation Dept.

personal-oriented service level specifically taking care of various customers' needs. While private banking refers to business aimed at HNWIs, traditional retail banking focuses on offering standardized products and services to a wide range of customers, where individual relationship is of less importance. One can think of mass affluent clients lying on a spectrum somewhere in-between retail and HNWIs.

The striking difference between serving retail and private banking relates to the much wider range of products and supplementary services available to the latter, that include: portfolio management, investment advisory services, estate planning, trust services and tax advice. Many of these services tend to be frequently organized in separate departments within a bank. As such, the private banking offering tends to involve a variety of different parts of a bank and for HNWI services there tends to be a blurring of distinction between various banking and investment services and a strong focus on develop 'wealth packages' to meet the needs of clients. Integral to this offering is the client focus of the bank – does it aim mainly at the mass affluent market or focus on various types of HNWI? Closely linked to this is the brand image of the institution[3].

As has already been suggested, private banking business can most easily be distinguished by the wealth or income of clients being served. Traditionally, private banks catered for individuals having more than $1 million in liquid assets.

[3] Taylor R, *Private Banking Renaissence*, 1990, p.X.

With the growth of mass affluent banking over the last decade or so, entry requirements have become more modest although there still remain private banking clients that focus on super wealth HNWI (like Goldman Sachs) where entry requirements are high.[4]

Not surprisingly, depending on the financial institution and entry requirements stipulated, the level and complexity of wealth management services can vary widely (See Exhibit 2). Note also that wealth management products need not only be provided by private banks. They can also be offered by a host of other firms including: universal, commercial and investment banks, trust banks, brokerage companies (e.g. securities firms), "financial boutiques", private banks (i.e. banks with traditional partnership structures), mutual fund companies, "special discounters" and "tailored ateliers", independent asset managers, intermediaries and life insurance companies. Exhibit 3 illustrates the types of firms offering private banking and wealth management services and the clients they typically target.

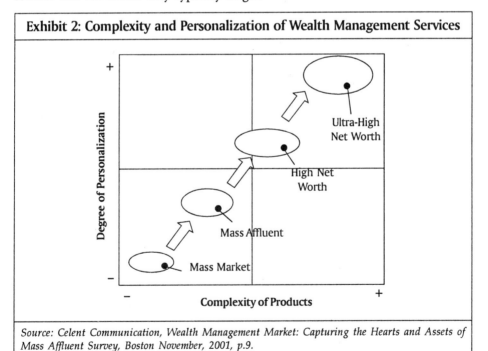

Exhibit 2: Complexity and Personalization of Wealth Management Services

Source: Celent Communication, Wealth Management Market: Capturing the Hearts and Assets of Mass Affluent Survey, Boston November, 2001, p.9.

---

[4]   Maude D and Molyneux Ph, *Private banking maximising performance in a competitive market*, Euromoney Publications, Great Britain, 1996, p.46.

The picture that evolves, therefore, is that private banking (or wealth management) industry is rather fragmented and is subject to intense competition. Traditional private banks vie with arms of commercial banks, investment banks, brokers, insurance companies and so on with a slice of the market. Like in other parts of the banking business, competition has increased putting substantial pressure on private banking participants to focus on managing their costs and revenue streams more effectively. The recent response to these pressures has been a significant degree of acquisition activity on the part of the largest wealth managers. The top Swiss banks, for instance, have acquired a significant number of relatively small, targeted, bolt-on acquisitions, mainly in the Asian markets and other acquisitions in the European onshore market (particularly in Spain)[5]. The consolidation trend is predicted to continue over the next few years.

Exhibit 3: Types of Private Banking Providers and their Targets

Providers	Presence		Service		Range		Targets:
	Local	Global	Standardised	Personalised	Narrow	Wide	
Category I							
Universal/Commercial banks		X	X			X	Globale clientele
Merchant/Investment banks		X	X			X	
Trust banks		x	X		X		
Traditional private banks	X		X			x	
Category II							
Financial boutiques	X		x		x		HNWIs UHNWs
Ateliers	X			X		X	
Independent asset managers	X			X	x		
Intermediaries	X			X	X		
Category III							
Mutual fund companies	x		X		X		Affluent
Life insurance companies	X	X	X		X		
Brokerage companies	x		X		X		
Special discounters	x		X		X		

X and x define a different strength of the item: X means strongly related to the item; x weak relation to the item.

Adapted from Svend E, International Private Banking, Zurich, Verlag Paul Haupt, 1997, p.104.

[5]   *Datamonitor*, Global Wealth Predictions 2005, pp.22-23.

Another interesting feature of the private banking business is that high net worth clients usually have multiple financial relationships. For example, a HNWI may have a relationship with his or her local retail bank for a simple checking account; with a full service broker for investment management; an insurance agent for life insurance and annuities; and a tax accountant for tax planning. The fact that private clients have multiple relationships means that suppliers of wealth management services are unlikely to have as complete a picture as they would like about their HNWI. This may make it difficult to leverage scale and scope economies from such relationships.

3. Customer Acquisitions and Retention

Client acquisitions, as well as, customer retentions are the main issues facing the wealth management industry today[6]. As the battle for new customers has intensified one resulting trend is that some wealth managers have become increasingly willing to waive their minimum investment thresholds for new customers, as we mentioned above. For example, in the US up to 50 per cent of private clients apparently fall below normally accepted minimum investment thresholds.[7] This situation occurred most noticeably during the late 1990s, when wealth managers sought growth through developing mass affluent market, drawing these clients into private banking services, and lowering their minimum account thresholds in the expectation of being able to cross-sell products and services.

The desire to attract new clients in this manner has been justified by the view that current wealth is not necessarily a good indicator of future wealth. Private client managers could build unprofitable current business with the prospects of these clients perhaps benefiting from inheritance or the sale of a company in the future. In addition, it is a fact that customer referrals from existing clients are one of the key means of client acquisition and some lower net worth clients may be valuable in terms of the customers they can bring in.

While some of these reasons may justify taking on lower net worth clients this should be weighed against the potential risks. The widening gap between the wealthiest and least wealthy clients implies a growing range of client needs that might not be well served by a single service proposition. Having said all

---

6   In accordance with Mercier Oliver Wyman: European Wealth Management Survey 2004.

7   *Datamonitor,* Customer Acquisition in Wealth Management Survey, September, 2002, pp-9.

this, client acquisition and retention is obviously a key feature of private banking business. The private bank obviously has to make a realistic assessment that considers which customer groups are attainable and which are not and the bank has to balance the costs of providing high levels of services and face-to-face contact (associated with HNWI clients) with the lower revenues available from the mass affluent sector.

Targeting the mass affluent segment has been a strategy of many financial intermediaries over the last decade or so. However, the mass affluent sector has already lost some of its allure, with many competitors increasingly moving up the wealth ladder to focus on higher net worth individuals, particularly those that that emphasise a wider range and more personal service. Many institutions found attracting new mass affluent clients was too costly, and they failed to adapt their level of services to reflect the margins achievable, and consequently these clients failed to meet their profitability targets.[8]

But while some private bankers and wealth managers have chosen to go up-market to pursue wealthier clients, there are others, such as Barclays in the UK, that have responded to the difficult mass affluent market conditions by pulling out of this segment altogether and instead have focused on increasing share of wealth management with among existing customers. Adopting such a strategy involves carefully selecting the relevant client segment and services and convincing existing clients of the extra value they will receive from adopting a new (or at least different) wealth management product set. The correct segmentation strategy should aim to ensure that there is a balance between the costs of serving investors likely to generate lower income that are apparent in current operating environment.[9]

Having said this, however, mass affluent clients are an important proportion of many wealth managers client base and a successful model for mass affluent banking should be able to generate good reward for those managers who are able to control costs, use technology effectively and manage lower service-level expectations. Wealth managers operating within retail banking groups are particularly well placed to succeed in this sphere by leveraging cross-sales based on their traditional retail operations. In this way they should be able to differentiate

---

[8]   See also PricewaterhouseCoopers, Competing for Clients Survey, Spring, 2004, p.6.

[9]   *Datamonitor*, Customer Acquisition in Wealth Management Survey, September, 2002, pp. 10.

products for the mass affluent market and keep a tight control over costs and provide apparently proactive service, using technology.

The identification of the mass affluent market was one (obvious) way that banks with large customer bases could develop private banking type activities and therefore generate greater fee and commission income.

However, to a certain extent this involved 'Balkanising' their established customer bases. Wealthy retail clients could be enticed from one part of the bank to another, or cross-sold investment and other services through the branch or traditional channels. By and large, targeting the mass affluent customer has resulted in a restructuring part of traditional retail banking activity but in most cases (as far as we are aware) has not resulted in large-scale acquisitions of new wealth management clients.

In addition to re-segmenting established customer bases there are also a wide variety of other potential sources of prospective customers. The ability to attract new clients, of course, depends on the bank's own internal capabilities as well as on various external opportunities. Various sources of prospective clients are illustrated in Exhibit 4.

Internal acquisition channels relate to the exploitation of the organizational structure including branches, representative offices, affiliates, as well as other business divisions. In the case of universal banks, substantial cross-selling potential is available through services that can be provided via the corporate and investment banking divisions to wealth management clients. Having said this, however, there is little empirical evidence to suggest that the potential economies of scope and other cross-selling advantages that purport to be a major feature of universal banking have resulted in noticeable performance gains – especially with respect to the cross-selling of products and services to private banking clients.

A private bank can develop its client acquisition strategy by focusing on both organizational issues as well as placing a greater emphasis on marketing based activity (See Exhibit 5). The marketing based approach focuses on acquiring clients via selling, promotional and various marketing activities. This approach, however,

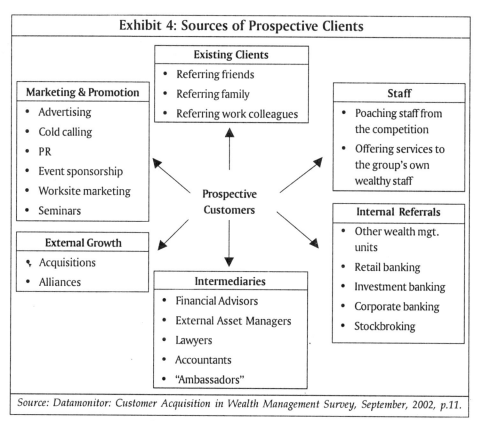

Exhibit 4: Sources of Prospective Clients

Existing Clients
- Referring friends
- Referring family
- Referring work colleagues

Marketing & Promotion
- Advertising
- Cold calling
- PR
- Event sponsorship
- Worksite marketing
- Seminars

External Growth
- Acquisitions
- Alliances

Prospective Customers

Intermediaries
- Financial Advisors
- External Asset Managers
- Lawyers
- Accountants
- "Ambassadors"

Staff
- Poaching staff from the competition
- Offering services to the group's own wealthy staff

Internal Referrals
- Other wealth mgt. units
- Retail banking
- Investment banking
- Corporate banking
- Stockbroking

Source: Datamonitor: Customer Acquisition in Wealth Management Survey, September, 2002, p.11.

has been shown to not always be effective by itself in the short run because of difficulties associated with potential client recognition and skepticism associated with a relatively financially sophisticated potential target market. A marketing based approach has to be developed in conjunction with a reorganization of the business organization so that prospective clients can be offered value relevant product and service propositions. Once a successful framework for client acquisition has been identified (easier said than done) private bankers/wealth managers should aim to convert the prospect to client and then develop a strong focus on customer knowledge to innovate its own client propositions.[10]

Customer retention is obviously an essential part of relationship development. The economic value of customer retention is widely recognised. It was found that customer retention has a more positive effect on profits than market share, scale

---

[10]   Mercer Oliver Wyman, European Wealth Management Survey 2004.

Exhibit 5: Sources of Client Acquisition	
Organization-based	**Marketing Activity-based**
• Senior management personal network	• Advertising
• Branches, representatives offices, affiliates	• Direct Marketing
• Other divisions, i.e., corporate banking, investment banking	• Cold calling
• Cooperation with complementary companies	• Media events
• Intermediaries (financial intermediaries, individuals with a professional network, individual with a social network)	• Sponsored events
• Existing clients – word of mouth	• Conferences, lectures
	• Sales presentations
	• Private luncheons
	• Cooperation with third-parties, e.g., clubs, organizations
	• Internal/external cross-selling
	• Purchase of addresses/mail shots
	• Database marketing
	• Internet access
	• Franchising/white labeling
	• Outsourcing peripheral services

Adapted from Svend E, International Private Banking, Zurich, Verlag Paul Haupt, 1997, p.124.

economies and other variables that are commonly associated with competitive advantage.[11] The problem is that once customers are lost, they are difficult to regain.

Financial institutions need to strive to keep defection rates low and retention rates high. A high customer defection rate makes the market attractive to new entrants since it makes easier for new players to acquire customers. Low defection rates increase barriers to entry and make the market less attractive for new entrants.

While there is strong agreement on the key issue of client retention, in practice it appears that there is too low an emphasis on client retention in the private banking/wealth management industry. According to the PricewaterhouseCoopers

[11]   Reichheld, F F and Sasser W E, "Zero Defections: Quality Comes to Services", in *Harvard Business Review*, Vol. 68, No.5, September/October, pp.105-111.

Survey (2005) on private banking operators in Europe, nearly 46% of industry respondents stated that they had no client retention process, and moreover, remarkably few wealth managers even collected and took any action on direct client satisfaction information. Clearly, significant attention should be given to both of these areas by wealth managers if they are to avoid losing clients.[12] So if they want to retain customers they have to develop retention strategies.

One of the difficulties for wealth managers is that while they claim to understand their individual clients' financial needs, preferences and behaviour quite well, they often have no way of tracking these features systematically. So they are not so good at extrapolating the insights of their customers in terms of developing new products and customer propositions aimed at building retention.

A more professional retention – marketing – scheme should help strengthen ties and also help support cross-selling possibilities. But banks need to be able to examine the nature of existing relationships and investigate the possibility of providing services that add value for the client, otherwise customers' requests cannot be satisfied and defections are likely to arise.

As customer loyalty declines with the growing presence of a wide array of service providers, the issue of client retention becomes increasingly important.[13] To overcome this threat, private banks and wealth managers can introduce a simple four-stage plan to foil defectors and boost retention rates.[14] The first step is to measure the current retention rate; then defection motives need to be ascertained; thirdly, an analysis of complaints/customer satisfaction issues need to be analysed and finally, financial institutions should attempt to erect barriers to customer exit. In this way wealth managers should be able to build on client retention helping to ultimately feed through into higher performance.

3.1 Loyalty and the Private Banking Relationship

As customer loyalty weakens among private clients[15], various industry participants are looking to ways to enhance loyalty – one such response is the increased offering

---

[12]   PricewaterhouseCoopers, Global Private Banking/Wealth Management Survey, 2005, p.11.

[13]   IBM, Wealth and Private Banking – Industry Survey 2003, IBM, London.

[14]   DeSouza G, "Designing a Customer Retention Plan", in *Journal of Business Strategy,* March/April, pp.24-31.

[15]   See: IBM, European Wealth and Private Banking Industry Survey, IBM, London, 2005.

of differentiating lifestyle services. While lifestyle services may provide part of the answer to the loyalty issue, they cannot substitute for getting the basics right in terms of understanding client needs, relationship management, investment reporting, product offerings and investment performance.[16]

In order to develop loyalty private banks have to be aware of the distinction between loyalty and trust. The word trust makes us think of how a person feels when he or she puts his/her trust in another one; it is the relaxed yet confident feeling a person or thing one can instil in another. On the other hand, loyalty refers to the precision with which we tend to our matters and keep our promises. The semantic origin of customer loyalty, therefore leads to two different meanings; one refers to a behavioural nature such as that of holding one's promises by making them come true while the other refers to an idealistic/ cognitive nature reflected in believing/having faith/feeling sure about someone/ something. Therefore, it is best first to focus attention on client trust before attention is paid to customer loyalty.[17]

Trust has been analysed from several different perspectives (economic, sociological, psychological, and organizational) and this has led to a multidimensional understanding of the word. Therefore, there are many differing definitions of trust. Economists favour a view of trust based on calculations regarding costs and benefits (Williamson 1993). Psychologists commonly focus their attention on individual traits that lead to a trust-based relationship (Williams 1988; Rotter and Tyler 1990). Organizational theorists, on the other hand, explore the role of trust in intra- and inter-organizational dynamics (Ring, Van De Ven 1994; Zaheer, Mcevilu, Perrone 1998). Sociologists study how trust can be woven into the network that ties interpersonal relationships between people and institutions (Granovetter 1985; Zucker 1986). For financial firms that wish to develop the trust of their clients a combination of the various aforementioned definitions are most likely to be used or emphasised.

Given that the trust of clients cannot be directly measured one has to introduce and recognize those resources where customer's trust comes from. They are

---

[16]   On this issue see also: Coyles S and Gokey T C, "Customer retention is not enough", in *The McKinsey Quarterly*, n.2., 2002.

[17]   See also: Griffin J, *Customer loyalty: How to earn it how to keep it*, Jossey-Bass, San Francisco, 2002.

represented by a set of important variables such as image, client loyalty and relations created by the bank/institution throughout the years. Every company has its own 'trust resources' that are the result of its past history, which no other company can copy. The very nature of trust resources represents both a competitive and lasting advantage for a company. Trust can therefore be described as the middle link of a chain that foresees customer satisfaction in regards to what the company offers, and looks back on customer loyalty as shown in Exhibit 6.

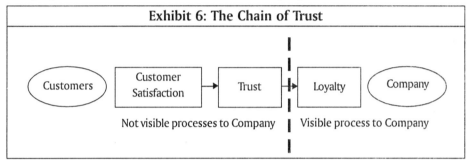

Exhibit 6: The Chain of Trust

Customers — Customer Satisfaction → Trust ┤├→ Loyalty — Company

Not visible processes to Company ┆ Visible process to Company

Customer satisfaction engenders trust in the value propositions of a company, which then leads to enhanced loyalty and the perpetuation of the buying process. But as noted in Exhibit 6, customer satisfaction and trust are customer's internal features, so they are not visible to a bank unless it undertakes studies to identify the trust embedded in customer satisfaction assessments of clients.

The link between trust and loyalty then has to be evaluated. Loyalty has two different meanings: first, it can refer to a behavioural nature such as holding one's promises by making them come true, while the second refers to an idealistic/cognitive nature reflected in believing/having faith/feeling sure about someone/something. For client retention purposes (obviously) the latter is the most important. Difficulties in measuring loyalty can arise as bankers typically assume that retention of clients equals loyalty – but there is no clear guarantee that because, say retention rates increase, that the private banking service offering is a reflection of any enhanced faith by clients. For example, clients retention may increase because of greater market uncertainty or volatility, or be confused about the complexity of alternative product offerings and so on.

This turns to be of some importance for managers because it suggests that existing measures of loyalty may be seriously flawed, and thus strategies developed on the strength of such measures may be inadequate. The very term loyalty implies commitment rather than just repetitive behaviour, which suggests that there is a need for a cognitive as well as a behavioural view. This has led many bankers to use various customer satisfaction measures as a proxy indicator of loyalty because it has been assumed that satisfaction affects buying intentions in a positive way. However, research indicates that it is overly simplistic to assume that dissatisfied customers will defect, and that satisfied customers will remain loyal. Indeed, despite being "satisfied" or "very satisfied" many customers still defect. Therefore there are two things to consider: the first is that attitudinal measures of satisfaction are poor predictors or measures of behaviour, and second, it casts some doubt on the concept of 100 per cent loyalty.[18]

When furthering our understanding of the word loyalty in private banking/wealth management industry, we have to face the fact that it is made up of two main assets. These are:

1. The image of the bank, as far as trust is concerned, is represented through the esteem, and the familiarity that the customer might summarize by saying: "I can trust my bank".

2. The coherence between bank image and behaviour, from which we may gather what relation exists between promising to place money in the bank and the bank keeping the promise to manage this money in an appropriate manner.

Customer loyalty, thus, is the result of a reciprocal relationship, in which there is some kind of equal exchange of interests; we can infer that in order to ask for/obtain loyalty it is necessary to offer loyalty.

As far as we are aware, little work has been undertaken on customer loyalty measures in private banking/wealth management and either on:

a. the value of trust; or

b. the value of user satisfaction which includes customer behaviour – his/her experiences with the private bank/wealth manager in terms of service, communication and access.

---

[18]   Omarini A, "Customers, retail banks and loyalty schemes", in *EfmaGazine* (on coming).

The former is represented through the ideal aspects of loyalty such as identity and the bank *brand* value. The current situation demonstrates that longstanding brands tend to survive thanks to their prestige; the new ones have not had time to consolidate themselves, while, there are some other brands that can rise in the consumer's mind such as those related to new value propositions proposed by brokers, wealth boutiques and so on.

So far much of what has been discussed focuses on loyalty from a clients perspective, but it is important to remember that in bank jargon "loyalty" is often used as a synonym for *cross-selling* and *retention*. Bankers generally view the degree of customer loyalty as the extent to which the customer turns to other providers to obtain services. Using this sort of definition, the difficulty lies in identifying whether loyalty is an attitudinal or a behavioural measure. Used loosely, as it usually is, the term "loyalty" conjures up various notions of affection, fidelity or commitment[19]. As we have already mentioned, this has led to the use of customer satisfaction as a proxy measure of loyalty because it has been assumed that satisfaction affects buying intentions in a positive way. However, research indicates that it is overly simplistic to assume that dissatisfied customers will defect, and that satisfied customers will remain loyal. Indeed, Reichheld (1994) found that despite being "satisfied" or "very satisfied" many customers still defect.[20] Then the very term loyalty implies commitment rather than just repetitive behaviour, which suggests that there is a need for a cognitive as well as a behavioural interpretation of the meaning of loyalty and more effective measures need to be developed to take this into account.[21]

Developing an affective commitment to both analyzing and promoting client loyalty is key to retention. In order to building loyalty private bankers/wealth managers need to act in an increasingly pro-active manner by investigating such things as: word of mouth recommendations, customer's purchase intentions, customer's price insensitivity and complaints (as well as procedures for dissatisfied clients). Once these are effectively analyzed then the private bank can focus on the issues of trust and loyalty.

---

[19]   McGoldrick and Andre, 1997, p.74.

[20]   Reichheld, 1994, p.45.

[21]   Assael, 1992, p.89.

4. Customer (Re-)Segmentation

The former features neatly lead onto some of the justifications for segmenting the HNWI customer base and the criteria used to differentiate clients. From the bank perspective, segmentation is all about maximizing value from every customer; so customers will pay more if they feel the product offering provides something special to them. This is particularly important in the context of private banking, as essentially the business model is based on the premise of high value clients and tailored services. Private banking clients, of course, have to value the service proposition on offer in both financial and psychic terms.

While a substantial proportion of retail banking and investment services are provided on a transactions basis, private banking is relationship-orientated. Clients and the wealth management proposition are heteregenous in nature. Despite this fact, clients of a private bank are often lumped together as one client group and do not always receive the tailored services they are promised at the outset of the relationship. True, they receive more individual attention, but their relationship manager has to be able to focus on a number of clients (however small) with very different needs and lifestyles. This can result in homogenisation of the product and service delivery mechanism that has the effect of not meeting client's needs. The following section outlines features of the segmentation strategy of private banks.

4.1 Ongoing Practices in Segmenting the Customer Base

In most cases wealth management customers are segmented by geography, demographics, wealth, income, asset class holdings and preferences, domicile, and so on.[22] But these criteria are becoming an inadequate denominator for customers' requirements as indicated in Exhibit 7 where it can be seen that customised segmentation for clients are being developed. However, it is still commonplace for clients and service offerings to be simply segmented on their level of wealth as shown in Exhibit 8.

Other widely used segmentation strategies focus on the source of wealth (e.g. inheritance, entrepreneurial activity etc.) and the risk preferences of clients.

---

[22]   See Maude, D and Molyneux Ph, *Private banking maximising performance in a competitive market*, Euromoney Publications, Great Britain, 1996, pp.49-51; PricewaterhouseCoopers, Global Private Banking/Wealth Management Survey, 2005, p.10; and Mercier Oliver Wyman, European Wealth Management Survey 2004, p.19.

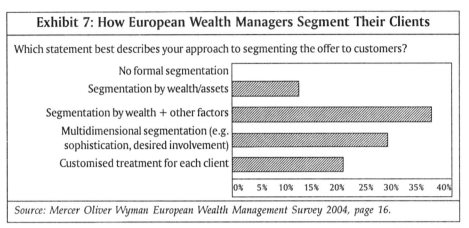

Exhibit 7: How European Wealth Managers Segment Their Clients

Which statement best describes your approach to segmenting the offer to customers?

Source: Mercer Oliver Wyman European Wealth Management Survey 2004, page 16.

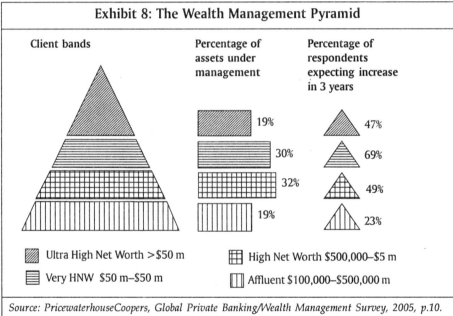

Exhibit 8: The Wealth Management Pyramid

Source: PricewaterhouseCoopers, Global Private Banking/Wealth Management Survey, 2005, p.10.

These ongoing practices outline a general lack of sophistication in the client segmentation process. As far as we can gather few wealth managers analyse individual client relationship profitability, demand elasticity of products and/or regular structured studies aimed at enhancing their client propositions or marketing techniques. A recent report[23] provides further evidence on the limitations of European wealth managers approaches to identifying the needs

---

[23]   Mercer Oliver Wyman, European Wealth Management Survey 2004, p. 15.

of their clients. The report found that only one third of respondents to a survey of wealth management firms said they undertook quantitative research into customer needs and preferences.

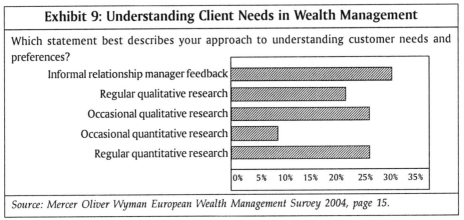

Exhibit 9: Understanding Client Needs in Wealth Management

Which statement best describes your approach to understanding customer needs and preferences?

Source: Mercer Oliver Wyman European Wealth Management Survey 2004, page 15.

Wealth managers do not always make good use of the information they already have about their customers. For example, the Mercer Oliver Wyman survey on European Wealth Management (2005) noted that survey participants said that their customers were more interested in service level, brand, privacy and "peace of mind" than in superior investment performance. But even if this ranking is broadly correct, many wealth managers still continue to sell themselves on their investment offering and performance rather than on other valued characteristics of service: so their current marketing is failing to exploit existing insight into customer preferences. This again suggests that much of the industry still works with relatively basic models of clients' needs, such as segmentation by wealth level or risk aversion.

At present, a single segmentation scheme used for both institutional and private clients is based on the concept of 'clients' professionalism'. A sophisticated client "buys" products and solutions; an unsophisticated client is "sold" products and services. Of course, a wealth manager usually proxies wealth for sophistication but this (obviously) is not necessarily the case. However, there has been a move by some of the larger private client wealth management firms to focus on the 'buying side' by bundling in an increasing number of lifestyle and other services – so the customer proposition is becoming a wider concept than the product offering alone. It is a promise to meet the clients' needs; the product is part of that solution, but not, in itself, the complete solution.

For instance, beyond the mechanical details of the service proposition (service intensity, frequency, coverage model and so on), and the asset classes and structure of investment management products, lie new selling opportunities in such under exploited areas as advice, delivery, ancillary services and branding, but also relating to developing new propositions, expanding product and service ranges to include non-traditional offerings such as tax, fine art and "concierge" services. As noted by the Mercer Oliver Wyman (2004) survey the vast majority of private bank/ wealth managers 85% said they were still looking to grow their product range while the remaining 15% were seeking to shrink their range selectively. The survey also noted that all the approaches implemented in designing customer propositions were largely unscientific. Around a sixth of the survey respondents use only informal procedures to improve their customer offerings. A further two-thirds focus on propositions designed around segments (with or without individual customisation), but the segmentation scheme used is usually very simply based on wealth; and as a consequence the resulting client propositions appears to be no more than weakly differentiated.

4.2 Some New Criteria for Re-segmenting the Client Base

It should be apparent that the existing client segmentation strategies pursued in European private banking/wealth management are simplistic and do not appear to map accurately into client requirements. This is somewhat surprising given that bankers very well know that an essential starting point for any financial services provider targeting HNWIs is to recognize their diversity and the important influences they have on their product/service demands and behaviour.

Of course the diversity of the HNWI population is important at much more than a purely conceptual level. It has to be translated into a range of very different product and service requirements and sometimes wealth managers may not have the appropriate business models to meet exacting demands. Indeed HNWIs appear to recognize their diverse nature much more than wealth managers. For instance, "Those people who have made money on a one-off opportunity and those that need to be consecutively successful with their investments have very different requirements".[24] (Quote from an Australian HNWI)

---

[24]   *Datamonitor*, Customer Segmentation in Australian Private Banking Survey, March 2005, p.10. And see also: *Datamonitor*, Customer Segmentation in Singaporean Private Banking Survey, April, 2005.

As with any individual, background and situation have a significant impact on attitudes and objectives. This is especially true when it comes to managing financial affairs. Many clients' requirements are not always born of practical choice, many are also based on individual interests and understanding. Furthermore there is the issue that complexity of service demands from individuals is often unique and increases with time and affluence. Various choices affecting the complexity of private client demands include:

- *Life choices.* These relate to employment and lifestyle preferences or the undertaking of key life events such as marriage, retirement or divorce. One notable example would be the decision to live abroad, which often adds several complexities to a HNWIs' financial situation in terms of tax and legal status issues.

- *Investment/product choices.* The greater the range of different asset classes and product categories into which clients place funds, the more complicated their management will become.

- *Provider choices.* These include the quality, type and number of providers selected by HNWIs in arranging and managing their financial affairs. Similarly, the stronger the element of self-direction and control over finances the greater the complexity in handling their financial situation.

These features mainly focus on the financial aspects of client demand while there are other dimensions that need to be taken into some considerations. To finish off, we propose a combination of segmentation approaches that we believe should be used by wealth management firms to more accurately identify client needs. These are illustrated in Exhibit 10 and emphasise segmentation strategies based on a combination of factors including:

1. Criteria based on the source of wealth;

2. Criteria based on client needs and sophistication;

3. Criteria based on the inherent advantages of lifestyle services;

4. Criteria based on price sensitivity; and

5. Criteria based on customer value.

Exhibit 10: New Criteria for Segmenting HNWIs		
Criteria Based on	Description of Sub-segments	Advantages
Source of wealth	The different segments are identified in terms of different sources of wealth (winning it; earning it; inheriting it ...)	This identifies similarities more effectively and information is relatively easy to obtain.
Needs and sophistication	The different segments are identified in terms of services to "non-professional" versus service to "professional" client segments	They have very different requirements so they should need different business models.
Inherent advantages of lifestyle issues	Sub-segments are identified in terms of value for customers such as trust, access, information...	Lifestyle issues must leverage on the existing segmentation strategies of the private bank to increase customer insight by monitoring the client's use of lifestyle services to glean knowledge of the clients behaviours and commitments in their general lives.
Price sensitivity	While pricing is one of the marketing mix variables, it can also be useful to segment the market	Price differentiation can be an effective way of promoting areas of core and non-core competencies by offering different pricing models to different sorts of client. Wealth managers should be aware of the price sensitivity of product offerings.
Customer value	The sub-segments are based on assessing the difference among a set of key indicators of value per customer (value of assets, value of liabilities, revenues, number of footings, duration of relationship, age...)	Identifying how value is distributed across the customer base can allow private banks to pinpoint the most attractive segments in targeting prospective clients and help to plan an approach to existing accounts by highlighting the priority areas/means by which it can extract additional value from its current clients.

5. Conclusions

The paper examines the features of private banking business in Europe and focuses on the key roles of client segmentation, retention and acquisition. There has been substantial growth in private banking business over the last decade or so as commercial banks have targeted both the 'mass-affluent' and more up-market high net worth individuals (HNWIs). The combined amount of investable assets at the disposal of these two groups amounts to around Euro 6 trillion and a wide range of banks, investment firms and other operators have focused on devising strategies aimed at grabbing a share of this potentially lucrative market. The private client wealth management industry in Europe remains relatively fragmented although a few major players have emerged and consolidation is an ongoing theme in the sector. Given the commercial opportunities afforded by this business area, the increased complexity of clients needs continues to be a critical strategic issue for industry participants. This paper illustrates important themes relating to the wealth management service proposition and focuses on client segmentation, retention and acquisition strategies. Overall, we find that private banks will have to adopt a more systematic approach to these areas and in particular will also have to pay greater qualitative and quantitative attention to client satisfaction, trust and loyalty issues if their client retention and acquisition strategies are to be successful.

The issue of client segmentation is the most important issue for customer retention and acquisition. It will always remain a central theme of private banking and wealth management. In devising new segmentation approaches the question may arise "where do you stop?" We would ague that, on the whole, the industry norm of using qualitative segmentation approaches based upon levels of wealth does not adequately address the issue of individual needs. There are a number of fundamental needs and sentiments that HNWIs have in common and we believe that these are not being appropriately gauged or addressed by European wealth managers.

Presuming that industry participants develop and use more appropriate client segmentation approaches, the next challenge is to develop a business model that can effectively and efficiently meet the diverse demands of clients. There is much talk about 'open architectures' and flexibility in the business model, although it is by no means clear the extent to which such structures are used, especially by the top firms who produce most of their products and services 'in-house'. Various specialist areas such as hedge funds, trust and fiduciary services are often outsourced as are certain lifestyle services. Small firms, of course, are much more dependent on offering third-party services to their clientele. There is also increasing discussion of the major players as 'producers' and the smaller operators as 'distributors' of wealth management services – note the analogy can apply to different divisions within the same organisation. This distinction is likely to become more polarised in the future.

(Philip Molyneux, SBARD, University of Wales Bangor, Hen Goleg, College Road, Bangor, Gwynedd LL57 2DG, United Kingdom, p.molyneux@bangor.ac.uk

Anna Omarini, Department of Business Administration, Institute of Financial Markets and Institutions "G. dell'Amore", Università Bocconi, via Sarfatti 25, 20136 Milano, anna.omarini@unibocconi.it.)

References

Abratt R and Russel J, "Relationship marketing in private banking in South Africa" in, *International Journal of Bank Marketing*, 17/1, 1999, pp.5-19.

Bloemer, J M and Lemmink, J G (1992), "The importance of customer satisfaction in explaining brand and dealer loyalty" in, *Journal of Marketing Management*, Vol. 8, pp. 351-64.

Capgemini Merril Lynch, World Wealth Report, 2004.

Citigroup, New Perspective on Wealth management. A Survey of the World's Wealthiest Families, January 2005.

Coyles S and Gokey T C (2002), "Customer retention is not enough", in *The McKinsey Quarterly*, n.2.

Datamonitor, Customer Segmentation in Australian Private Banking Survey, March, 2005.

Datamonitor, Customer Segmentation in Singaporean Private Banking Survey, April, 2005.

Datamonitor, Global Wealth Predictions Survey, March, 2005.

Datamonitor, Building a Customer Value Framework in Wealth Management, August 2004.

Datamonitor, Client retention strategies for the next wealth generation: A global perspective on practices, August 2004.

Datamonitor, Customer Acquisition in Wealth Management Survey, September, 2002.

DeSouza G, "Designing a Customer Retention Plan", in *Journal of Business Strategy*, March/April, pp.24-31, 1992.

Dimitrios K Koutouvalas, George J Siomkos, John Mylonakis, "Perceived service quality management and loyalty in public versus private banks operations: some empirical evidence" in *International Journal of Services and Operations Management* 2005, Vol. 1, No.2, pp. 101-122.

Dirk R Dreux IV and Bonnie M Brown, "Marketing Private Banking Services to Family Businesses" in *International Journal of Bank Marketing*, Vol. 12, No. 3, 1994, pp. 26-35.

Gale, B T, *Managing Customer Value, Creating Quality and Service That Customer Can See*, The Free Press, New York, 1994.

Granovetter M S, "Economic Action and Social Structure" in *American Journal of Sociology*, n.91, 1985.

Griffin J, *Customer loyalty: How to earn it how to keep it*, Jossey-Bass, San Francisco, 2002.

Grönroos, C, "From marketing mix to relationship marketing: Towards a paradigm shift in marketing" in *Management Decision*, 1997, Vol. 32, No.2, pp. 4-20.

Gronroos C, "Quo vadis marketing? Toward a relationship marketing paradigm" in *Journal of marketing management*, n.10, 1994.

IBM, European Wealth and Private Banking Industry Survey, IBM, London, 2005.

IBM, Wealth and Private Banking Industry Survey, IBM, London, 2003.

KPMG, Private Bank Acquisition Survey, 2005.

KPMG, Private Bank Acquisition Survey, 2004.

Maslinski M, "Flying the flag of convenience", in *Private Banker International*, Lafferty Publications, Dublin, 1995.

Maude, D and Molineux Ph, *Private banking maximising performance in a competitive market*, Euromoney Publications, Great Britain, 1996.

McGoldrick and Andre, 1997.

Mercer Oliver Wyman, European Wealth Management Survey, 2004.

Mercer Oliver Wyman, Wealth Management Strategies for Success Survey, 2005.

Omarini A, "Customers, retail banks and loyalty schemes", in *EfmaGazine* (on coming).

Omarini A (2004b), "Loyalty programs in retail banking" in Sda Bocconi – Research Division, Working Paper Series, n. 125/04, December.

PricewaterhouseCoopers, Global Private Banking/Wealth Management Survey, 2005.

PricewaterhouseCoopers, Competing for Clients Survey, Spring, 2004.

Reichheld, F F and Sasser, W E, "Zero Defections: Quality Comes to Service" in *Harvard Business Review*, Vol. 68, No.5, September/October, 1990, pp. 105-111, 1990.

Ring P S Van De Ven A H, "Developmental Processes of Cooperative Inter-Organizational Relationships", in *Academy of Management Review*, Vol.19, n. 1, 1994.

Rotter J B, "A New Scale for the Measurement of Interpersonal Trust" in *Journal of Personality,* n.35, 1967.

Svend E, International Private Banking, Zurich, Verlag Paul Haupt, 1997.

Taylor R, *Private Banking Renaissance*, Lafferty Publications, Dublin, 1990.

Williams K C, *Psicologia peril marketing*, Il Mulino, Bologna, 1988.

Williamson O E, "Calculativeness, Trust and Economic Organization", in *Journal of Law and Economics,* n.30, 1993.

Zaheer A Mcevily B and Perrone V. "Does Trust Matter? Exploring the Effects of Interorganizational and Interpersonal Trust of Performance", in *Organizations Science*, Vol. 9, n.2, 1998.

Zucker L G, "Production of Trust: Institutional Sources of Economic Structure, 1840 to 1920", in *Research in Organizational Behavior*, n.8, 1998.

Private Banking in Switzerland

Switzerland has been the cradle bed of private banking for over three centuries. Banking is the sector of prime significance for the Swiss economy, with 14% contribution to the fiscal revenues, of which 50% comes from Swiss private banking. The two private bank majors UBS and Credit Suisse have a market share of 50%, while the 150 foreign banks operating in Switzerland claim 20% of the market share. Such is the significance of private banking in the country. Characterized by extreme conservatism, the traditional Swiss bankers possessed professional expertise in international asset management for their clientele. In its Financial System Stability Assessment, 2002, the International Monetary Fund (IMF), noted 'Professionalism, reliability, and client confidentiality' as comparative advantage factors of Switzerland for private banking. This assessment comes in support of the financial regulatory system prevailing in Switzerland in an era of mounting pressure for transparency in financial dealings.

Swiss private banking has been leading the field of wealth management worldwide. Almost 30% of private assets invested across the world are managed in Switzerland, estimated at about US$2.6 trillion. The private banking industry is highly fragmented in view of the high degree of personalization that the nature of business calls for. This is supported by the fact that the top ten private banks in the world hold a cumulative market share of less than 12%. UBS is the market leader and holds about 2–3% of the world market share.

With the developments in information and technology and international politics, more specifically in Europe, the globalization trend and the change in the private banking client profile and their expectations, Swiss Private banking has undergone radical transformation. This is vividly depicted in the Figure 1.

Figure 1: The Forces of Change in Swiss Private Banking

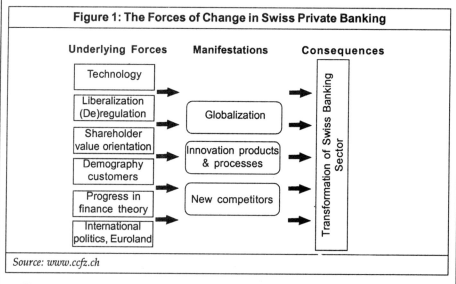

Source: *www.ccfz.ch*

The changing regulatory terrain and the demand for new financial services have forced the banks in Switzerland to innovate and design new products that cater to the specific requirements of the various client classes. With the increasing sophistication and demand specialized services becoming the norm, the value chain is heading towards decomposition and banks are not averse to outsourcing tailor made to partners in the value chain (Figure 2).

Contd...

Contd...

Figure 2: The Value Chain in Private Banking			
Distribution	Wealth planning	Customizing products	Transaction & reporting
• Prospect contacting and client acquisition • Needs analysis • Sales of services and products (including stocks and bonds) • Maintaining of relationship	• Investment planning • Financial planning • Tax planning • Retirement planning • Estate planning	• Bank accounts, custody accounts, retirement accounts • MM, FX, bonds, stocks, futures, and options • Loans • Mutual funds • Discretionary asset mgmt. • Structured products • Alternative investment • Insurance products • Trusts, foundations	• Funds transfer • Clearing & settlement • Custody • Brokerage • Collateral management • Document handling • Reporting

Source: *www.ccfz.ch*

The basic criteria underlying the private banks segmentation strategy are the clients' risk preferences, size of investment and domicile. This would in turn determine the asset allocation and product portfolio for the client, keeping in mind the tax and inheritance laws applicable.

Notwithstanding the pressure from financial regulators and anti-money laundering laws, client privacy will still remain the mainstay of Swiss private banking industry. The industry has to transform into an international financial centre through aggressive growth in onshore operations across borders. In an increasingly sophisticated, high-cost and competitive environment, adaptation of new and improved models of business will hold the key to the success of Swiss private banking in the years to come.

References
1. Hans Geiger & Harry Hurzeler, *The Transformation of the Swiss Private Banking Market*, *www.ccfz.ch*

Compiled from various sources.

15

Wealth Structuring for Latin American Clients

Richard J Hay and Robert L Reymond

In Latin American countries, tax was imposed only on income derived from domestic source. Tax systems are changed to increase revenue from direct taxation. Implementation of worldwide taxation has an impact on the structuring for offshore investments maintained by wealthy families in Latin America. The article reviews the technical chnges and the private banking opportunities in Mexico, Argentina, Venezuela and Brazil. Latin governments continue to develop their tax systems and hence there is an exciting period ahead for all parties involved in private banking operations.

Many Latin American jurisdictions have turbulent political and economic environments. Instability increases client appetite for investment diversification and fuels demand for international private banking services.

Tax regimes in Latin America are transforming as governments in the region respond to local and international pressures to upgrade their tax systems. International private banks are following these changes closely in order to provide their clients with the sophisticated structuring required to pursue the attractive opportunities in the region.

This article reviews the impact of worldwide taxation on structuring for offshore investments maintained by wealthy families resident in Mexico, Venezuela, Argentina and Brazil. Implications and strategies for the international banks providing services to private clients in the region are also reviewed. Finally, lessons from the experience in the region are considered for their impact on the strategy for institutions with global private banking businesses.

Local Private Banking Environment

Latin America is a heavy net importer of both private and public capital. Government attitudes toward foreign investment in the region have necessarily become more benign over the last decade. Many of Latin America's family businesses have been sold to international and corporate investors, generating vast pools of liquid wealth. Tax systems in the region are, in general, not effectively redistributive so that wealth is very unequally held. For better or worse, these and other factors mean that Latin America has many substantial private banking clients.

American and European financial institutions, particularly the New York and Swiss banks, have been active in servicing the needs of Latin American private clients for decades. Families in the region have used these services to export wealth to mitigate home country political risk and enhance personal security by making wealth less visible. Private bankers have provided investment management services for these funds, which were traditionally held either directly or in simple structures such as an offshore company. Occasionally a revocable trust held the company to facilitate personal estate planning or political risk mitigation objectives.

Latin American tax systems historically had a territorial focus, so that tax was imposed only where the income arose from a domestic source. In a strict territorial system, common in the region before the gradual introduction of worldwide taxation in the late 1990s, tax is not imposed even on remitted income or gains from a foreign source. Consequently, no planning was required in the past to facilitate tax-free accumulation for funds, other than moving the situs of the assets offshore. This situation has now changed.

This paper considers the political and economic drivers for the changes. The changes are summarised at a technical level and some avenues for planning in response are noted.

The following table provides an indication of the relative size of the various national markets which are the subject of this paper.

Comparative Economic Data for 2005[1]				
	Mexico	**Venezuela**	**Argentina**	**Brazil**
Population (million)	106.3	26.70	39.44	184.4
Total GDP (US$ billion)	677.9	107.21	163.67	706.4
GDP per head (US$)	6377	4015	4150	3831
Annual inflation (%)	4.2	15.0	7.5	5.5
Total external debt (US$ billion)	158	29.6	145	181
Total external debt as % of GDP	23.3	27.6	88.6	25.6

Pressures on Latin American Tax Systems

Latin American countries are seeking to expand taxing capability to meet public investment and social welfare objectives. International pressures also play a growing role in changing tax systems.

Countries with worldwide tax systems, including the US, have been reluctant to enter into double taxation treaties with Latin American countries with territorial tax systems. For example, the US had negotiated and signed a tax treaty with Brazil and Argentina, in the mid-90s but was unwilling to bring either treaty into force.[2] This has placed pressure on Latin jurisdictions to reform their tax systems to encourage high tax jurisdictions to enter into tax treaties in order to facilitate essential inbound foreign investment. Tax treaties would also encourage foreign investment as they provide some tax certainty in a dynamic environment.

The US also waited to enter into a tax treaty with Venezuela until Venezuela had adopted legislation concerning a worldwide system. Thus, the US/Venezuela tax treaty had been under negotiation for many years but entered into force on

---

[1]   Source: Mexico, Venezuela, Argentina and Brazil statistics – *Latin America Monitor*, Business Monitor International (Venezuela, Argentina and Mexico figures are estimates).

[2]   Joseph H Guttentag, "An Overview of International Tax Issues", *University of Miami Law Review*, April 1996, Vol. 50, No. 3 at p.451. The only Latin American countries with which the US currently has a treaty are Mexico and Venezuela.

January 1, 2000, two months after Venezuela adopted proposals to move to worldwide taxation.

Treaty partners also scrutinise perceived deficiencies in the design of tax systems and enforcement efforts. A major study by the OECD, for example, concluded that Mexico's 15% level of tax revenues relative to gross domestic product is the lowest among OECD countries.[3] (The next lowest, Turkey, has a 25% rate.) The report also notes that personal income in Mexico is considerably lower and more unequally distributed than in any other OECD country, except Turkey. Although the report notes an "environment of non-compliance", it lauds Mexico for an increasingly organised tax bureaucracy, resulting in dramatically improved enforcement of tax laws. The report notes, in particular, that the number of taxpayer audits has increased dramatically and is now on a par with some Western European nations.

The Move to Worldwide Taxation in the Key Jurisdictions

Latin American governments commenced adoption of worldwide tax regimes in the early 1990s. In most cases these early steps were not accompanied by companion rules providing for taxation of controlled foreign companies, so the provisions for worldwide taxation were largely toothless. Thus, worldwide tax was easily avoided by holding income producing assets in a foreign company established in an offshore centre, which facilitates deferral as long as the profits are not distributed. Outright avoidance was also possible in such scenarios, to the extent that profits were spent by the company rather than distributed to the shareholder.

The main development, accordingly, has been the recent adoption of CFC type rules for foreign companies established or controlled in prescribed low tax jurisdictions. These make provisions for worldwide taxation practically effective as profits accruing in such companies are attributed to controlling shareholders on a current basis. CFC rules have now been adopted in Mexico, Venezuela, Argentina and Brazil. Brazilian CFC rules are not yet applicable to individuals (they are limited to corporations) but local tax policy is moving towards that goal.

---

[3]   Thomas Dalsgaard, "The Tax System in Mexico: A Need for Strengthening the Revenue-Raising Capacity", the Organisation for Economic Co-operation and Development, Economics Department at p.8.

Mexico

Mexico adopted CFC rules in late 1996, with effect from January 1, 1997. Until 2005 Mexico's CFC rules generally provided that income arising in listed low-tax jurisdictions must be[4] accrued into the income of a Mexican resident. Such income was taxed on a current basis where the Mexican resident exercised control, directly or indirectly, over the investment or entity in a TPTR. Control was presumed for these purposes subject to the taxpayer rebutting the presumption.

The government of Mexico adopted sweeping changes to its CFC rules in its 2005 tax reform which took effect on 1 January 2005.[5] The new rules have abandoned the blacklist approach in favour of an objective test to identify low tax structures.

The new regime subjects Mexican residents to tax and reporting on income earned through foreign entities and trusts controlled directly or indirectly by Mexican residents where the income is taxed at less than 75% of the Mexican rate. The Mexican tax rate in 2006 is 29%, so effectively catching controlled foreign structures taxed at less than 21.75% (22% from an administrative perspective). Where income is earned indirectly, tax paid by each intermediate entity is taken into account. Again, control is presumed for these purposes subject to the taxpayer rebutting the presumption. Income subject to the new CFC regime is referred to as income from a "preferential tax regime".

As under previous rules, Mexican residents are obliged to file an information return in February on income earned in a preferential tax regime during the previous year. This also applies to all income of an entity established in a jurisdiction on the current Mexican blacklist.

An additional component of the new CFC rules is enhanced reporting in respect of transactions "performed through" a foreign "fiscally transparent" entity or vehicle. The tax reform deems foreign entities or vehicles to be "fiscally transparent" where such entities or vehicles are not taxpayers in the country in which they are constituted or resident for tax purposes and their income is taxed at the level of their members.

---

4   Mexico has released a comprehensive list of countries which are considered to be TPTRs (prior to 2002, these were referred to as low tax jurisdictions). The current list is attached in Appendix A.

5   The tax reform was approved by Congress on 13 November 2004 and published in the Official Gazette on 1 December 2004.

The new CFC regime also seeks to tax capital distributions from controlled foreign structures by applying the domestic capital reduction rule to distributions from any entity in the foreign structure. The capital reduction rule deems profits, retained earnings or other accrued (but unrealised) gains reflected on the balance sheet of a controlled foreign entity to be distributed prior to capital.

A presidential decree relating to the new CFC rules was released on 26 January 2005. Under the decree, a reduced tax rate applies for income from preferential tax regimes repatriated to Mexico. Only 25% of such income would be taxable, resulting in an effective tax rate of 7.25%. In order to benefit from this, repatriated assets must, in some cases, be maintained in Mexico for 3 years. The decree also permits payment of tax in Mexico on income from preferential tax regimes through a domestic financial institution on an anonymous basis, though the Mexican financial institution must keep taxpayer information in Mexico.

On 3 October 2006, Mexican rules were amended again to provide that the CFC regime does not apply to a direct interest in a foreign entity of less than 10% of the capital (or patrimony) of the foreign entity, provided the Mexican resident does not control the administration of the entity. The amendment also provided that a foreign entity taxed at a rate of at least 22% in the jurisdiction in which it is established or administered will not be considered as subject to a preferential tax regime.

Venezuela

Venezuela has historically operated a strict territorial regime, taxing residents only on local source income. Even remitted foreign income was excluded from the tax base.

Rules in a new Income Tax Law[6] (ITL) effective January 1, 2001, made Venezuelan residents subject to tax on both domestic and foreign source income.[7] A unilateral tax credit will generally be granted for taxes paid in foreign jurisdictions. Non-residents continue to be subject to tax on Venezuelan source income but pursuant now to

---

[6]   Official Gazette of the Republic of Venezuela, Issue No. 36.813, October 22, 1999 [hereafter the "ITL"].

[7]   Pursuant to the worldwide regime, a taxpayer will have two pools of income: (i) Venezuelan source income and (ii) offshore income. A Venezuelan's income will be calculated separately according to these types of income and tax allowances and deductions will also apply to each type of income (see Miguel Valdés, "Venezuelan Tax Reform: Worldwide System of Taxation Adopted", Practical Latin American Tax Strategies February 2000, Vol. 3, No. 2 at p.4).

expanded rules. In this respect, the ITL has introduced a definition of "permanent establishment" and Venezuelan-source income.

In a related development, a general anti-avoidance rule was also adopted for tax-driven transactions. Article 95 of the ITL, adopted in October 1999, provides the Integrated National Service of Tax Administration ("SENIAT") with the power to disregard contracts, the incorporation of companies and generally legal forms and procedures where the fundamental intention of such transactions is to evade, elude or reduce the effect of the application of the ITL. The Organic Tax Code was also recently amended to increase the powers of the Venezuelan tax administration in this respect.

Venezuela has adopted controlled foreign company type legislation in a form similar to the rules adopted in Mexico in 1997. There were, however, a number of important differences, both in the general design of the tax systems and in the detail in the new rules. The changes require reporting of income and impose reporting obligations on Venezuelan residents with a direct or indirect investment located in a low tax jurisdiction (LTJ).[8] These requirements apply where a Venezuelan resident has control over the distributions from, or exercises management and control over, such LTJ investments. The required control is presumed subject to the taxpayer rebutting the presumption (see Article 101 ITL). These rules would generally not apply where over 50% of the total assets of an investment are fixed assets used to carry on an enterprise in a LTJ.

The following investments or entities are deemed to be located in a LTJ:

(i)   accounts or investments of any kind in institutions located in a LTJ (when a taxpayer opens such an account for the benefit of a spouse, concubine, ascendant or descendant, the account is deemed to be an investment of the taxpayer);

(ii)   entities with a domicile or P.O. box in a LTJ;

(iii) entities with their main administrative headquarters or place of actual or principal management or administrative office or permanent establishment in a LTJ;

---

[8]   On 28 March 2001, SENIAT released a list of LTJs in an administration ruling (published in Official Gazette No. 37.168). The current list is attached in Appendix B.

(iv) entities with a physical presence in a LTJ;

(v) entities created under the laws of a LTJ; or

(vi) entities whose business is conducted, regulated or formalised under the laws of a LTJ.

Venezuelan residents will be required to file information returns within 3 months after the end of their fiscal (normally calendar) year in respect of direct or indirect controlled investments made or maintained in LTJs in the preceding taxation year.

Pursuant to these rules, Venezuelan residents must include in their income the gross income earned in a controlled LTJ investment. A deduction for expenses incurred at the level of the investment will not be allowed unless the accounting records of the LTJ investment are made available to the SENIAT and the Venezuelan resident files the information return described above.

The Venezuelan tax haven blacklist was revised to provide that jurisdictions with which Venezuela has a double tax treaty which includes provision for information exchange will not be subject to the rules applicable to low tax jurisdictions even if they meet existing criteria (essentially taxing income at a rate of less than 20%). In addition, the following countries have now been deleted from the original list: the Netherlands Antilles, Jamaica, Marrakech, Tonga, Botswana, Cameroon, Ivory Coast, Costa Rica, El Salvador, Guatemala, Guinea, Lithuania, Maldives, Namibia, Nicaragua, South Africa, Zaire, Zimbabwe, Paraguay, Senegal and St.Kitts.

The Venezuelan government has proposed to adopt a wealth tax to replace inheritance and gift taxes. A draft of the Individual Assets Tax Law has been released and SENIAT announced that it should be enacted in 2007 with effect from 2008. This tax will apply to worldwide assets at a rate of 1% of the gross value of an individual's assets, without deduction for liabilities or expenses.

Argentina

Argentina adopted CFC rules on December 31, 1999[9], effective for fiscal years beginning as of December 31, 1999. Argentine rules are very brief and give the

---

[9]   See Article 133(a) of Tax Reform Law No. 25,239.

impression of extreme haste in their design, which is not surprising as they became effective less than a month after the newly elected Alliance government took office. Though the policy objective is similar, Argentina's rules differ significantly from those adopted by Mexico and Venezuela.

Argentina's rules are more limited as they apply solely to directly held corporations created or located in low tax countries or in countries which do not levy a tax. Trusts, partnerships and other types of entities are not made explicitly subject to the CFC regime. However, the Argentine rules are broader than those of Mexico and Venezuela as there is no requirement that an Argentine resident control the LTJ entity.

The new regime only applies to income derived from interest, dividends, royalties, rents or other similar passive taxable income specified in the regulations. Thus, where an Argentine resident holds shares in a corporation created or located in a LTJ, passive income earned by the corporation will be allocated to the Argentine resident on an annual basis, irrespective of whether the Argentine resident controls the LTJ company.

Decree 290/2000 implements Law 25,239 that was adopted on December 31, 1999. The Decree was effective April 3, 2000 and applies retroactively to the effective date of Law 25,239. Prior to the Decree, there was some uncertainty as to whether Argentina's new CFC rules applied to foreign corporations in any jurisdiction or only to corporations in LTJs. Section 1(q) of the Decree clarifies that the CFC regime will only apply to corporations located in LTJs. A list of LTJs was released in Decree 1037/2000[10], effective from 14 November 2000, and is attached in Appendix C.

Argentina also imposes a tax on personal assets, and so that country differs from Mexico and Venezuela, which have gift and death taxes but not wealth tax. The rate of tax is 0.75% and 1.5% for assets located in Argentina that are held by an LTJ entity. Law 25,585[11], effective as of 31 December 2002, expands this tax to apply, at a rate of 0.5%, to all non-Argentinian resident companies that hold equity interests in Argentinian companies. Other Argentinian sited assets

---

[10]   This Decree was published in the Official Gazette on 14 November 2000.

[11]   This law was published in the Official Gazette on 15 May 2002.

held by LTJ companies continue to be subject to a 1.5% tax. The existence of this tax significantly enlarges the planning needs over those considered in Mexico and Venezuela.

Brazil

Brazilian resident individuals have been subject to tax on their worldwide income since 1939. From January 1, 1996 corporations in Brazil also became subject to a worldwide tax system.[12] The 1996 tax reform also introduced CFC rules applicable to Brazilian corporations.

Initially, Brazil's CFC regime provided that the undistributed income of a controlled[13] or associated[14] foreign company would be attributed to the Brazilian corporate shareholder and taxed annually. This regime was far reaching as there were no exceptions. Furthermore, the regime did not distinguish between income earned in LTJs or high tax jurisdictions.

Shortly thereafter, however, the Brazilian Federal Revenue narrowed the scope of the CFC regime in Normative Instruction n. 38.[15] Article 2 provided that profits earned abroad would only be included in the income of a Brazilian company when such profits were made available to the Brazilian company. Profits are considered to be made available when paid or credited to a Brazilian company. Thus, the rules no longer attributed income from the CFC to a company in Brazil. In August 2001, the CFC rules were again amended, in favour of a more expansive CFC regime. The new rules provide that income of a CFC is taxable to the Brazilian parent company on 31 December of each year, irrespective of whether the Brazilian parent receives a dividend from its CFC.

There are other anti-deferral regimes in Brazil which apply specifically to entities in LTJs. These include a higher withholding tax on payments of income made to

---

[12] Law No. 9.249 published in the official Gazette on December 27, 1995.

[13] Generally, control is ownership of more than 50% voting shares. However, the Brazilian company must control the foreign company's policy and elect directors or managers. Therefore, it is possible that a holding of less than 50% would result in the required control.

[14] Generally, a Brazilian company is associated with a foreign company if it holds at least 10% of the foreign company's capital and influences corporate activities. See Teresa C. Mello de.Almeida Prado, "Brazil Moves to Worldwide Tax on Corporate Income", FT World Tax Report March 1996 Vol. XXI at p.44. and Nélio Weiss and Joseph Wolf, "Brazil's 1999 Tax Year in Review", Tax Notes International, January 3, 2000, at p.19.

[15] Published on June 28, 1996.

LTJs and, for purposes of Brazil's transfer pricing rules, a taxpayer that transacts with a company in a LTJ is subject to the transfer pricing rules irrespective of whether they are related or not. For the purposes of both these rules, a LTJ includes a country which has no income tax or imposes a tax rate of less than 20%. These LTJ rules and the CFC rules currently applicable to corporations provide insight as to how Brazil might adopt a CFC regime applicable to individuals.

Brazil is edging towards a regime applying CFC rules for individuals, adopting broad powers to determine the moment when foreign revenue and income become available, and therefore taxable to Brazilian residents. Rigid constitutional constraints forbidding the taxation of unreceived income mean that any new rules introduced will be subject to considerable litigation.

Individuals are already obliged to provide disclosure concerning worldwide assets in their tax return. The Central Bank of Brazil is now compiling its own list of foreign assets. Brazilians were required to file a list of assets owned abroad by the end of the first quarter, 2002 with the Central Bank. Ongoing disclosure is now required to both the tax authorities and the Central Bank.

Response of the Private Banks to the New Regimes

Historically, structures established by Latin private clients were located in listed LTJs, for the obvious reason that such structures do not attract tax in the host jurisdiction. The new CFC rules in Mexico, Venezuela and Argentina mean that income and gains arising in such LTJ structures are now liable to local tax where the controlling shareholder resides in one of those Latin countries. Structures in blacklist jurisdictions need to be redesigned to avoid reporting obligations and tax exposures.

Most private bankers have become tax-sophisticated in order to develop structures to capture (or retain) the lucrative investment management business sought by the financial institutions. A minority have not done so. Should those bankers simply continue with existing LTJ structures and leave it to the clients to sort out local tax issues?

The UK and US governments, the OECD and the UN have pressed offshore jurisdictions to adopt legislation to criminalise conduct where retention of the proceeds of crime is facilitated by a local financial institution or professional. In some cases the legislation explicitly extends to proceeds of foreign tax evasion. Where such legislation does not currently extend to foreign tax evasion, there is a good prospect that it will do so in future.

Many banks have now had painful experiences in attempting to jettison business that looked acceptable at the time it was taken on (i.e., lucrative despite the risks), but which was subsequently perceived as dangerous, limiting to the objectives of another part of the bank, or simply too resource intensive to maintain. Thus, a bank expanding into an onshore location from which poorly evaluated business was accepted in the past is apt to regret past failures to properly price risk in its client portfolio. Banks, particularly American ones, also find it embarrassing to respond to local treasury officials concerned about portfolios filled with tax evading clients.

Highly visible or careful clients will want to restructure at the outset. Less scrupulous clients are likely to be dragged along in due course by country club chatter or visible teeth in government enforcement efforts. Timely restructuring usually confers the additional advantage of maintaining lost basics or, even better, re-basing assets at current value in the new structure with significant consequent tax advantages for future distributions on the ultimate dissolution of the structure. For all these reasons, any responsible institution is likely to see it as being in its own, and certainly the client's, best interests to move now to structures compliant with the new rules.

Need for Proactive Strategy

Reformatting existing offshore structures requires attention both to local law and international tax planning opportunities. Most local Latin American professionals experienced in moving money across borders will have been concerned primarily with importing private capital for local investment. In territorial tax systems, returns from money invested abroad are simply not taxable, with the result that local professionals have been consulted infrequently where resident clients were exporting or repatriating funds held offshore. In consequence, with a number of notable exceptions, Latin American tax professionals have traditionally had little need to follow international tax planning structures and opportunities.

The pool of professional talent familiar with both local and international requirements is small, particularly considering the current high demand for help. For international private bankers, this is a fundamentally distinguishing characteristic in the Latin American market. In Asia, the market that entranced private bankers over the 1990s, local professional advice on capital export was readily available and since most structures were structured for pre-immigration planning for migration to high-tax countries such as Canada, the US and Australia, sophisticated international advice was readily available. In that environment, banks normally took the view that they were largely passive facilitators of structures designed by professionals acting for the client (i.e., they were not responsible for the efficacy of the planning advice).

In the Latin American context, bankers that wait passively for clients to come to them with "fully cooked" plans for offshore structures may wait forever, and find that their existing client base is cannibalised by other institutions in the meantime. The structures are complex and there simply is not enough experienced professional talent to make one-off structuring practical for the number of clients who need immediate advice in view of the rapid and complex changes in the local environment. In consequence, banks with a serious interest in the region have been active in considering their own tax sensitive structures to respond to local client needs.

Designing Compliant Structures for the New Regimes

Client Planning Objectives

What considerations need to be taken into account in the design of such structures? Clients are concerned about limiting information lodged in (insecure) government databases for personal security reasons. Clients also seek to externalise wealth to achieve investment diversification and limit local political risks such as foreign exchange controls and devaluations.

From a tax perspective, foreign structures holding client assets should be designed to mitigate local income, gains, gift, estate and wealth taxes, as well as reporting obligations, all in a compliant fashion. The foreign structure should be constructed so as to avoid similar exposures and reporting obligations in the jurisdiction where it is established, resident or holding assets. Reformatting out of existing arrangements into a new structure should also be conducted in a manner which does not create any new tax liabilities.

Many private clients are used to exercising control over investments held in their structures. Such arrangements need to be examined for their potential to create local tax exposures under new laws. Where securities are to be held in onshore countries such as the US, care must be taken to ensure that the new structure does not create US estate tax liabilities on the death of the local owner, or settlor of a (typically revocable) trust where one is used. The structure should also anticipate the prospect of tax-efficient distributions or ultimate payout on termination, and so should be designed to mitigate local income, gift and estate tax liabilities when funds leave the structure.

Trust and Company Structures

Many existing and more new structures will use a trust, normally revocable, in order to facilitate estate planning, tax and confidentiality objectives. The use of trusts in civil law jurisdictions inevitably raises characterisation and possible transparency issues with fiscal consequences.

Most new structures will also include an onshore company, or possibly a hybrid (between partnership and corporate status) or possibly a straight partnership. Such structures need to be established and run outside a prescribed LTJ, but ideally will not attract tax or reporting obligations in the high tax jurisdiction where they are established and managed.

The point of the LTJ lists adopted by national Latin governments is to preclude the use of foreign tax-free structures. Most onshore structures (i.e., those in countries not on the prescribed list) are, of course, taxable. Irish non-resident companies were widely used as an immediate response to the Mexican changes, but virtually all were unwound by September 1999 when the Irish government established that date as the deadline after which such companies would no longer be insulated from local Irish tax. Popular substitutes involved use of companies in high tax jurisdictions that were not taxable for one reason or another or structures which were tax transparent (and so not taxable) where established but recognised as separate legal entities under the law of the relevant Latin American jurisdiction.

Traditional onshore corporate entities have the considerable advantage of being conventional and therefore readily comprehensible to clients and the bankers who operate them. However, such structures are often established under relatively arcane general law (i.e., nothing like the operating flexibility of a modern offshore international business corporation statute). Winding up such structures on termination is also complex and costly. Striking off is a possibility on ultimate termination, though that procedure leaves "long tail" liability for directors.

Local corporate law often requires public filings disclosing directors, officers, shareholders and full or abridged financial statements. Such filings are accessible to any member of the public for payment of a nominal fee. Information on structures established in treaty jurisdictions may also be available through exchange mechanisms provided by bilateral tax treaties.

Tax transparent structures located in high tax jurisdictions (such as Scottish partnerships) have also been deployed as investment vehicles for Latin American families. These are contractual, so that the constitution and operation of such structures is not subject to the detailed regulation invariably applicable to companies. The consequent flexibility in design of these vehicles facilitates the complex arbitrage of the tax requirements of the various jurisdictions involved in the structure. Information available on partnerships is generally more limited than that available on corporate registers. In some circumstances even local registration may not be required with the perceived advantage that no information at all may be available to local authorities. Contractual vehicles are also cost efficient to maintain and easy to wind-up on termination.

Life Insurance

Use of life insurance is an attractive option in several countries including Mexico, Venezuela and Brazil as the payment of proceeds on death is tax free. Issues to explore with life insurance include the level of death cover necessary to preserve characterisation of payments as being from life insurance, tax and reporting on withdrawals and regulatory issues.

Selling life insurance is a regulated activity and so financial institutions and foreign insurers must ensure they do not contravene domestic regulation. Such regulations usually provide a 'mobility' exception permitting residents to buy insurance outside the country. Mexico, and to a certain extent Brazil, have 'mobility' exceptions in their regulations; whereas Venezuela requires that a foreign insurer be authorised to insure the life of a Venezuelan resident irrespective of where the policy is taken out. These regulations are usually enforced, with the encouragement of local institutions conscious of the activities of foreign competitors.

In Mexico, survival insurance is interesting as it permits tax free payments after the life insured survives to 60 years of age where the policy has been in place for 5 years and the insured paid the premium (such a policy would also pay out in the event of the early death of the life insured).

New Private Banking Opportunities

This section reviews opportunities for private bankers in the Latin American region which have arisen in recent developments.

Mexican tax legislation adopted at the end of 2001 removed the existing reporting obligation for structures established in blacklisted jurisdictions (TPTRs) where the structure did not have income. Accordingly, a portfolio which can be structured to give rise to no income could be held in a structure established in a TPTR, with no Mexican reporting obligation or tax exposures. This continues to be the case under the new CFC rules.

In Argentina, clients' concerns have expanded to include political risk. Private bankers should consider, in particular, the use of bilateral investment protection treaties (BITs). BITs are similar to tax treaties, in that they are entered into on a sovereign-to-sovereign basis, and they are designed to protect persons in one signatory state investing in the other signatory state. BITs do not generally contain "limitation of benefits" articles.

BITs typically provide protection from foreign exchange controls, in the form of guarantees for the repatriation of profits, capital gains, dividends and royalties including, generally, provision for such payments at prevailing exchange rates in a freely convertible currency. Argentina has concluded more than 40 of such treaties and clients who have invested in domestic assets in Argentina (including clients resident in the country) should consider the use of such treaties to mitigate political risk. The Argentinian Government has recently established an agency to better defend itself against claims under BITs, indicative of the substantial successes enjoyed by many investors concerned about government interference with their assets.

In the Brazilian context, private bankers are finding that while offshore structures are still technically effective to facilitate tax-free accumulation of income and gains for individuals, there is increasing reluctance to use offshore structures established in "traditional" offshore centres. As noted above, Brazil has moved to a worldwide taxation of companies, now with a reasonably effective CFC regime. Proposals to extend such taxation to foreign structures controlled by individuals are under active consideration (as noted in the technical section above). Accordingly, bankers are finding a ready client appetite to restructure existing tax haven arrangements to take account of likely future developments.

No immediate changes are in prospect for the existing Venezuelan taxation of low tax jurisdiction structures, patterned after Mexican rules applicable before 2005. However, Venezuela is proposing to adopt a wealth tax with effect from 2008 (reviewed above). Also, increasing perceptions of instability in the government have increased client appetite for offshore (including political risk) planning and the overall market for private banking services.

Future Developments

Domestic tax systems invariably become much more complex once the decision is made to track and tax worldwide income of resident taxpayers. The experience of other countries which have moved to worldwide taxation with complementary CFC rules suggests that years of painstaking effort on the part of tax authorities will be necessary to adjust the system to tax international income in a fair and effective manner.

Mexico was the first Latin American country to adopt a system for worldwide taxation with complementary controlled foreign company rules. As noted above, Mexico has now adopted a "second generation" set of rules to enforce policy goals. Such rules may well cascade down to other Latin American countries.

External and internal pressures to reduce fiscal deficits will incentivise Latin governments to continue the work now commenced to improve tax compliance and upgrade the international dimension in local tax systems. This suggests an interesting and dynamic period lies ahead for the private banks, their clients and their advisers, as all parties seek to adjust and adapt offshore structures to the new regimes now underway.

(Richard Hay is the international tax partner in the London office of Stikeman Elliott, Canadian and International lawyers. He is admitted to practice in Ontario, New York and England. Prior to entering practice Mr. Hay was Law Clerk to the Chief Justice at the Supreme Court of Ontario and an Assistant Professor and Lecturer on the Law Faculties at The National University of Singapore and the University of Ottawa in Canada. Mr. Hay is Co-Chair of the STEP International Committee.

Robert Reymond is a Canadian and international tax lawyer in the London office of Stikeman Elliott. His practice focuses on tax and international estate planning for high net worth families, particularly those in Latin America, Canada and Europe.)

APPENDIX A

Mexico

Prescribed List of Territories with Preferential Tax Regimes

In the Americas

Anguilla; Antigua and Barbuda; Aruba; the Bahamas; Barbados; Belize; Bermuda; the British Virgin Islands; the Cayman Islands; Costa Rica; Dominica; Grenada; Guyana; Honduras; Montserrat; Puerto Rico; St. Kitts and Nevis; St. Pierre and Miguelon; St. Vincent and the Grenadines; the Netherlands Antilles; Trinidad and Tobago; the Turks and Caicos Islands; Uruguay and the US Virgin Islands;

In Europe

Albania; Andorra; Azores; Campione d'Italia; Canary Islands' special zone (ZEC); the Channel Islands; Cyprus; the Falkland Islands; Greenland; Gibraltar; the Isle of Man; Liechtenstein; Macau; Madeira; Malta; Monaco; Ostrava Free Zone; San Marino; St. Helena; Trieste and Tristan da Cunha;

In Africa and the Middle East

Angola; Bahrain; Cape Verde; Djibouti; the United Arab Emirates; Jordan; Kuwait; Liberia; Mauritius; Oman; Qatar; Qeshm Island; the Seychelles; Swaziland; Tunisia and Yemen;

In Asia and the Pacific

American Samoa; Brunei; Christmas Island; the Cocos or Keeling Islands; Hong Kong; Guam; Norfolk Island; the Cook Islands; Kiribati; Labuan; Maldives; the Marshall Islands; Nauru; Niue; Belau; Pitcairn; French Polynesia; Western Samoa; the Salomon Islands; Svalbard Archipel; Sri Lanka; Tonga; Tokelau; Tuvalu and Vanuatu.

APPENDIX B

Venezuela		
Prescribed List of Low Tax Jurisdictions		
Albania	Guyana	Qeshm Island
Andorra	Honduras	San Marino
Angola	Hong Kong	Salomon Islands
Anguilla	Isle of Man	Samoa (American)
Antigua and Bermuda	Jordan	Samoa (Occidental)
Aruba	Keeling Islands (Cocos)	Seychelles
Ascencion Island	Kiribati	Sri Lanka
Bahamas	Kuwait	St. Cristabel
Bahrain	Labuan	St. Helena
Belize	Lebanon	St. Pierre and Miquelon
Bermuda	Liberia	St. Vincent and the Grenadines
British Virgin Islands	Liechtenstein	Svalbard Archipelago
Brunei Darussalam	Luxembourg	Swaziland
Campione D'Italia	Macau	Tokelau
Canary Island's Special Zone (ZEC)	Malta	Tristan da Cunha
Cape Verde	Marshall Islands	Tunisia
Cayman Islands	Mauritius	Turks and Caicos Islands
Channel Islands	Monaco	Tuvalu
Christmas Islands	Monserrat	US Virgin Islands
Cook Islands	Nauru	United Arab Emirates
Cyprus	Nevis	Uruguay
Djibouti	Niue	Vanuatu
Dominica	Norfolk Island	Yemen
Dominican Republic	Oman	
Falkland Islands	Ostrava Free Zone	
French Polynesia	Pacific Islands	
Gabon	Panama	
Gibraltar	Patau	
Greenland	Pitcairn Island	
Grenada	Puerto Rico	
Guam	Qatar	

APPENDIX C

Argentina		
Prescribed List of Low Tax Jurisdictions		
Albania	Isle of Man	Qeshm Isle
Andorra	Jordan	Samoa (American)
Angola	Keeling Islands	Samoa (Occidental)
Anguilla	Kiribati	San Cristobal
Antigua and Barbuda	Kuwait	San Marino
Aruba	Labuan	Seychelles
Ascension	Liberia	Solomon Islands
Azores Islands	Liechtenstein	Sri Lanka
Bahamas	Luxembourg (1929	St. Helena
Bahrain	Holding Company)	St. Lucia
Barbados	Macao	St. Pierre and Miquelon
Belize	Madeira	St. Vincent and the Grenadines
Bermuda	Maldives	Svalbard archipelago
British Virgin Islands	Malta	Swaziland
Brunei Darussalam	Marshall Islands	Tokelau Islands
Campione D'Italia	Mauritius	Tonga
Cape Verde	Monaco	Trieste
Cayman Islands	Montserrat	Trinidad and Tobago
Channel Islands	Nauru	Tristan da Cunha
Christmas Island	Netherlands Antilles	Tunisia
Cook Islands	Nevis	Turks and Caicos Islands
Cyprus	Niue	Tuvalu
Djibouti	Norfolk Island	US Virgin Islands
Dominica	Oman	United Arab Emirates
French Polynesia	Ostrava	Uruguay
Gibraltar	Pacific Islands	Vanuatu
Greenland	Panama	Yemen
Grenada	Patau	
Guam	Pitcairn Island	
Guyana	Puerto Rico	
Hong Kong	Qatar	

APPENDIX

DEBATE

RBI' Draft Guidelines on Private Sector Banks

A Muralidhar and Ashok Bhattacharya

The RBI's draft guidelines on several corporate governance issues concerning private sector banks has resulted in stir in the market. The think tanks of almost all these banks are already on the move.

Treasury Management has solicited the opinion of two experts on some of grueling issues relating to the same.

- The recent RBI draft guidelines brought in certain norms in terms of minimum net worth in case of private sector banks. These guidelines have landed many new private sector banks in the problem zone. Elucidate your views on this sudden decision been taken by the government?

A Muralidhar (AM): The RBI draft guidelines on ownership and governance of private sector banks, which was placed in the public domain for discussion and feedback during July 2004, is a step towards making the ultimate ownership and control of private sector banks well-diversified. It only wants to ensure that the undesirable elements do not remain in the system.

The draft guidelines said that all private banks should have a net worth of Rs.300 cr at all times. Where the net worth falls below Rs.300 cr, it should be restored within reasonable time. This will trigger a major shakeout in old private banks, most of which have a lower capital base. They will be required to indicate a time-table to push up their capital base to the stipulated level. Minimum net worth criteria will ensure sustainability of banks and protection of depositor's money. However, it may also induce consolidation in cases where smaller banks are unable to mobilize additional required capital.

Ashok Bhattacharya (AB): The current policy framework for ownership and governance in private sector bank's announced by Reserve Bank of India seeks to diversify ownership, make it "fit and proper" and improve systemic stability as some private sector banks which were opened during recent times are facing serious problems. RBI appears to have taken a mid-stream correction to signal a politically correct image in the given situation. This decision may have been triggered by GTB episode which was kept at the back burner for quite some time.

- **The draft RBI guidelines have capped the promoter stake of private banks to 10%. Most of the promoters of private banks have a higher stake. How are the private banks going to be affected by it and what are they planning to do?**

AM: Under draft guidelines, promoters' stake is to be brought down to 10% within three years. At present, promoters are allowed to hold up to a 49% stake in a new private bank and the voting right of stakeholders is capped at 10%, irrespective of the holding of an entity. If an individual entity's maximum stake is capped at 10%, there will not be any need to free voting rights. Promoters of new private sector banks like Kotak Mahindra, Yes Bank and others, including HDFC Bank, will be required to bring down their stakes to 10%. Kotak Mahindra Bank started operations last year with the condition that the promoters could hold up to 49% stake for five years. Similarly, ICICI Bank will also have to bring down its stake in both Federal Bank and South Indian Bank, in both of which it holds more than 15%. Smaller banks need capital to grow. While larger banks can access capital through the stock markets, smaller players have to rely on private equity investors. Promoters shall be given three years time to bring down the stake. Hence, it shall not affect the valuation of private banks adversely.

AB: The promoters of private sector banks which are having more than 10% of paid up capital need to reduce it under a time bound program and their problems can be manifold with falling prices of bank-scrips plus requirements of raising fresh capital. As many things in our country do not take place in a transparent manner, the real promoters of private sector banks may attempt concealing their ownership. HSBC's acquisition of UTI Bank, HDFC's holding in HDFC Bank, ICICI Bank's 1)lding in Federal Bank, South Indian Bank—all may come under pressure.

- FII and FDI stake by single or group of related entities have been capped at 10%. As per the increased capital requirements due to Basel II implementations, how the banks are going to be affected by it?

AM: The draft guidelines emphasized that the aggregate foreign investment in private banks from all sources (FDI, FII, NRI) could not exceed 74%, and at all times, at least 26% of the paid-up capital of the private bank would have to be held by residents. An objective assessment will reveal that the RBI is only moving towards internationally accepted best practices in banking. It only wants to ensure that undesirable elements are kept out of the dynamic financial system. The excess stake of FII/FDI will be replaced by the other entities. Banks having deficient capital to meet Basel II requirements can infuse capital into it by other means like issuing subordinate bonds.

AB: Even before Basel II implementation many private sector banks may have a capital adequacy problem. With continuous erosion of prices of bank shares, the capital market and prospects of FDI investments looks bleak if the situation does not turnaround. Banks now also need to examine more expensive route of Tier II capital.

- Recently, more than 50 institutional investors have registered with SEBI. With reference to the FII holding directive, how do you perceive the effects on the listed banks and on the capital markets in terms of liquidity because of this move on the part of the central banks?

AM: Higher participation of FIIs in the capital market will only increase the liquidity and strength of the market. Their participation in the market or liquidity of the capital market *per se* shall not be affected by reduction of FII holdings. Banking is one among the many segments of the capital market in which FIIs have shown interest. Their continued participation will be broadly based on how the different sectors of the economy perform and not on a particular sector.

AB: The registration of institutional investors with SEBI under policy of acknowledgment of holding in private sector banks will definitely have a negative cascading effect on bank's ability to raise Tier I capital. Erosion of market capitalization, market-related losses on inventory of fixed income investments, dilution of controlling interest, rising inflation etc., will adversely affect the cost-effectiveness of maintaining liquidity, especially for private sector banks.

- **Private and foreign bank's (operating in India) holding in another bank have been capped at 5%. In the situation, where all the sectors are opened up, the political overtone may sometimes undermine the economic implications. Comment on this.**

AM: The objective behind the move is to ensure that there is real capital formation while preventing crossholding by other banks or by connected entities. The shareholding should be broadbased in accordance with the international best practices ensuring that the important shareholders (shareholding of 5% and above) are "fit and proper," and the directors and CEOs who manage the affairs are "fit and proper." Such a move is meant to minimize the influence of a particular promoter or a group of persons on working and functioning of a bank.

AB: The political compulsions of UPA government are different from that of earlier NDA government. As regulators like RBI/SEBI are finally controlled by GoI, more than 90-degree turn on rules, procedures and proclamations cannot be avoided.

- **Certain times the political overtones undermine the economic implications, is it so?**

AM: The draft guidelines are essentially in the larger interest of the banking sector and not too different from internationally accepted best practices. I think it has an economic rationale and not just a political overtone. Definitely, long-term political consensus is also for strengthening the financial sector and bringing a fool-proof mechanism to ensure that vested interests do not cause instability. Anyway, this draft was just a discussion paper and the RBI will come out with another discussion paper soon after considering the comments received from banks, media and other parties.

- **The RBI guidelines have stated that not more than one member of a family or a close relative or associate to be on board of a bank. How is the corporate governance going to be affected by this move, when the industrial groups enter the market?**

AM: This will be a qualitative step towards ensuring that vested individual interests do not lead to any such incidents, which could hamper the functioning of the banks. The 'board of directors' should have diversity in terms of area of specialization, representation rather than excessive importance given to persons of similar professional interests and background. Therefore, I think the proposal, of barring more than one member of a family or a close relative or associate on the board, shall ensure better corporate governance in the banks.

AB: Reserve Bank of India prescription regarding corporate governance in banks need not be taken very seriously as of now. Restricting family members etc., appear to be a very mechanistic way of dealing with corporate governance in banks. It is indeed unfortunate that "important" shareholders of bank need to be "fit and proper", while directors appointed under BR Act are to be given "need-based training". Thus, scope for deficiency in corporate governance continue to exist.

(A Muralidhar, General Manager, Corporate Planning Department, Andhra Bank.

Ashok Bhattacharya, General Manager, State Bank of Mysore, Bangalore.)

INDEX